The Politics of Crime Control

The Politics of Crime Control

edited by

Kevin Stenson and David Cowell

⑤ SAGE Publications
London ● Newbury Park ● New Delhi

Editorial arrangement © Kevin Stenson and David Cowell, 1991
Chapter 1 © Kevin Stenson, 1991
Chapter 3 © John Bright, 1991
Chapter 5 © Neil Boyd and John Lowman, 1991
Chapter 6 © Chris R. Tame, 1991
Chapter 7 © Jock Young, 1991
Chapter 8 © Phil Scraton and Kathryn Chadwick, 1991
Chapter 9 © Jill Radford and Elizabeth A. Stanko, 1991
Chapter 10 © Willem de Haan, 1991

First published 1991

Chapter 2 is compiled from extracts from *Confronting Crime: An American Challenge* by Elliott Currie and from responses by James Q. Wilson which appeared in *Dissent*, Spring 1986. The former © 1985 by Elliott Currie and is reprinted by permission of Pantheon Books, a division of Random House, Inc. The latter © James Q. Wilson 1986 and is reprinted by permission of *Dissent*.

Chapter 4 by Michael King first appeared in 1989 as 'Crime Prevention à la Thatcher' in *The Howard Journal of Criminal Justice* 28 (4): 291–312. © the Howard League 1989. The chapter is reprinted with kind permission of Basil Blackwell.

SAGE Publications Ltd
6 Bonhill Street
London EC2A 4PU

SAGE Publications Inc
2455 Teller Road
Newbury Park, California 91320

SAGE Publications India Pvt Ltd
32, M-Block Market
Greater Kailash – I
New Delhi 110 048

British Library Cataloguing in Publication data
The politics of crime control.
I. Stenson, Kevin II. Cowell, David
364.4

ISBN 0-8039-8341-7
ISBN 0-8039-8342-5 pbk

Library of Congress catalog card number 91-053149

Typeset by GCS, Leighton Buzzard, Bedfordshire
Printed in Great Britain by Biddles Ltd, Guildford, Surrey

Contents

Preface

As teachers of criminology on a variety of courses, we have often felt frustrated by the difficulty of providing students with brief and digestible accounts of the main alternative perspectives on the nature of crime and related approaches to crime prevention and control. We particularly wanted students to read arguments presented, with some passion, by committed proponents of the various approaches, rather than dry and sometimes doubtful *Reader's Digest*-style textbook summaries. Good teaching materials are often scattered in inaccessible journals. In addition, important arguments can be buried in inaccessible prose, heavy with jargon – fatal given the brevity of our attention spans in this TV-zapped age. Furthermore, we felt that many otherwise excellent edited collections and textbooks are marred by concentrating on narrow spans of the criminological spectrum. State-sponsored criminologists of orthodox views, financed by large research grants, can be very snooty about radical voices on the sidelines. In consequence, the 'mavericks', as we have dubbed them, rarely rate a mention by the great and the good in our discipline. In fact sometimes their books and journals are not even ordered for prestigious university libraries, let alone get much recognition on reading lists.

However, the mavericks can be just as narrow minded. Radical texts and edited collections tend to get revenge on the snooty by citing theory and research mainly within the radical academic networks; mutual citation being the surest sign of academic affection. For the new student the resulting differentiation between schools, inaccessibility of key pieces of the jigsaw puzzle and the disturbing lack of genuine debate across the major boundaries between schools can be very confusing and disappointing.

Thus, as naive idealists we conceived of a text which would provide signposts for the student but allow the proponents of alternative approaches to present their own arguments. In practice, as with most edited collections, it produced its share of headaches, including persuading authors who would not normally do so to share the same platform. We hope that the reader will share our view that the results are worth the effort, particularly given the international flavour of these contributions from two continents. Although we should not underestimate the importance of different historical legacies in criminology and systems of crime control, at the same time we live in a shrinking world. Local conditions can vary, but the cross-fertilization of ideas between societies has been considerable and will undoubtedly grow.

The bonds of sentiment and common language have been of particular significance for British and US criminology. But in recent years, the moves towards European integration, with the usual convivial conference junketings in a variety of exotic locations from Islington to Florence, have created new friendships. These are helping to break down Anglo-Saxon insularity and open up the barbarism of British criminal justice and corrections to European innovations in theory and practice. We hope that this book may play some small part, too, in breaking down the insularity of US criminology. Although US criminology is well financed and at the cutting edge in many areas, not least in the application of criminological research to sentencing policy and decision making, there are many European ideas and practical innovations which deserve more attention in North America. We have not covered all criminological flavours in this book, but hope to whet the reader's appetite for more. To have attempted full coverage in the book would have increased its size and price, putting it beyond the pocket of the diverse students of criminology and criminal justice who we hope will buy it.

Thanks must go to James Q. Wilson and Elliott Currie, respectively, the leading figures on the new conservative Right and the liberal democrat Left of US criminology, for allowing us to reprint the debate between them. This first appeared (well spotted, Jock!) in *Dissent*, the New York journal, in 1985 and 1986. Thanks also to the editors of *Dissent* for permission to reprint and for acting as go-betweens. Without this, the book probably would not have got off the ground. Thanks also to the editors of the *Howard Journal* and to Basil Blackwell for permission to reprint, in updated and modified form, Michael King's chapter, which originally appeared there in 1989. Thanks to the Dutch Ministry of Justice for reinforcing their reputation for kindness to criminologists.

In addition, of the people who have helped in the production of the book, the following, particularly, deserve a mention: Gillian Stern at Sage for kind encouragement and staying with it, Frances Heidensohn, Todd Clear, Jean Murtagh, Keith Doughty, Mike Musheno, Nigel South, Nigel Brearley, Anne Beech, Joanna Lane for invaluable help in the final stages and Janina Paszkowska for the bear.

Kevin Stenson
David Cowell

Notes on contributors

Kevin Stenson teaches criminology and sociology at Buckinghamshire College and is a visiting lecturer at Goldsmiths' College, University of London. He has published many articles and reviews in the fields of criminology, social work and discourse analysis. He is currently engaged in an ethnographic study of the relations between young people and the police in London.

David Cowell is Head of sociology and criminology at the Polytechnic of Central London and editor, with Trevor Jones and Jock Young, of *Policing the Riots* (1982).

Elliott Currie teaches criminology at the University of California, Berkeley. He is a critic of conservative approaches to criminal justice and a leading voice on the liberal democrat Left of US criminology. His many publications include the seminal *Confronting Crime: an American Challenge* (1985).

James Q. Wilson is a Professor of Government at Harvard and also at the University of California, Los Angeles. He has been an adviser on crime and justice issues to the US government and to state legislatures, and has been a leading conservative figure in international criminology. His many publications include the very influential *Thinking about Crime* (1975) and, with Richard Herrnstein, *Crime and Human Nature* (1985).

Michael King is Reader in Law at Brunel University, London. He has extensive experience of research in criminal justice issues in both the UK and France. His publications include (with Christine Piper) *How the Law Thinks about Children* (1990).

John Bright is Director of Field Operations for 'Crime Concern', the (UK) National Crime Prevention Development Organisation. He has pioneered multi-agency approaches to crime prevention and community safety in public housing. His publications include *Crime in America: a British Perspective* (1991).

Neil Boyd teaches criminology at Simon Fraser University, Burnaby, BC, Canada. His many publications include *The Last Dance: Murder in Canada* (1988) and *The Social Dimensions Of Law* (1986).

John Lowman, with a background in social geography, teaches criminology at Simon Fraser University Burnaby, BC, Canada. His many publications include *Transcarceration: Essays on the Sociology of Social Control* (1987), co-edited with R. Menzies and T.S. Palys.

Chris Tame is secretary of The Libertarian Alliance, a leading New Right intellectual pressure group. He has published many scholarly articles on libertarian themes, was a consultant for the UK Television series, 'The New Enlightenment', and edited *The Bibliography of Freedom*, London, Centre for Policy Studies.

Jock Young is Professor of Criminology at Middlesex Polytechnic, London. The leading figure in the Left Realist school, his many publications include (with Ian Taylor and Paul Walton) *The New Criminology* (1973), (with John Lea) *What is to be Done about Law and Order?* (1984) and (with Roger Matthews) *Rethinking Criminology*, vols I and II (1991).

Phil Scraton is Professor of Criminology at Edge Hill College, Lancashire, and a leading figure in European critical criminology. His many publications include *The State of the Police* (1985) and, with J. Sim and P. Skidmore, *Prisons Under Protest* (1991).

Kathryn Chadwick teaches criminology at Edge Hill College and has published many articles, particularly in the field of feminist research on criminal justice. She is co-author of *In the Arms of the Law* (1987).

Jill Radford is a feminist activist and researcher. She works for 'Rights For Women' and teaches criminology and women's studies for the Open University in London. She is co-editor, with J. Hanmer and E. Stanko, of *Women, Policing and Male Violence: International Perspectives* (1989).

Elizabeth A. Stanko teaches criminology at Brunel University, London and has been a pioneer of feminist criminology on both sides of the Atlantic. Her many publications include the influential *Intimate Intrusions: Women's Experiences of Male Violence* (1985) and *Everyday Violence: how Women and Men Experience Physical and Sexual Danger* (1990).

Willem de Haan teaches criminology at the University of Utrecht in the Netherlands and has had extensive experience in critical teaching and research in several European countries. His publications include, *The Politics of Redress: Crime, Punishment and Penal Abolition* (1990).

Organization of the Book

The introductory chapter, by Kevin Stenson, will first examine the scope of crime: how far there have been changes in behaviour and the rising rhetoric of law and order. It will examine the problems involved in defining the key terms of crime, crime prevention and control and politics, and will present a perspective on the nature of scientific truth as applied to criminology, which derives from the work of Foucault. Using this perspective, it will account for the role of the maverick radical voices on the sidelines of the discipline, before going on to examine their links with the major debates between liberals/social democrats and conservatives. The chapter concludes by examining the problems facing the liberals/social democrats in seizing the high ground of criminology from the conservatives and in redefining the agenda of criminology.

Part One of the book examines the formation and implementation of official crime prevention and control policy and major debates surrounding them.

The second chapter reproduces a rare debate, which first appeared in the US journal *Dissent*, between Elliot Currie, the leading voice of the liberal democrat Left and James Q. Wilson, the leading voice of the new Conservative Right in US criminology and a former adviser to the Reagan administration and state legislatures. Focusing on Wilson, Currie attacks the dominance of conservative thinking and policy making since the late 1970s, and the allegedly disastrous consequences, by international standards, for US crime and incarceration rates. Wilson replies by distancing his own from punitive, value-based conservative approaches. He emphasizes the failure of earlier liberal democratic policies to deal effectively with crime problems and under-lines the difficulties in explaining national differences in the crime rate. This is followed by a rejoinder by Currie.

John Bright, a leading crime prevention practitioner and adviser, then provides a detailed account of recent shifts in crime prevention programmes and activities in Britain, within the orbit of local and national government and by the police and the voluntary, 'not for profit', sector. With his critique of UK policy, Bright, echoing Currie's work, argues that there is a shift in paradigm towards a concern with social crime prevention and away from the narrow concentration on crime control issues. Whereas the transatlantic influences in the 1980s were mainly conservative, now they may be moving in a more social democratic, interventionist direction once more.

The fourth chapter, by Michael King, argues that crime is a socially constructed problem, constructed and sustained on behalf of a range of interest groups, stretching from party politicians to the mass media to professionals in the crime prevention and control industry. This thesis is developed via a comparison of the ideological underpinnings and mechanics of the French, social democratic approach to crime prevention strategies with young people and the British New Right strategies which developed during the 1980s.

In the fifth chapter, Neil Boyd and John Lowman examine the varieties of control strategies in contemporary Western societies for dealing with what they describe as 'tainted hedonisms'. Focusing on drugs and prostitution, they argue that the criminal law and law enforcement strategies are underpinned by a range of moral scripts, interacting with public health concerns. Distinguishing between the legal models of prohibition, decriminalization and legalization of drugs, they draw particular contrast between the drug control policies of the United States and the Netherlands. Similarly, they use international contrasts in distinguishing between strategies of criminalization, regulationism and legalization in the control of prostitution. They also point to the need to understand these issues within the framework of the wider political economic relations within and between societies.

Part Two deals with the maverick, radical alternative approaches - on both the Left and Right – to the definition of crime, and proposals for crime prevention and control.

Chris Tame offers an insider's account of the varieties of approaches to crime and crime control, which can broadly be termed Right. Distancing the Right from the extremes of racism, fascism, religious fundamentalism and biological reductionism, Tame distinguishes between: natural rights liberalism or libertarianism; the application of liberal, free market economics of the University of Chicago school; traditionalist conservatism and the 'New Realist', pragmatic and scientifically based conservative critics of liberal approaches to crime control. This category includes James Q. Wilson.

It is debatable whether the seventh chapter, by Jock Young, on the Left Realist approach, belongs in Part One or in Part Two. With its roots in the maverick radical criminology of the 1970s, European Left Realism, in an echo of Currie's liberalism, is moving towards the mainstream of debate with the conservatives. In this account, Left Realism tries to absorb the lessons of the conservative New Realist approaches, with their scientific monitoring of crime control strategies and their stress on the importance of community controls. Furthermore, within the framework of a social democratic social policy programme to deal with poverty, unemployment and so on, Young tries to steer a path between the narrowness of conservative concerns with crime control and the exaggerated emphasis on the oppressiveness of the systems of control, by the neo-Marxist left.

Rejecting the one-sidedness of most theories, Young aims for a comprehensive explanation of crime and victimization and control, with the goal of providing a better service for the neglected poor. In this there is much reliance on the role of local surveys as a democratic instrument for charting the scope of crime and the citizens' priorities for crime control. At the core of this approach is the view that, despite flaws and distortions, legal conceptions of crime are not just labels imposed on the flux of events, but denote the prevailing codes of public morality in interaction with the objective reality of human suffering. The second part of the chapter explores the implications of this approach for the development of multi-agency programmes of intervention.

In the eighth chapter, Phil Scraton and Kathy Chadwick claim a continuity between earlier approaches within radical criminology, linking their emphases on the role of the criminal justice system in regulating class conflict and reproducing exploitative relations of production, with newer versions of conflict theory. These newer approaches also recognize a range of other structures of oppression, including the reproduction of unequal gender and sexual relations and also the 'neo-colonialist' structures of racial domination. Scraton and Chadwick stress the interrelationship between these structures in the various strategies of control. Here the emphasis is not so much on the explanation of crime in its usual legal senses. Rather, these conceptions are subjected to a critical deconstruction and the focus is on the processes involved in the 'criminalization' or stigmatization of subordinate groups and the need for effective resistance against oppression. This version of radical criminology emphasizes its distance from the centre left reformism of the Left Realists.

Like Scraton and Chadwick, in chapter nine, Jill Radford and Elizabeth Stanko reject and deconstruct the conventional legal definitions of crime. These are said to reflect the patriarchal and racist assumptions incorporated in the male-dominated and white-dominated institutions of the police, criminal justice and penal systems. They emphasize the need for women to name their own troubles in dealing with the effects of male violence, in the complex social contexts in which they occur. Furthermore, they question the benefits accruing to women in the new interest being shown, internationally, by police forces and professional social services agencies, in regulating the domestic sphere. By contrast, they stress the need for women to develop their own strategies of self-protection and resistance, in effect, self-organized strategies of 'crime' control.

Willem de Haan, in Chapter 10, like other mavericks, rejects and deconstructs the concept of crime. This deconstruction operates within the framework of the left libertarian, abolitionist movement, which developed internationally through the prison reform movement. The ultimate goal is the abolition of prison and the diminution of the criminal justice system. In direct opposition to Left Realism, the category of crime is seen as a historical myth which serves to uphold dominant power relations and to justify the expansion of intrusive networks of control. This deflects attention from great social problems. For the more serious social and economic problems, social and economic policies are usually more appropriate interventions than the divisive and stigmatizing processes of criminal justice. With respect to interpersonal and intergroup relations, it is seen as usually counter-productive for the criminal justice system to intrude on the inevitable conflicts of everyday life. Rather, the goal should be to develop alternative means of social redress, including mediation schemes and so on, within a climate conducive to the maintenance of rational dialogue between citizens.

1

Making Sense of Crime Control

Kevin Stenson

THE SCOPE OF CRIME AND PROBLEMS OF DEFINITION

The Scope of Crime

A volume on the politics of crime control would seem never to be of greater relevance, given the mounting alarm registered in media reports and the speeches of politicians on the issue of law and order. This is nowhere more apparent than in the United States, where the most sensitive indicators are officially recorded rates of homicide and other crimes of violence. In July 1990, the *New York Times* reported that after the false dawn of falling homicide rates in the mid-1980s, by the close of the decade most cities were reporting dramatic rises. A new record of more than 23,000 murders were reported in 1990. The 'murder capital', Washington DC, with 703 homicides, experienced the third consecutive year in which records had been broken. Sensational trials like the 'jogging trial' in New York in 1990, in which a group of African-American youths were accused of the violent multiple rape of a wealthy white woman focused worldwide media attention. In addition, reports of growing fiscal crises, homelessness and other major social problems, help to create the impression that American cities are out of control, perhaps in terminal decline (*New Statesman and Society*, 25/1/91, 1/2/91).

Problems of violent crime do seem to be relatively worse in the United States than elsewhere (see Chapter 2). For the year 1989–90, in the USA, males between 15 and 24 were 73 times more likely to die a violent death than their counterparts in Austria, 44 times more likely than in Japan, 24 times more likely than in Britain (Currie, 1990). These problems bear most acutely on poor African-American males in the cities, among whom homicide is now the most common cause of death. Moreover, nearly one-quarter of African-American males between the ages of 20 and 29 are in prison or in some way enmeshed in the criminal justice system (Currie, 1990). Yet while these figures make European criminologists gasp, the trends elsewhere seem also to be upward, and foreign interest in the US crime figures stems from an awareness that, in a world which increasingly resembles a homogenized global village, New York and Washington DC may be seen as metaphors for the future of the great cities in other advanced industrial societies, East and West. For example, the city riots of 1981 and 1985 have dented Britain's image as a peaceful, law-abiding society. And this is reinforced by the news that, despite the recruitment of 15 per cent more police officers and consistent real increases in the law and order budget, there was a 79 percent increase in officially reported crime between Mrs Thatcher's accession to power in 1979 and 1990 (*Guardian*, 28/3/91).

Complaints about the growth in violent crime, the spread of corruption and a decline in respect for the law, especially among the young, are sometimes accompanied by visions of a descent into anarchic chaos, with honest citizens afraid to walk the streets and united only in mutual hostility and suspicion. The spectre traverses both the public and private domains, with people seen as living under siege conditions behind bars, protected by savage dogs and, for those who can afford it, by expensive security systems. The feminist variant of this vision presents women and children locked away in this spuriously protected space, and cut off from female networks, thus being made ever more vulnerable to oppression by their violent menfolk (Hanmer and Saunders, 1984).

However, for generations, politicians and moral arbiters have complained about a decline in public morality related to the growth in crime. Whatever the base point, the usual complaint has been that crime has been getting worse over the previous 20 years (Pearson, 1983). Perhaps the role of the criminologist should be to offer a sober alternative to political exaggeration and emphasize underlying continuities rather than superficial changes? There is not the space here to provide more than a cautious answer to this question, but we can note some of the complex issues involved. The problem with presenting snapshot or headline statistics in the way we have just done, and the way that they are usually presented in the media, is that they become part of routine rhetoric about a society. That is, they, along with *Miami Vice* and other action-packed TV shows and movies, can paint a rather misleading picture of a whole society. The United States, in this case, is represented by its cities – as exciting but crime ridden.

However, official statistics on crime are notoriously difficult to interpret, both as indices of changes over time and as bases for comparing societies (see the debate between Currie and Wilson in Chapter 2). Methods of recording crime vary widely and change over time. In the USA, for example, the Uniform Crime rates, which the Department of Justice has published since 1930, unlike the British figures, are based on voluntarily supplied sample, rather than comprehensive, statistics from local law enforcement agencies (Heidensohn, 1989). In addition, public tolerance of crime can change, affecting readiness to report crime, or even to recognize it in the first place. This is particularly true of male crimes against women and children, or more generally, parental crime against children (see Radford and Stanko, Chapter 9). A central point here is that crime statistics are *moral statistics*, they record both human conduct and the shifting professional and public perceptions of that conduct (see Chapter 7). It is, for example, feasible that the extent of criminal behaviour has increased, that public tolerance of it has diminished, as has the capacity of informal and formal controls to check it – if true, this would be a potent brew.

In order to overcome the problems of relying only on official figures, criminologists have conducted victim surveys; these involve interviewing large samples of citizens about their experience of crime and assessing their priorities for crime control. Regular national crime surveys were initiated in the USA in 1972, followed by Canada, Britain, Holland and other countries (Hough and Mayhew, 1985; Mayhew et al., 1989). These have been supplemented by feminist surveys (Hall, 1985; Hanmer and Saunders 1984) and by intensive local surveys (Crawford et al., 1990; and see Chapter 7). Even here, however, differences in methodology employed can make comparison of results difficult. Yet, it has been argued that various sources of data show upward trends, implying that the changes are real and internationally based (van Dijk, 1991). It is significant that despite these differing practices in recording and in social surveys, and variations in police and criminal justice organizations between countries, the advanced democracies have experienced steady rises in overall crime rates in the past three decades. In Europe, for example, 1955 seems to be a watershed point, with steady rises in most countries from that year, while in Sweden, the upward trend began immediately after the Second World War (van Dijk, 1991: 31).

In an effort to provide the basis for more accurate international comparison over time, a series of comparative victim surveys has been launched involving 17 countries (van Dijk et al., 1990). This confirms that the USA has markedly higher than average levels of violent crime, but is closely followed by Australia, another society founded on immigration and with a heterogeneous population. Moderately high levels of violent crime were also noted in Finland, the Netherlands, the Federal Republic of Germany, Spain, Canada and Scotland. While the picture may not look as lurid as that in the American cities, in Europe by the end of the 1980s 'crimes like theft, burglary, simple assault and indecent assault place[d] a heavy burden on the inhabitants of the larger European cities in particular' (van Dijk, 1991: 31).

However, it is becoming clear from victimization studies that global generalizations comparing nation states in relation to overall levels of crime can be misleading. Not surprisingly, general levels of reported victimization are related to the degree of urbanization in a country. While the large American cities compare badly with cities elsewhere, the lives of the many millions of Americans living in leafy suburbs and small towns and villages are no more likely to be touched by crime than their counterparts in other advanced societies. In fact,

> *average* risks of many many crimes across the USA are not especially greater, and even lower than in other countries . . . risks of assault with force in the USA were similar to those in England and Wales and Scotland, and lower than those in the Netherlands. (van Dijk et al., 1990: 108)

But the interpretation of these various sources of data is a never-ending process and this fuels the debates, particularly between liberals and conservatives, over the appropriate diagnosis of the 'crime problem' and ways to deal with it (see Chapter 2). If we had to rely on the survey data and official figures alone, it would still be difficult to justify the claim that the crime problem is worsening. However, other historical and sociological argument and evidence does lend tentative support. One should always treat with caution stories about happier times gone by, since they can paper over evidence of deep social conflict and dissent in the past. Nevertheless, it is plausible to argue that the interaction of modes of informal community control of disruptive behaviour – at least in the public sphere – and the developing institutions of policing, criminal justice and corrections from the mid-nineteenth century to the early post-Second World War era, helped to transform the experience of city life in the advanced societies.

The degree to which control agencies achieved public acceptance and legitimacy varied widely. In Britain, for example, the gradual, if grudging, acceptance of locally organized policing by the working classes (Reiner, 1985; Brogden et al., 1988) was reinforced by the growing discipline of factory organization and the related development of the disciplines of the labour movement. This helped to create a 'respectable' artisan working class, with highly developed forms of self-organization and social control, and with a vested interest in the formal and informal repression of the 'disreputable' poor (Cohen, 1981). In the United States too, professional police forces, with a degree of public acceptance, and based initially on the British model, were an important cog in the machinery of urban administration by the end of the nineteenth century (Monkkonen, 1981). By contrast, in much of continental Europe, while the labour disciplines were also developing, the highly centralized and intrusive police institutions have never achieved the same level of public legitimation. The social distance between police and public was reinforced by the co-option of police agencies by the Nazi occupying powers during the Second World War (Mawby, 1990).

However, in interaction with less formal, community-based organization and control, the establishment of professional police forces and modern criminal justice and penal systems did much to transform the dangerous, crime-ridden Victorian cities into relatively safe zones for 'gentlefolk' and the new, 'respectable' artisan working classes. More generally the professionalization of crime control in conjunction with sophisticated modes of community control (Foucault, 1977), the restraint of violent emotional expression and the dissemination of 'gentle' codes of manners, could be seen as part of the 'civilizing process' (Elias, 1939/1982). Perhaps the growth in crime since the late 1950s, and the relative ineffectiveness of the crime control systems to check it, could be seen as a *decivilizing* process, though this process probably has differential effects on different social classes.

And while it would be wrong to reduce this complex process to the economic dimension, it does place firmly on the agenda the social effects of deindustrialization in the cities of the advanced societies since the 1960s and its associated ripple effects. These would include the decline in 'breadwinning' paid work for men, the erosion of the labour movement and associated changes in individual, family and community organization (Currie, 1990; Box, 1987; Taylor, 1990; Wilson, 1987). Again, these social changes have had a disproportionate impact on the urban poor and in Paris, London and other European cities, on those poor people who have, as in an echo of Victorian town planning (Jones, 1971) been steered towards bleak public housing in satellite towns, away from the tourist gaze. Sophisticated French crime prevention programmes (see Chapter 4) have not prevented major recent disturbances in such districts outside Lyons and Paris.

Law and order rhetoric in high profile

These real changes in behaviour have been accompanied by changes in both political and academic discourses about crime, law and order. Perhaps the watershed came in the early 1970s, with the US administration of President Nixon and Spiro Agnew. They promised to reverse the soft approach to crime control, allegedly practised by 'bleeding-heart', 'do-gooding' liberals under Democratic administrations. The attempt to rehabilitate offenders would be replaced by tougher policing and sentencing policies. The 'War against Poverty' would be replaced by a 'War against Crime'.

Through murky political codes, artfully playing on racial fears and tensions, this rhetoric was part of an attempt to win white working class voters over to the Republicans. These people were allegedly disillusioned with liberal democratic policies and enraged by the growth of crime. Though conservative approaches to crime control are now more sophisticated, the familiar codes were evident during the Bush/Dukakis presidential contest. The Republicans held out the prospect of a liberal nightmare under the Democrats, with the liberal Massachusetts corrections policies generalized to the whole country and violent criminals turned loose on the people.

This form of political discourse held wide international appeal on the political Right and, by the mid-1970s, had already been imported into parts of Europe (Hall et al., 1978). In Britain, it formed a major plank of Mrs Thatcher's successful campaign against the Labour Party in 1979. Familiar litanies of complaint can now be heard in virtually every modern society, including the capitalist West, Latin American countries in the grip of drug barons and the emerging democracies of the old Soviet bloc in Eastern Europe. While it was widely claimed that crime rates were lower under the old communist regimes (Bienkowska, 1991), there are fears, as yet only expressed through journalistic reporting, that part of the price of liberation from communist tyranny is a loosening of the old Stalinist social controls, an explosion of envy and greed and, therefore, of crime.

Like China, the USSR discovered that the new mix of planning and capitalism produced a rise in street crime in addition to the mafia-style black marketeering and protection rackets which have long greased the wheels of creaking collectivist economies (Walker, 1989). The lag between the disintegration of the KGB apparatus and Kremlin planning machinery and the formation of efficient markets, creates a vacuum filled by gangsters. But goods reaching mob-controlled markets are often beyond the pocket of average citizens and the police ill-resourced to handle the situation (Vitaliev, 1991). As elsewhere (Pearce, 1976), organised crime may find natural allies on the populist Right and become one of the greatest threats to fledgling democracies of the post-Soviet republics.

The Chinese version of the war against crime includes, according to Amnesty International reports, mass sentencing rallies and public executions. After parading offenders through the streets they are executed en masse, for crimes including murder, robbery and rape. China now has over 40 offences which carry the death penalty, a significant increase since the introduction of the criminal code 10 years ago. Moreover, families of offenders are also usually billed for the bullets used (Guardian 2/1/1991).

The problem of definitions

So the view that crime is a political issue, rising up the agenda, may seem self-evident. But that depends on what we mean by crime, crime prevention and control and politics. There have long been maverick voices on the sidelines of criminology, who have attempted to challenge and/or extend the usual stereotypical definitions of crime and have, in consequence, proposed changing the priorities for crime prevention and control. It is a major concern of the second part of this volume to spotlight these academic mavericks and their attempts to penetrate the major official discourses about crime, its prevention and control. This will complement the first section which involves an exploration of the more familiar terms of debate between conservatives and liberals within the major circuits of power.

Before studying the more complex issues relating to the meaning of crime, let us examine the term crime control. It is sometimes used to refer to all the measures developed to prevent and control crime. For those radicals who see the measures of the criminal justice system as largely ineffective, or even crimogenic, the most effective forms of crime control are those which deal with the deep social and economic causes which supposedly cause crime. By the same token, for those who see such social policy measures as irrelevant, quite apart from the less official controls operating within the community, effective *official* crime prevention can only operate through efficient detection and punishment. From this point of view, crime control could be seen as the most effective form of crime prevention. Additionally, for radicals who are concerned to challenge the operations of the criminal justice system, fine distinctions between preventive and control measures may be of little meaning; they become more meaningful to policy makers and professional practitioners who have a direct stake in developing the various strategies. It may be more important for radicals to focus on self-organized strategies of prevention and control (see Chapter 9).

One of the clearest conceptual models is provided by Patricia Brantingham, who presents a criminal process model of crime prevention along a continuum, stretching from more general social policy interventions towards crime prevention in the narrower sense of police practice to control criminal acts themselves (Brantingham, 1989). This could be extended to encompass the trial and subsequent, correctional stages of crime control. With the focus in the 1970s shifting away from traditional attempts to deal with the deeper alleged causes of crime, towards more precisely focused crime prevention and control programmes and strategies (see Chapter 3) it has made sense for both criminologists and practitioners to draw increasingly precise distinctions between different stages of prevention and control.

Yet we should resist the temptation to view these issues as 'technical' concerns, bound up with the scientific evaluation of alternative means to deal with problems, which everyone agrees are evils to be eliminated from the body of society. It is precisely the goal of the maverick voices to break up, or to use fashionable French jargon, to 'deconstruct' this cosy technical discourse, which would largely leave crime prevention and control to the expert academic and salaried crime prevention and control practitioners.

Expanding the political

Let us now look more closely at the term politics. There is not the space here to examine complex political science models and it is not clear that such an investigation would, for our purposes, bear much fruit anyway. Instead let us begin with the common-sense meaning of politics. It is the pursuit of power by those given the title of politician. While the picture is clearly different in authoritarian societies like Iraq, our focus here is mainly on the advanced liberal democracies. In these societies, politicians are those who run for elected office at local or national level and market policy proposals which resonate with enough voters to get them elected, and maybe stay elected. Thus, it is not surprising that politicians, senior police officers and judges, who also enter the political firing line, tend to highlight those crimes which regularly make headlines. There is certainly debate about crime in the mainstream of public life, but there is a predictable quality to much of this debate. To enter this arena and retain credibility, it helps if one speaks within the familiar terms of debates within the conservative camp and between conservatives and mainstream, 'respectable' liberals.

But it must be stressed that these common-place depictions of 'Big Politics', operating from the arena of City/Town Hall to the national and international stages, are not neutral representations which can be taken at face value. In fact this language of politics, which dominates the media, has a reflexive relation to the political process. By assuming that the everyday, overt struggles and rituals of democratic politics constitute the true sites of political action, the political language focuses public energy and attention on this sphere, helps to legitimate common-sense meanings of politics and implicitly or explicitly de-legitimizes more maverick notions of the nature and sites of politics (see Laclau and Mouffe, 1985; Clegg, 1989). But as we shall see, mavericks of various colours encourage us to think of politics and the sites of struggle in more diverse, less stereotyped terms.

It is worth noting at this stage that the terms 'liberalism' and 'social democracy', which recur throughout this text, have variable meanings in different countries. Without the space to investigate the complex issues involved, the term liberalism will be used in its US, rather than its various European senses. It refers to progressive approaches to social and economic policies, which accept a measure of collective governmental responsibility for the provision of universal public services and, in particular, stresses the need to take effective action to improve the lot of the poor. Thus its adherents are the modern inheritors of the philosophy represented by Roosevelt's New Deal in the 1930s and 1940s. European social democracy overlaps with this tradition considerably. But, while rejecting the authoritarian Soviet models of socialism, European social democrats, of varying shades, have been defenders of the more highly developed labour movements and welfare systems which developed in Europe. These features are held to distinguish West European societies from both the US and Soviet social models. However, social democracy has suffered its own crises of faith and, in a period of renewal, there is a search for new more democratic and participative models which give greater recognition to the individual freedom and choices of the citizen (Hirst, 1986).

The liberals and social democrats may not always be liked by right-wing political elites and the elites within the justice systems, but their positions are usually accorded the legitimacy of analyses and policy proposals worthy of serious consideration. Perhaps this is because the liberals' views, while often rather more open than those of their principal, conservative opponents, to the ideas of the mavericks, do not deviate too far from the more orthodox legal conceptions of crime. It is accepted that these notions of crime are the ones most worthy of attention. Moreover, they harmonize with most citizens' moral codes and conceptions of what constitutes troublesome conduct; whereas there is less public agreement or strength of feeling about the damaging effects of the crimes of the privileged (Hagan, 1987). The major debates are over how to prevent and control behaviour which most people regard as threatening, and which is responsible for the overwhelming bulk of cases processed routinely through the courts.

The more orthodox conceptions of crime are broadly accepted and prioritized by the criminal justice agencies, mainstream politicians, the news media, Hollywood and other organs of popular culture. These social institutions legitimate each others' notions of what crime is, and which crimes are most worthy of attention, in mutually reinforcing and self-fulfilling circles (Chapman, 1968; Box, 1983). Predictably, these are the crimes of the poor and the working class, including: public order offences, particularly where they erupt into riot or insurrection; routine property offences; crimes against the person and low-level frauds, involving the passing of stolen cheques and use of stolen credit cards; drug-related offences and so on.

This institutional focusing tends to reinforce at any one time popular imagery which makes particular groups into scapegoated targets, or what Stan Cohen calls 'folk devils' (Cohen, 1980). These folk devils collectively signify criminality (Matza, 1969; Hall et al.,

1978), to some extent whether or not their behaviour patterns warrant the stigmatization. The list would, for example, include: in the USA, African-Americans of the ghetto (rather than the middle-class suburbs) and – in part due to Hollywood keeping alive old stereotypes – working-class Italian-Americans; travelling people (or, pejoratively, 'Tinkers') in Ireland, Gypsies in much of Europe and so on. In most societies this produces a rich folklore about the actual or fantasized behaviour of these groups and has stimulated academic controversy about variable ethnic disposition to crime (Wilson and Herrnstein, 1985; Galliher, 1989; Lea and Young, 1984; Gilroy, 1987; Keith and Murji, 1990; Junger, 1989; Bowling, 1990b; Albrecht, 1991). Some would consider it indecent even to mention these stigmatized groups, though trying to enforce an academic taboo will not make one of the key issues of criminology disappear.

But, without wanting to enter that debate here, it can be argued that, in large measure, the ease with which 'outcaste' groups are made to signify or represent criminality in general is not just a function of how they behave and/or are treated by the police and the courts, but is also a function of the narrowness of the images and definitions of crime which operate within popular culture and the criminal justice agencies. The new definitions of crime and troublesome behaviour provided by the mavericks may not, sadly, displace these folk devils, but at the least they may supplement them with a new cast of rogues, drawn from more privileged social positions. To follow this logic, crime and strategies for dealing with it are not just political issues in the terms of conventional political rhetoric, they are political in a deeper sense. They are struggles over how we define crime in the first place, what is meant by crime and crime prevention and control, and over the priorities for research and social policy.

By contrast, the mavericks on the sidelines of criminology and the politics of crime and crime prevention and control, go beyond the more usual common-sense understandings of politics. The political struggles over crime operate in a range of social contexts, in the streets, in business circles, on picket lines, in new social movements, in the academy and so on, which go way beyond the formal local and national political institutions. At the heart of these struggles lie conflicts over the definitions of crime itself, *struggles over what counts as knowledge and truth.*

THE POLITICS OF TRUTH –
A FOUCAULTIAN PERSPECTIVE

The struggle to define the meaning and truth of crime, and strategies to deal with it has also been explored in a literary context by Tom Wolfe's nightmare tale of New York City *(The Bonfire of the Vanities)*. In the light of recent New York history, he presented a remarkably prescient account of the way that criminal justice can be one more political battlefield, where questions of guilt or innocence and legal rationality are transformed into weapons of bitter and emotionally charged group warfare. 'Proving' the truth of a legal case is simply one element in a larger, ongoing struggle. 'Truth' is not simply a casualty of this warfare; it becomes another missile. Wolfe's is a partisan view from the political Right and the world of the poor is portrayed as generally threatening and barely differentiated into its complex ethnic and class components (Kornblum, 1991).

Would not a criminological perspective on crime reject such partisanship, with the detached academic a servant to no master other than objective truth? Certainly this has been the dream of the scientific, positivist criminologists from Lombroso onwards, who take their model of science from the natural sciences (Dahl, 1985; Wilson and Herrnstein, 1985; Eysenck, 1977; Fishbein, 1990); yet this does not provide a simple solution. It is the concern of this volume to illustrate that, in many ways, conflicts about the definition of crime and how to control it are central to criminology as a discipline, and there can be no simple escape into a world of antiseptic, disinterested science. Science provides no refuge from politics.

The view of knowledge as an instrument of power was originally associated with the German philosopher Friedrich Nietzsche (Minson, 1985), Max Weber came close to this view also in arguing that there is no all-encompassing 'God's eye' view of the social world. Rather, knowledge always springs from an active and situated stance in society. Though Weber recommended that we do not subordinate scholarship to tub-thumping political prejudice, nevertheless, we cannot study without presuppositions or values; they give us a stake in the knowledge we produce and determine the meaningfulness of our objects of investigation (Weber, 1949).

More recently Michel Foucault has taken this further. For him, the criminologist, like the doctor, the teacher and other accredited professional workers, is a new type of 'specific' intellectual. The old-style 'universal' intellectual claimed to give voice to the otherwise inarticulate masses, being the conscience of the nation or perhaps of all humanity; his or her truths were presented as universal and binding

(Foucault, 1980a: 131). By contrast, the 'specific' intellectual, more modestly, produces knowledge within specific, delimited sectors. The production of truth by 'specific' intellectuals is best understood as a socially co-ordinated, technical process. This may offend our common sense because our dominant cultural images tend to present truth as *discovered* by the fearless *seeker*: the religious prophet, the brave, honest journalist or Sherlock Holmes-style detective hunting for clues. For Foucault, however, we should focus on the criteria which become established and legitimated for deciding on what *counts as truth* and *who has the right and status to speak it with acknowledged authority*. For example, the special authority of the professional truth makers is reinforced every time an expert in crime, economics, pollution or whatever, is wheeled on to the TV screen to give an instant comment on the media issue of the moment.

> 'Truth' is to be understood as a 'system of ordered procedures for the production, regulation, distribution, circulation and operation of statements'. (Foucault, 1980a: 133).

> 'Truth' is linked in a circular relation with systems of power which produce and sustain it.' (Foucault, 1980a: 133).

In this view, knowledge and power are twin sides of the same coin. All strategies which try to control the world around us involve the production of forms of knowledge; and all forms of knowledge, no matter how innocent or disinterested they may appear at first sight, are accompanied by strategies of control or power (Stenson and Gould, 1986).

Any attempt to produce an analysis of the *current* production of knowledge by criminologists as 'specific' intellectuals can only provide a tentative, broad-brush picture. It is clear that an exhaustive investigation of modern criminology as a knowledge-producing industry is beyond our scope here and more a topic for the historian with the benefit of long hindsight. Already impressive work in this vein has been done on the creative period of early criminology and the foundations of modern forms of penality and criminal justice, from the Victorian period to the First World War (Dahl, 1985; Garland, 1985, 1988). Foucault himself was less concerned with the narrow discipline of criminology than with explaining new forms of punishment. In particular, he was concerned with how the modern prison illustrates the emergence of new forms of power/knowledge based on systematic surveillance, and the attempt to transform the character and behaviour of the offender. This approach marks a significant move away from strategies of crime control in pre-modern, or less developed societies – for example in the Islamic world – which usually involve inflicting pain on the human body (Foucault, 1977; Souryal, 1988).

Criminology emerged as a part of this new penal process, particularly associated with programmes of liberal reform. Foucault's view of criminology as a 'learned' discipline was unflattering (Foucault, 1980b: 47). Its theories of criminal types, crime causation and so on and the associated reform programmes were inevitably associated, down the years, with 'failure' in the efforts to transform the criminal. Yet each failure became the occasion for new theories and new reform programmes. The real underlying function of these programmes and strategies was to make possible and to rationalise the ever extending reach of patterns of control through strategies of justice and welfare (Foucault, 1980b: 48; Cohen, 1985: 36).

Foucault's targets were the more traditionally 'scientific' forms of criminology. Yet his own studies and other work critical of the more naive goals of liberal reformism have given rise to a body of work more self-conscious of the history and present role of criminological knowledge and practice (Cohen, 1985; Garland, 1985, 1988; Harris and Webb, 1987). These applications of Foucault's theories resonate, from the libertarian Left, with the new conservative criminology's deep scepticism about any liberal reform programme (see Chapters 2, 3, 6 and 7). The pessimism generated by Foucaultian ideas, about any liberal reform measure, can have a paralysing effect which is not always justified, and the general thesis has been extensively debated (Garland and Young, 1983; Bottoms, 1983; Matthews, 1989b). This is not the place to repeat that debate or engage in interpretations of Foucault's texts in the manner of biblical scholarship, which would in any case be against the spirit of his lively and irreverent work. However, we should stress two points here.

First, the recent debates about the relevance of Foucault's theories have tended to equate the extension of crime control measures with a nightmare vision of a monolithic state, ever extending its tentacles of control. Stan Cohen's work excepted, this use of Foucault often consists of grafting his theories on to Marxist or neo-Marxist theories of the state. These theories tend to explain crime and criminal justice in terms of deeply institutionalized oppression in the social structure; the roots of the domination are envisaged to be the ruling capitalist class, patriarchy, institutionalized racism, heterosexism or some combination of all of them (Steinert, 1985; Scraton, 1990; Chapter 8; Sumner, 1990). This is odd, since Foucault specifically rejected this type of theorizing about power (Foucault, 1977, 1980a; 133; Stenson, 1986; Miller and Rose, 1988).

These neo-Marxist theories tend to identify power with a ready-made monolithic force, or *structure* of oppression. Knowledge or ideology are then seen as logically separate from and largely a reflection of that great structural force. These theorists, in essence, view knowledge, the way we make sense of the world, as an *effect* of power. On the contrary, it is precisely Foucault's argument that power and knowledge are inseparable. In this sense, Foucault opened the way to *post-structuralist* theories in social science. From this perspective, power is not seen as rooted in ready-made structures, but rather is an unfolding process in its own right. There are no simple engine rooms of power, whether in reified conceptions of the ruling class, patriarchy and so on. Rather, power is dispersed, it exists in the capillaries, the nooks and crannies spread across the whole terrain of society. Instead of a monolith of power, or coherent structure of oppression, we may equally envisage an increasing diversification and pluralization of the circuits of power, and an ever-increasing recognition and encouragement of individualization (Rose, 1990: 257–8; Stenson, 1989).

Secondly, the debates focus on images of power in its *negative* forms, in the forms of repression, oppression and censorship, plus the resistances against them. Certainly, this is one side of power, but Foucault was also anxious to stress the other side of power, that it is also *productive*. It creates new ways of making sense of the world and acting within it. The liberal forms of criminological theorizing and practice, like their new conservative counterparts, did not just offer a new way of interpreting what was happening, but also helped to change the world we live in, whether or not we welcome these changes.

In turn, radical and critical forms of theory and practice have had to adjust to those changing circumstances and in producing their own 'truths' and forms of political resistance, they have created their own circuits of power and knowledge. Thus our emphasis here is on the diverse ways that criminology creates truths, without necessarily endorsing the thesis that modern societies are coming to represent a prison writ large, or that our lives are tightly governed by an overarching, integrated *system* of oppressive power. The real world is more messy and capricious than any such model will allow for. And while many may feel that they are caught behind the bars of an unchanging cage, a Foucaultian perspective emphasizes how relations of power and knowledge produce a restless striving and constant change within modern societies. But let us consider more specifically the political frameworks within which modern criminology creates its forms of knowledge.

Criminology and circuits of power

Foucault argues that the sectors, or power circuits, where the criminologist (or any other 'specific' intellectual) produces knowledge are threefold (Foucault, 1980a; 132). In the first place there is his/her class position, for example whether they work in the service of the state, or in the United States particularly, for the major foundations like Rand or Ford which, with the National Institute for Justice and other government bodies, provide the major funding for research and hence for academic departments of criminology. Their counterparts in Europe, including for example the British Home Office and the Dutch Ministry of Justice, similarly provide the economic framework for the careers of criminologists and crime prevention and control practitioners and therefore secure the livelihoods of their families. This framework provides the most prestigious and probably the most financially rewarding route for the young hopeful of orthodox views.

However, the liberals and mavericks have their alternative, if more precarious, sectors, in which the ambitious can establish their careers and create their own status hierarchies. Included here are the think tanks and conference circuits of the New Right and their corporate sponsors (see Chapter 6). In addition there are, on the radical left and centre left, the institutions of higher education, particularly outside the elite universities, which provide a base for radical scholars. From these bases, they ally with radical progressive forces in organized labour, radicalized ethnic minority organizations, the women's movement and elsewhere (Young 1988a; Chapters 7, 8 and 9). This has been specially significant in Britain, where radical criminology has bloomed and where left and centre left urban local authorities, run by the Labour Party, have financed local victim surveys, and critical research on the police and justice system (Young, 1988a).

Foucault's second sector includes the criminologist's conditions of life and work as an intellectual. That is the field of research, the intellectual's place in the academy, the political and economic demands to which he/she submits or against which he/she rebels, in the university or other place of work (Foucault, 1980a; 132). While connected to political processes in the outside world and in the criminal justice systems, the academic world has its own arenas of political struggle, where knives flash in the deadly competition for survival and success. As in other professions, there is a tendency for people to coalesce into tribe-like groupings, with tribal chiefs and followers, key – sacred – texts, lines of patronage and gatekeeping (Becher, 1986). The forms of social organization are complex, but let us briefly note that the mavericks, who feel excluded from the mainstream power brokers in the elite academies, professional associations, conference trails and the more prestigious, refereed journals, respond by creating their own academic power circuits. These include their own journals, conferences, series of radical texts (in which friends reference each others' work) and in more subtle ways, their own networks of friendship and professional influence to assist in the advancement of their careers. They also include the now-familiar black and women's caucuses at mainstream conferences. These aim to break down resistance to stigmatized groups and stigmatized, radical forms of social science knowledge.

Radicals have to pay their bills like everyone else and have the same range of human emotions. It is doubtful that they are less egocentric, or less motivated by the drive for academic success, than are orthodox criminologists. For example, Radford and Stanko (Chapter 9) warn of the way in which radical scholarship can be parasitic on feminist struggles outside the academy.

Foucault's third sector is, more broadly, the politics of truth in the wider society. The assumption is that any society has a dominant

> regime of truth, its 'general politics' of truth: that is, the types of discourse which it accepts and makes function as true; the mechanisms and instances which enable one to distinguish true and false statements, the means by which each is sanctioned; the techniques and procedures accorded value in the acquisition of truth; the status of those who are charged with saying what counts as true. (Foucault, 1980a: 131)

These three sectors are arenas of conflict. The struggles to define what is real and true and about who has the status and clout to be taken seriously are never-ending. This applies within myriad, localized areas of knowledge, as well as in the general, public context. It is the third sector which provides the greatest prize for the criminologist. It is here, in the broad public arena, that it may be possible to influence the public's understandings of the nature of crime and how it might be dealt with.

For criminology to take and maintain its place within the dominant regime of truth, it must meet essential formal criteria. In modern society, to gain credibility, the knowledge of the specific intellectual must conform with the rubrics of science. High status knowledge often assumes a mathematical, quantitative form. To get past the referees, who are the gatekeepers of the major journals, and also the mass media, it helps if research reports analyse data from respectable-sized samples, using currently acceptable statistical techniques, theories and methods of proof (Cohn and Farrington, 1990). This kind of work is expensive and requires funding from the major agencies. Having one's research proposals accepted usually means getting past gatekeepers drawn from the same intellectual community who draw up those criteria in the first place; and best favoured will be the proposals from those who make those rules, in a spiralling, self-validating circle (Clear, 1991). However, while particular schools may predominate at any one time, knowledge is rarely sewn up on a permanent basis. We are currently witnessing a great struggle between the new conservatives who have had the upper hand since the mid-1970s and the emerging liberal/social democratic consensus on both sides of the Atlantic who, once more, wish to seize the high ground and define the meaning of crime and the agenda for its control (see Chapters 2, 3 and 7; Currie, 1989).

But what are the implications for understanding the production of truth in academic criminology and in the processes of criminal justice? It is important not to see the relation between the former and the latter in terms of a relation between theory and practice, with the academic intellectual providing the theory and the professional practitioner engaging in unreflective practice on police patrol, or making law in the courtroom and other arenas. Rather, theory and practice are inter-woven in all these contexts. The intellectual and practical production of the truths of crime operate in the academy and in every dimension of criminal justice.

To give one example, Hobbs' graphic account of policing in London's East End shows how, collaboratively, detectives turn their experiences of complex real-life events, like chasing a burglar or getting a confession from a thief or fence, into legally acceptable, homogenized and effective paper documents (Hobbs, 1988: 193). This intellectual work is a vital linkage which helps to legitimize the whole process of criminal justice. It feeds through into later stages of the power circuits of the justice 'system': the district attorney (or equivalent prosecuting authority), the courts and corrections.

How might this power/knowledge model apply to the criminology of the academy, considered in its more narrowly theoretical sense? Before considering the major debates between liberals and conservatives, let us focus on the mavericks on the sidelines. Not only do they try to open up our common-sense notions of what constitutes crime and crime control, but they also create different ways of conceptualizing the criminal *and* victims as human subjects (Walklate, 1989).

Criminological mavericks

In the 1940s, Sutherland urged that criminology devote more attention to white-collar crimes, particularly committed in the course of work within the corporate hierarchy. Such activities as black marketeering, fraud, anti-trust violations, violations of factory safety codes, in-dustrial pollution and so on are often regulated – or self-regulated – by administrative or civil, rather than criminal, law. But given the damage they do to the social fabric, they merit the same level of attention by criminologists as the crimes of the poor (Sutherland, 1983). There has been a growth in academic interest in this field in recent years (Box, 1983; Braithwaite, 1984; Levi, 1989, 1991; Hagan, 1987; Clarke, 1990). Moreover, the landmark prosecution of the Ford Motor Company for reckless homicide over the affair of the unsafe Ford Pinto (Cullen et al., 1987) and recent trials on both sides of the Atlantic of junk bond kings, insider traders and other stock market fraudsters, have indicated a growing readiness by regulatory authorities to use the criminal sanction against high-status offenders and the corporations themselves as legal entities. Yet, given the preoccupation of the criminal justice systems of the advanced societies with low-status offenders, the moves against white-collar and corporate crime remain sporadic and un-crystallized (Cullen et al., 1987: 353). However, in challenging the usual ways in which white-collar crime is normalized away, they open up the possibility of seeing 'respectable' citizens and corporations as criminal or deviant subjects. This is a subversive redrawing of the boundaries between saints and sinners.

However, these particular maverick discourses involve *extending the reach of the criminal law*, as do some versions of feminist discourse (see Chapter 9) which have helped stimulate greater recognition by the law of 'crimes' within the hitherto designated 'private' spheres of domestic and sexual relations. This has redefined and put the official spotlights on child abuse, assaults on homosexuals, sexual harassment, rape and, more generally, male violence. Traditionally, male-dominated police institutions were reluctant to tread into this psychologically threatening minefield. Yet most maverick discourses are concerned to *restrict the reach of the criminal* law. The more libertarian strands of feminism react sceptically to the new interest by officialdom in the USA, Canada, the UK and elsewhere, in these areas of behaviour. In addition to insisting on the right of women to devise their own methods of response, we can also see here a feminist challenge to mainstream criminological conceptions of the subjectivity of both victims and offenders. Rejecting traditional views which accept the abnormal irrationality and pathology of rape and other forms of male violence, now male violence is seen as part of a *rational* technology of control, normal within patriarchy (Brownmiller, 1975; Hanmer et al., 1989). In addition, rather than seeing female victims as eliciting violence, the blame is placed squarely on men.

A parallel debate has emerged over the recognition of and attempts to control racial attacks on ethnic and racial minorities, particularly in Britain and mainland Europe, where consciousness of such attacks is escalating, as is criticism of allegedly inadequate police response to such attacks (Bowling, 1990a; Albrecht, 1991). This provides an echo of similar concerns in the 1930s and 1940s and indeed the present, over anti-Semitic attacks (Factor and Stenson, 1989). We can see here a recurrent theme in much maverick discourse, which stresses the rationality of both victim and offender, in contrast to more traditional, determinist, 'scientific' approaches to the explanation of offending vulnerability to victimization (Walklate, 1989).

As the initial summaries of the chapters of this volume have indicated, many mavericks, on both the Right and Left, in different ways reject the alchemy of legal conceptions of crime, that they somehow correspond to a homogenized field of threats, which have to be dealt with through the institutions of law and criminal justice. Most mavericks, like the abolitionists, prefer to manage social problems and conflicts within the social contexts in which they emerge (see Chapter 10). In this sense, they reflect the growing disillusionment across the political spectrum in most of the advanced societies in the 1970s and 1980s about the effectiveness of 'top-down', centralized controls and policies, created by politicians and 'experts' for public consumption and implementation. Libertarians on the New Right (see Chapter 6), the libertarians and other radicals of the new social movements for emancipation of women, gays, ethnic minorities and so on, and dissident intellectuals of the communist bloc, borrowed each others' intellectual clothes in arguing for a diminution of the powers of the state and centralized, unresponsive bureaucracies.

The notions that 'small is beautiful' and that social control, the provision of social care, economic development and other essential processes could often be better performed by and within the 'community' of creative, free citizens, came to enjoy wide appeal. This individualism which flowered so colourfully in the 1960s, unleashed a major revival of the subterranean but still vigorous traditions of nineteenth-century anarchist thought. These ideas are difficult to classify in the familiar Left–Right – or socialist versus capitalist – political categories bequeathed to us by the French revolutionaries of 1789 and nineteenth-century socialist movements (Taylor, 1982).

The abolitionists of the Netherlands and Scandinavia (see Chapter 10) illustrate the anarchist dimension of maverick discourse most clearly. For the most radical abolitionists, the logical aim is a decentralized, anarchistic utopia, where social policy and community initiatives replace criminal justice and the destructive effects of incarceration altogether. But, in practice, that is recognized as an elusive dream; rather, the strategic goals should be the erosion of criminal justice through decriminalization, diversion, mediation and restitution (see Chapter 10; Matthews 1988; Pelikan, 1991). To this end, it can be argued that social crime prevention, especially with young people, would be more effective than crime control strategies in the narrow sense.

In this book, Boyd and Lowman, in discussing the varieties of crime control strategies for dealing with prostitution and mind-altering drugs, provide a critique of the mainstream criminalization of these behaviours, which echoes the libertarianism of the abolitionists. In the search for alternatives to the 'war against drugs' with its military and punitive connotations and singular lack of tangible success (Dorn and South, 1991), considerable interest is being shown in decriminalization strategies, particularly as practised in the Netherlands (see also Chapter 10). This approach, while falling short of full legalization, tries to regulate drug use and distribution, and provide health care and education from the public purse for those in trouble.

What underlies this strategy, and similar strategies for controlling prostitution, is a left libertarian belief that the law should interfere minimally, if at all, with personal hedonism and the individual rights to self-expression. In a better world, should these behaviours be classified as crimes at all? In this vision, the rational and expressive individual is seen as logically and morally prior to social relations. This is a view which echoes strongly among libertarians of the right, as Tame (Chapter 6) demonstrates. In disentangling the complex strands of political discourse, conventionally labelled as the 'New Right', Tame distinguishes the 'natural rights' libertarians, who insist on the fundamental rights of the individual to self-actualization and property. This leads to a view of what may legitimately be defined as crime, and presumably this criterion may be applied as a critical tool and litmus test to any existing legal system. Crime should only be defined in terms of an invasion of property or person, for example through violence. This provides a warrant for decriminalizing or legalizing a range of victimless crimes (logically not crimes at all), including the distribution of pornography and drug use and trading.

The gap between right and left libertarianism becomes evident in the right-wing insistence on retributive punishment for 'real' crimes and a denial of social science explanations for crime. In fact the crime explosion is largely blamed on the 'excuse-making' industry of social science and social welfare. But the implications for crime control are not exhausted by draconian state retribution. Since the state should retreat to a minimal role and eschew welfare, there is much scope for private law enforcement, restitution, privatized prisons and so on (Matthews, 1989a). However, much store is placed on a remoralization of society; in other words, a reliance on effective moral education and self-discipline, replacing 'state power' with 'social power'.

From a more explicitly neo-Marxist standpoint, Scraton and Chadwick (Chapter 8) reinforce critiques of American and British New Right rhetoric on crime, which evolved during the years of the Reagan and Thatcher administrations. Like the libertarian mavericks, they also see the notion of 'crime' as an ideological mask which abstracts from wider social problems. These are seen to emanate from the crises of advanced capitalist societies. Their focus on the way that a variety of minority groups are stigmatized through 'criminalization' draws on the libertarian ideas crystallized in the labelling theories of the 1960s.

However, while this neo-Marxist perspective shares with libertarian mavericks allied to the radical social movements and the New Right a view of the individual as expressive and rational, it does smuggle in an important qualification.

This is the view, which can be traced back to Marx himself, that there is nothing very rational about crime (particularly intra-class crime) by the poor and the working class. For example, street crime is the result of brutalization, is reactionary, divisive by race and gender and a betrayal of the true interests of the proletariat (Quinney, 1977). The libertarian insistence on the rationality of the criminal and this Marxist recognition of irrationality remains a contradiction.

The perspective represented by Scraton and Chadwick is an uncompromising challenge to official conceptions of crime and crime control. Additionally, in claiming to carry the torch of the radical criminology tradition, the neo-Marxists are sharply critical of their erstwhile colleagues in the Left Realist school (see Chapter 7), who have moved to a gentler, reformist middle ground within the political mainstream. They accuse the Left Realists of being seduced by the law and order crusade and accepting the dominant legal conceptions of crime and the picture of crime presented by the official statistics (particularly in relation to black crime rates) too uncritically.

However, with the Left Realists, we are moving here to the bridge between maverick discourses and the liberal and social democratic centre ground of mainstream criminological debates. Since, for criminologists to be taken seriously, to gain access to the mass media and the ears of the policy makers in government and the major political parties, to obtain *serious* funding for research and, perhaps incidentally, to enhance their careers and earning potential, it helps if they speak a language which is intelligible to the key decision and policy makers, and within the terms of the major alternative political discourses of democratic society (Norton, 1984).

Debates of the mainstream

The politics of crime prevention and control, in its everyday sense, has mainly revolved around well-worn arguments about how best to deal with the crimes of the poor and especially of violent, young males. Debates about what to do about crime, have for many years, followed familiar political divisions on the left–right continuum. Where crime causation is still of interest – and interest waned during the 1970s and 1980s – conservatives tend to emphasize biological factors, poor parenting, especially by single parents, and a collapse or blurring of the major moral boundaries, particularly linked with the decline of religion (Wilson and Herrnstein, 1985). The liberals on the centre left are more likely to emphasize economic and social deprivation and the oppressive treatment of the poor and powerless by the criminal justice agencies.

However, this gloss on a complex debate hardly does justice to subtle shifts which have occurred and are occurring in the liberal and conservative positions. The rare debate we reproduce in this volume, between, respectively, the most influential voices on the liberal democratic Left and the conservative Right of American criminology, Elliott Currie and James Q. Wilson, provides an excellent entry point to a difficult but important debate. This author hesitates to summarize the debate, since the arguments are incisively put by the two eminent criminologists. Rather than enter this dangerous ring, it is wiser to let readers judge for themselves. But it is, perhaps, worth providing some of the background. Wilson emphasizes his distance from the traditional punitive, conservative approaches to crime, exemplified by Nixon's law and order rhetoric, in addition to what he sees as the failed liberalism of the 1960s. He only advocates punishment which is fitting to the crime and effective. Thus, the priorities are police effectiveness and the certainty of punishment. But government and the criminal justice system should humbly accept the limitations of official intervention. Informal community controls are more important than official ones and, where the local community structures have crumbled, official intervention should be directed towards bolstering community controls (Wilson and Kelling, 1982).

It is important to stress that these ideas did not develop in an academic vacuum. The key new architects of conservative theory, including von Hirsch (1976) and Wilson himself, were also active participants in the power circuits in the state legislatures, within the funding agencies and elsewhere, in shifting policy away from rehabilitation and indeterminate sentencing, towards a tighter relationship between crimes and particular, deterrent and incapacitating tariffs of punishment (Clear, 1991). This illustrates the close interconnections of power and criminological knowledge at the highest levels and how scientific fact and theory is produced by a political process (Latour and Woolgar, 1979). In Britain, too, during the Conservative 1980s, the Home Office (the ministry responsible for criminal justice) became almost the monopoly supplier of funding for mainstream research. This led to frequent complaints that this was distorting the shape of criminological knowledge; more open-ended enquiry was driven out by research tied to the policy agenda of the Conservative government.

This new conservative climate, in shifting the focus away from large-scale inequalities, also shifted attention towards individual differences and the factors which allegedly distinguish the most anti-social 'career criminals' from other citizens (Blumstein et al., 1987). Where liberal policies are off limits, it is politically useful to depict the criminal subject as radically different from the respectable subject; it raises the possibility of more precisely focused and cost-effective crime prevention and control policies. In the US, as in much of Europe, this move is associated increasingly with the creative expansion of the relatively cheap range of sanctions between prison and probation (Morris and Tonry, 1990; Lilley, 1990).

Furthermore, this focusing on the individual offender has created innovations of major significance. Now, in many US states, decision making in jails, probation departments and in the courts is based on scientific assessments of the predicted behaviour of defendants. On the basis of individual records and wider criminological research, offenders are assessed in terms of their vulnerability to victimization, amenability to treatment, suicide proneness and so on (Gottfredson and Tonry, 1987). All these criminological developments have been influential on policy during the Reagan and Bush years – perhaps with the major exception of the 'war against drugs' – and given Wilson's prestige within British policy-making circles, the influence of some of these ideas can clearly be seen in recent British crime prevention and control policies.

The emphasis has been on reducing the opportunities for crime through 'target hardening' and other situational factors (see Chapter 3), in addition to the stimulation of more natural and organic controls within the community (Young, 1986, 1988b and Chapters 3 and 4). But, of course, these are strategies proposed by groups at various points of the political spectrum, *not just by the Right*. Already by the mid-1980s Stan Cohen was able to demonstrate expertly the complexities of the shift towards community crime prevention and control and the difficulties of explaining those changes in terms of traditional categories or polarized debates (Cohen, 1985). We should not underestimate the cross-fertilization of thinking which has impacted on these policy innovations. Yet, more pertinently, the desperate search for solutions to unprecedented waves of prison riots and the enormous expense of incarceration have been an important check on the more traditional conservative 'flog 'em and lock 'em up' approach to crime control.

As we have begun to see, but have not the space to explore fully here, the twists and turns and cross-fertilizations of criminological discourses do not always fit neatly into the slots provided by traditional political argument. This must be disappointing for those who want criminological discourses to line up neatly into two moral universes, as in an old western movie, with the white and black hats confronting each other over a clearly drawn boundary. As Chapters 5 and 10 make clear, traditionally liberal Dutch penal policy – which cannot be characterized as abolitionist – is particularly open to a range of libertarian policy initiatives (see also Downes, 1988). In Britain, while there has been no mass conversion to abolitionism or right libertarianism within the Conservative administration, some themes which have crept into criminal justice policy and practice do not look out of place in abolitionist or libertarian right discourses. Mediation, diversion, community service and restitution are now vogue terms (Marshall, 1988, 1990). The new Criminal Justice Bill, currently going through parliament, proposes a 'twin-track' policy for sentencing: tough, retributive and deterrent sentences for serious, particularly violent, criminals, and as far as possible, lighter and preferably non-custodial sentences for the mass of trivial offenders, who currently pack the crumbling Victorian prison system.

But while innovative in certain fields, by the late 1980s, the new conservative criminology, which had supplanted the allegedly failed liberal theories of the 1960s, was itself beginning to acquire the taint of failure. According to Currie and Young (Currie, 1989; Young, 1988a and in this volume), the dramatic rises in crime rates, manifested both in official crime rates and in national and local crime victim surveys, in continued rises in the rates of incarceration (but see Pease, 1991; Schlesinger 1987), the continued epidemics of drug use and associated gang wars, have all demonstrated the failure of the new conservatism. It is alleged that this failure is part of a much deeper failure of New Right social and economic policies (Currie, 1989, 1990), perhaps throughout the English-speaking world, where these policies were adopted with most enthusiasm during the 1980s and whose great cities are now paying a heavy price in terms of economic and social dislocation (Taylor, 1990; Wilson, 1987).

Conclusion – Redefining the liberal/social democratic agenda

However, the changes wrought by the new conservative criminology also demonstrated the need to reconstruct and update liberal models, in the light of available research on what does and does not work. Whereas the new conservative model, dubbed by Young (1986, 1988a, 1988b) 'administrative criminology', led to a gloomy view that for the most part official interventions do not work, the revamped liberalism is more optimistic. Currie recognizes that, in fragmentary form, the conservatives have some good arguments. Old-style liberalism was often blind to the role of the individual and the family. It sometimes failed to see the dangers in drug abuse and failed to recognize the importance of a good, supportive family environment in protecting children from engaging in anti-social conduct and helping them to achieve at school. Taking these insights on board would involve, for example, proper collective funding for pre-school programmes of proven worth, for parents and children (Currie, 1985, 1989).

But, a traditional liberal theme of continued relevance, is the need for economic regeneration in the cities to combat deindustrialization, rather than relying on capricious market forces. The latter have at best provided dead-end, low-paid jobs for the poor. They will not provide a breadwinning wage, nor dignity for the potentially violent young male. In all, the agenda moves way beyond the narrow issue of crime control, in the hands of self-interested professionals, towards a multi-faceted strategy of prevention and control interventions, from the individual and family levels to social and economic policies which tackle the larger inequalities held to provide fertile soil for criminality (Currie, 1989: 11).

There are close parallels in the work of the British Left Realists (see Chapter 7; and Schwartz, 1990). They are committed to the close monitoring of crime prevention and control schemes, particularly those which operate through local, democratically elected government. They have pioneered the use of local crime victim surveys in radical local authorities, as a democratic means to uncover local priorities for crime control, and have, with the police, local authorities and a range of other agencies, engaged in action research crime prevention and control projects in London and elsewhere. But the emphasis on well-co-ordinated, multi-agency interventions indicates that the concern with crime control is only one element in a wider programme of policies to deal with the family and community disorganization. Moreover, as committed and influential advisers to the British Labour Party, their crime prevention and control policies are only part of a much larger agenda of redistributive social democratic policies (Lea and Young, 1984). As with Currie's own shifts since the early days of 1960s radicalism, Young and the other left realists have moved towards the centre ground of reformist politics. This signals a challenge to the claims that conservatives now articulate the prevailing moral consensus; social democrats hold out the prospect of the conservatives losing their grip on the hearts and minds of the majority (Stenson and Brearley, 1991).

In competing for the high ground of the criminological *regime of truth* – the criminological and social policy consensus, where the stakes are high indeed – there is an emerging intellectual consensus between liberals in Europe and in North America. But there are rocks on which this consensus might founder. Developing European integration will create new challenges for crime prevention and control, particularly in the ethnically sensitive areas of immigration and border control (Kattau, 1990). So far, this is a terrain dominated by the policies of the Right, responsive as they are to the fears of the white, European working classes, about possible 'invasion' and criminal attack by peoples from impoverished countries to the east and south. For the social democratic Left to enter the big league of policy making, may draw it inexorably towards the Right in this and other areas.

But this will surely widen rifts between them and some of the more maverick voices we have been considering. We have already noted the criticisms of the neo-Marxists (Chapter 8). Radical feminists and the remaining communitarians, in particular, will baulk at the way that a positive programme of support for the nuclear family is steadily ascending the liberal/social democratic policy agenda. Will this reinforce, if inadvertently, the right-wing view that the single parent family nurtures the violent and disturbed street criminal? But more profoundly, the move towards a new liberal/social democratic consensus may necessitate a shift away from a utilitarian individualism shared by policy makers and criminologists in the English-speaking world (Marquand, 1988).

This individualism is shared in varying forms across the political spectrum, and includes the maverick Right, some traditional conservatives and left libertarians. At root, the individual criminal is depicted as making a rational, moral decision in engaging in a criminal act. But like the pioneer social scientists of Chicago between the world wars (Bulmer, 1984), liberals and social democrats now recognize the crucial interplay between the home and wider community environment in influencing the formation of character and the predisposition towards crime. This indicates that they may be moving away from the rational and expressive view of the criminal subject shared by libertarian mavericks, both right and left. Furthermore, this signals a return to the recognition that much crime is symptomatic of personal and social pathology, in relation to the norms of conduct required in a civilized society (Stenson and Brearley, 1991). This may apply as much to upperworld as to lowerworld deviancy. The guilt-free narcissism and worship of greed among the new-money elites of the 1980s, which was neatly captured in the movie 'Wall Street', were essential counterparts to the Reaganite and Thatcherite espousal of the 'enterprise culture'. Perhaps this kind of unbridled, macho egoism is what binds the mugger in the street with the sharply dressed fraudster.

Moreover, in a number of countries, the libertarian reluctance to view human conduct as pathological and in need of treatment and control, has played a part in the dismantling of institutional care for the mentally disturbed, along with other factors, such as shifting residential patterns and cuts in welfare budgets by conservative administrations. 'Community care' provisions have not kept pace with these changes and governmental and professional responsibilities for the plight of these unfortunate people are often ill-defined and confused. This has produced a growing population which drifts between mental hospitals, prisons and homelessness on skid row (Scull, 1984; Dear and Wolch, 1987). The emerging liberal/social democratic consensus prioritizes the need for a more coherent, integrated collective response to these problems.

The concern with multi-agency interventions can be seen as a – hopefully less patronizing – echo of policies pursued with the poor earlier in this century. The combination of social insurance, welfare/ social work and correctional policies were an attempt to create new types of civilized and self-directing citizens (Garland, 1985; Miller and Rose, 1988; Stenson, 1989). The nettle to be grasped by social democrats is that it is too dangerous to leave the production of individual character to the whims of parents alone or other unaccountable educators. In various ways social collectivities, from ethnic organizations to the state, must assume more responsibility for the task (Dingwall et al., 1983) and also pick up more of the tab at a preventive stage. This would be sound investment, given the community costs caused by crime further down the line.

As King reminds us (Chapter 4), French versions of social democracy are founded on a social myth which contrasts with Anglo-Saxon individualism. Instead of the individual being the logical starting point for society, rather *society,* conceived of as a reality which goes beyond the individuals which make it up, is the true starting point, and our individual characters are, to a degree, a product of this society. This view, the legacy of Rousseau and Durkheim (Stenson and Brearley, 1991), emphasizes that we are not floating social atoms. Rather – and despite the competition between us – we are all bound up in each others' lives, rich and poor, black and white, male and female. Moreover, we bear a moral responsibility for each others' welfare and behaviour. As King argues, in Britain, Conservative rhetoric presents the young criminal as evil and separate from the body of society. By contrast, in the more progressive French crime prevention programmes, in the hands of local bodies representative of varied community interests, the wayward young are seen as within the fold, a problem to be dealt with within, so to speak, the family of society. A criminology guided by this social myth would view with suspicion academic and control strategies whose main function is to create, in symbols and reality, a population of folk devils, cast out from the community of saints.

References

Albrecht, H. (1991) 'Ethnic minorities: crime and criminal justice in Europe', in F. Heidensohn and M. Farrell (eds), *Crime in Europe*, London/New York: Routledge.

Becher, T. (1986) *Gatekeeper, Academic Tribes and Territories, Intellectual Enquiry and the Cultures of Disciplines.* Milton Keynes: Open University Press.

Bienkowska, E. (1991) 'Crime in Eastern Europe', in F. Heidensohn and M. Farrell (eds), *Crime in Europe.* London/New York: Routledge.

Blumstein, A., Cohen, J., Roth, J.A. and Visher, C.A. (eds) (1987) *Criminal Careers and 'Career Criminals'* Vol. 1. Washington DC: National Academy Press.

Bottoms, A (1983) 'Neglected features of contemporary penal systems', in D. Garland and P. Young (eds), *The Power to Punish.* London: Heinemann.

Bowling, B. (1990a) 'Racial harassment and the process of victimisation: methodological implications for the local crime survey'. Paper presented to the Realist Criminology Conference, Simon Fraser University, Vancouver, Canada, May.

Bowling, B (1990b) 'Conceptual and methodological problems in measuring "race" differences in delinquency – a reply to Marianne Junger', *British Journal of Criminology*, 30(4): 483–92.

Box, S. (1983) *Power, Crime and Mystification.* London: Tavistock.

Box, S. (1987) *Recession, Crime and Punishment.* Basingstoke: Macmillan.

Braithwaite, J. (1984) *Corporate Crime in the Pharmaceutical Industry.* London: Routledge and Kegan Paul.

Brantingham, P.L. (1989) 'Crime prevention: the North American experience', in D.J. Evans and D.T. Herbet (eds), *The Geography of Crime.* London/New York: Routledge.

Brogden, M., Jefferson, T. and Walklate, S. (1988) *Introducing Policework.* London: Unwin Hyman.

Brownmiller, S. (1975) *Against Our Will: Men, Women and Rape.* London: Secker and Warburg.

Bulmer, M. (1984) *The Chicago School of Sociology.* Chicago: Chicago University Press.

Chapman, D. (1968) *Sociology and the Stereotype of the Criminal.* London: Tavistock.

Clarke, M. (1990) *Business Crime, Its Nature and Control.* Cambridge: Polity.

Clear, T. (1991) 'American criminologists and the offender control movement of the 1980s'. Paper presented to the Department of Social Science and Administration Seminar, London School of Economics, February 1991.

Clegg, S.R. (1989) *Frameworks of Power.* London: Sage.

Cohen, P. (1981) 'Policing the working class city', in M. Fitzgerald et al. (eds), *Crime and Society, Readings in History and Theory.* London: Routledge and Kegan Paul.

Cohen, S. (1980) *Folk Devils and Moral Panics. The Creation of the Mods and Rockers.* Oxford: Martin Robertson.

Cohen, S. (1985) *Visions of Social Control.* Cambridge: Polity.

Cohn, E.G. and Farrington, D.P. (1990) 'Differences between American and British criminology. An analysis of citations', *British Journal of Criminology*, 30(4): 467–82.

Crawford, A., Jones, T., Woodhouse, T. and Young, J. (1990) *Second Islington Crime Survey.* London: Centre for Criminology, Middlesex Polytechnic.

Cullen, F.T., Maakestad, W.J. and Cavender, G. (1987) *Corporate Crime under Attack. The Ford Pinto Case and Beyond.* Cincinnati: Anderson.

Currie, E. (1985) *Confronting Crime: An American Challenge.* New York: Pantheon.

Currie, E. (1989) 'Confronting crime: Looking toward the twenty-first century', *Justice Quarterly*, 6(1): 5–25.

Currie, E. (1990) 'Crime and market society – lessons from the United States'. Paper delivered to the Crime and Policing Conference, London Borough of Islington, November 1990.

Dahl, T.S. (1985) *Child Welfare and Social Defence.* Oslo: Norwegian University Press.

Dear, M. and Wolch, J. (1987) *Landscapes of Despair - from Deinstitutionalisation to Homelessness,* Cambridge: Polity.

van Dijk, P. (1991) 'More than a matter of security: trends in crime prevention in Europe', in F. Heidensohn and M. Farrell (eds), *Crime in Europe.* London/New York: Routledge.

van Dijk, P., Mayhew, M. and Killias, M. (1990) *Experiences of Crime across the World. Key Findings from the 1989 International Crime Survey.* Deventer/Boston: Kluwer Law and Taxation Publishers.

Dingwall, R., Eekalar, J. and Murray, T. (1983) *The Protection of Children, State Intervention and Family Life.* Oxford: Blackwell.

Dorn, N. and South, N. (1991) 'After Mr Bennett and Mr Bush: US foreign policy and the prospects for drug control', in F. Pearce and M. Woodiwiss (eds), *Global Connections.* London: Lumière/Macmillan.

Downes, D. (1988) *Contrasts in Tolerance.* Oxford: Clarendon Press.

Elias, N. (1939/1982) *State Formation and Civilization - The Civilizing Process,* Vol. 2. Oxford: Blackwell.

Eysenck, H.J. (1977) *Crime and Personality.* London: Routledge and Kegan Paul.

Factor, F. and Stenson, K. (1989) 'Community control and the policing of Jewish youth'. Paper presented to the British Criminology Conference, Bristol Polytechnic, July.

Fishbein, D.H. (1990) 'Biological approaches in criminology', *Criminology,* 28(1): 27-72.

Foucault, M. (1977) *Discipline and Punish.* London: Penguin.

Foucault, M. (1980a) 'Truth and power', in C. Gordon (ed.), *Michel Foucault, Power/ Knowledge - Selected Interviews and Other Writings 1972-1977.* Brighton: Harvester.

Foucault, M. (1980b) 'Prison Talk' in C. Gordon (ed.), *Michel Foucault, Power/ Knowledge - Selected Interviews and other Writings 1972-1977.* Brighton: Harvester.

Galliher, J.E. (1989) *Criminology: Human Rights, Criminal Law, and Crime.* New York: Prentice-Hall.

Garland, D. (1985) *Punishment and Welfare.* Aldershot: Gower.

Garland, D. (1988) 'British criminology before 1935' in P. Rock (ed.), *A History of British Criminology.* Oxford: Clarendon.

Garland, D. and Young, P. (eds) (1983) *The Power to Punish.* London: Heinemann.

Gilroy, P. (1987) *There aint No Black in the Union Jack.* London: Hutchinson.

Gottfredson, D.M. and Tonry, M. (eds) (1987) *Prediction and Classification Criminal Justice Decision-making, Crime and Justice, A Review of Research,* Vol. 9. Chicago: University of Chicago Press.

Hagan, J. (1987) *Modern Criminology - Crime, Criminal Behaviour and Its Control.* New York: McGraw-Hill.

Hall, R. (1985) *Ask any Woman: A London Inquiry into Rape and Sexual Assault.* Bristol: Falling Wall Press.

Hall, S., Critcher, C., Jefferson, T., Clarke, J. and Roberts, B. (1978) *Policing the Crisis.* London: Macmillan.

Hanmer, J.J. Radford and Stanko, E. (1989) *Women, Policing and Male Violence - International Perspectives.* London: Routledge.

Hanmer, J. and Saunders, S. (1984) *Well Founded Fear.* London: Hutchinson.

Harris, R. and Webb, D. (1987) *Welfare, Power and Juvenile Justice.* London: Tavistock.

Heidensohn, F. (1989) *Crime and Society.* Basingstoke: Macmillan.

von Hirsch, A. (1976/1986) *Doing Justice: the Choice of Punishments.* Evanston: Northeastern University Press.

Hirst, P.Q. (1986) *Law, Socialism and Democracy.* London: Allen and Unwin.

Hobbs, D. (1988) *Doing the Business – Entrepreneurship, the Working Class, and Detectives in the East End of London.* Oxford: Oxford University Press.

Hough, M. and Mayhew, P. (1985) *Taking Account of Crime: Key Findings from the Second British Crime Survey.* Home Office Research Study No. 85. London: HMSO.

Jones, G. Stedman (1971) *Outcaste London: A Study in the Relationship between Classes in Victorian Society.* Oxford: Clarendon Press.

Junger, M. (1989) 'Ethnic minorities, crime and public policy', in R. Hood (ed.), *Crime and Policy in Europe.* Oxford: Centre for Criminological Research, University of Oxford.

Kattau, T. (1990) '1992 – Europe without frontiers'. Paper delivered to the Crime and Policing Conference, London Borough of Islington, November 1990.

Keith, M. and Murji, K. (1990) 'Reifying, legitimising racism: policing, local authorities and left realism', in W. Ball and J. Solomos (eds), *Race and Local Politics.* London: Macmillan.

Kornblum, W. (1991) 'Mean streets', *New Statesman and Society,* 3(135).

Latour, B. and Woolgar, S. (1979) *Laboratory Life.* Beverly Hills: Sage.

Laclau, E. and Mouffe, C. (1985) *Hegemony and Socialist Strategy.* London: Verso.

Lea, J. and Young, J. (1984) *What Is to Be Done about Law and Order?* London: Penguin.

Levi, M. (1989) 'Fraudulent justice? Sentencing the business criminal', in P. Carlen and D. Cook (eds), *Paying for Crime.* Milton Keynes: Open University Press.

Levi, M. (1991) 'Developments in business crime control in Europe', in F. Heidensohn and M. Farrell (eds), *Crime in Europe.* London/New York: Routledge.

Lilley, J.R. (1990) 'Tagging reviewed', *Howard Review,* 29(4): 229–45.

Marquand, D. (1988) *The Unprincipled Society.* London: Jonathan Cape.

Marshall, T.F. (1988) 'Informal justice: the British experience', in R. Matthews (ed.), *Informal Justice?* London: Sage.

Marshall, T.F. (1990) 'Mediation, reparation and criminal justice: the findings of the Home Office research project'. Paper delivered to the British Society of Criminology, October.

Matthews, R. (ed.) (1988) *Informal Justice?* London: Sage.

Matthews, R. (ed.) (1989a) *Privatizing Criminal Justice.* London: Sage.

Matthews, R. (1989b) 'Alternatives to and in prisons: a realist approach', in P. Carlen and D. Cook (eds), *Paying for Crime.* Milton Keynes: Open University Press.

Matza, D. (1969) *Becoming Deviant.* New Jersey: Prentice-Hall.

Mawby, R. (1990) *Comparative Policing Issues, The British and American Experience in International Perspective.* London: Unwin Hyman.

Mayhew, P., Elliot, D. and Dowds, D. (1989) *The 1988 British Crime Survey – Home Office Research Study No 111.* London: Her Majesty's Stationery Office.

Miller, P. and Rose, N. (1988) 'The Tavistock programme: the government of subjectivity and social life', *Sociology,* 22(2): 171–92.

Minson, J. (1985) *Genealogies of Morals. Nietzsche, Foucault, Donzelot and the Eccentricity of Ethics.* Basingstoke: Macmillan.

Monkkonen, E. (1981) *Police in Urban America, 1860–1920.* Cambridge, Mass.: Cambridge University Press.

Morris, N. and Tonry, M. (1990) *Between Prison and Probation, Intermediate Punishments in a Rational Sentencing System.* New York and Oxford: Oxford University Press.

Norton, P. (ed.) 1984) *Law and Order and British Politics.* Aldershot: Gower.

Pearce, F. (1976) *Crimes of the Powerful.* London: Pluto.

Pearson, G. (1983) *Hooligan, A History of Respectable Fears.* London and Basingstoke: Macmillan.

Pease, K. (1991) 'The calculation of imprisonment rates'. Paper presented to the British Criminology Society, January.

Pelikan, C. (1991) 'Conflict resolution between victims and offenders in Austria and in the Federal Republic of Germany', in F. Heidensohn and M. Farrell (eds), *Crime in Europe.* London/New York: Routledge.

Quinney, R. (1977) *Class, State and Crime.* London: Longman.

Reiner, R. (1985) *The Politics of the Police.* Brighton: Wheatsheaf.

Rose, N. (1990) *Governing the Soul – The Shaping of the Private Self.* London: Routledge.

Schlesinger, S.R. (1987) *Imprisonment in Four Countries.* Bureau of Justice Statistics Special Report, US Department of Justice.

Schwartz, M. (1990) 'US as compared to British left realism', *Critical Criminologist,* 2(2): 5–12.

Scraton, P. (1990) 'Scientific knowledge or masculine discourses? Challenging patriarchy in criminology', in L. Gelsthorpe and A. Morris (eds), *Feminist Perspectives in Criminology.* Buckingham: Open University Press.

Scull, A. (1984) *Decarceration: Community Treatment and the Deviant: A Radical View.* New Jersey: Rutgers University Press.

Souryal, S.S. (1988) 'The role of the Shariah law in deterring criminality in Saudi Arabia', *International Journal of Comparative and Applied Criminal Justice,* 12(1): 1–25.

Steinert, H. (1985) 'The development of 'discipline' according to Michel Foucault: discourse analysis vs social history', *Crime and Social Justice,* 20: 83–9.

Stenson, K. (1986) 'Foucault, policing and the body.' Paper presented to the National Deviancy Conference, Central London Polytechnic, March.

Stenson, K. (1989) 'Social work discourses and the social work intereview'. PhD thesis, Brunel University, London.

Stenson, K. and Brearley, N. (1991) 'Left realism and the return to consensus theory', in R. Reiner and M. Cross (eds), *Beyond Law and Order – Law and Order into the 1990s.* London: Macmillan.

Stenson, K. and Gould, N. (1986) 'A comment on "A framework for theory in social work"'. *Issues In Social Work Education,* 6(1): 41–5.

Sumner, C. (1990) 'Foucault, gender and the censure of deviance', in L. Gelsthorpe and A. Morris (eds), *Feminist Perspectives In Criminology.* Buckingham: Open University Press.

Sutherland, E. (1983) *White Collar Crime: The Uncut Version.* London: Yale University Press.

Taylor, I. (ed.) (1990) *Free Market Policies – an International Text.* Brighton: Harvester-Wheatsheaf.

Taylor, M. (1982) *Community, Anarchy and Liberty.* Cambridge: Cambridge University Press.

Vitaliev, V. (1991) *Dateline Freedom.* London: Hutchinson.

Walker, M. (1989) *The Soviet Union.* London: Collins.

Walklate, S. (1989) *Victimology.* London: Unwin Hyman.

Weber, M. (1949) *The Methodology of the Social Sciences.* New York: Free Press.

Wilson, J.Q. and Herrnstein, P. (1985) *Crime and Human Nature.* New York: Simon and Schuster.

Wilson, J.Q. and Kelling, G. (1982) 'Broken windows', *Atlantic Monthly,* March: 29–38.

Wilson, W.J. (1987) *The Truly Disadvantaged: The Inner City, the Underclass and Public Policy.* Chicago: Chicago University Press.

Young, J. (1986) 'The failure of criminology: the need for a radical realism', in R. Matthews and J. Young (eds), *Confronting Crime*. London: Sage.

Young, J. (1988a) 'Radical criminology in Britain: the emergence of a competing paradigm', in P. Rock (ed.), *A History of British Criminology*. Oxford: Clarendon Press.

Young, J. (1988b) 'Recent developments in criminology', in M. Haralambos (ed.), *Developments in Sociology*. London: Causeway.

PART ONE

CONTROL AND PREVENTION IN PRACTICE

2

The Politics of Crime: The American Experience

A debate between Elliott Currie and James Q. Wilson

ELLIOTT CURRIE

Crime and the Conservatives: how their Analyses miss the Problem

To understand why we've arrived at our present impasse in dealing with crime, we must first reconsider the assumptions that have guided the dominant policies on crime in America through most of the past decade. This means taking a hard look at the conservative argument about the causes of crime.

At first blush, that may seem a contradiction in terms; during the 1970s, conservatives often ridiculed the very idea of searching for the causes of crime. James Q. Wilson took this stance to its most adamant extreme in his influential book, *Thinking about Crime*. To those who contended that crime could be dealt with only by attacking its root causes, Wilson said he 'was sometimes inclined, when in a testy mood, to rejoin: stupidity can only be dealt with by attacking its root causes. I have yet to see a root cause,' he continued,

> or to encounter a government program that has successfully attacked it, at least with respect to those social problems that arise out of human volition rather than technological malfunction. But more importantly, the demand for causal solutions is, whether intended or not, a way of deferring any action and criticizing any policy. It is a cast of mind that inevitably detracts attention from those few things that government can do reasonably well and draws attention toward those many things it cannot do at all. (Wilson, 1975: XV)

On closer inspection, however, it's clear that Wilson's statement confuses two quite different arguments. The first is that it makes no sense to talk about the social or 'root' cause of crime at all, either because such causes do not exist or because no one knows what they are or how to find them. The second is an essentially political, rather than conceptual, argument – that government either cannot or should not intervene in the conditions that many criminologists had held to be root causes of crime. The first argument is difficult to take seriously; after all, it is hardly possible to say anything very compelling about crime – or any other social problem – without working from some assumptions about why the problem exists. And, in fact, beneath their rhetoric about the futility of looking for the causes of crime, conservatives have offered at least the elements of a causal theory.

That theory has never been carefully articulated, but it is always some variant of the idea that crime is caused by inadequate 'control,' that we have a great deal of crime because we have insufficient curbs on the appetites or impulses that naturally impel individuals towards criminal activity. Most conservative writers regard these lurking appetites as a fundamental part of 'human nature'. As Wilson puts it in *Thinking about Crime,* a 'sober' or 'unflattering view of man' tells us that 'wicked people exist' and that 'nothing avails but to set them apart from innocent people' (Wilson, 1975: 235).

The difficulty with this as an explanation for crime is not exactly that it is untrue – but that, at this sweepingly general level, it is unhelpful. No one would deny that wicked people exist or that human beings have destructive and predatory impulses against which others must be protected. But such generalizations cannot help us to understand why crime is so much worse at some times or places than others. Why are people in St Louis so much more 'prone to crime' than those in Stockholm or, for that matter, Milwaukee? Why are people in Houston not only far more likely to kill each other than people in London or Zurich, but also much more likely to do so today than they were 25 years ago?

Faced with these questions, the criminological right has countered with a number of intellectual ploys. One is simply to ignore or deny the difference between our crime rates and those of other industrial societies. Thus, in *Thinking about Crime,* Wilson made a point of caricaturing the belief that crime was 'an expression of the political rage of the dispossessed, rebelling under the iron heel of capitalist tyranny'; that this view was thoroughly misguided, he asserted, was proved in part by the fact that 'virtually every nation in the world, capitalist, socialist, and communist, has experienced in recent years rapidly increasing crime rates' (Wilson, 1975: xiii).

One problem with this statement is that, stated so flatly, it is simply untrue. Several countries did *not* experience rapidly rising crime rates in the 1960s and 1970s, most notably Japan and Switzerland; and in at least one 'socialist' developing country, Cuba, the rates of criminal violence fell rather dramatically (Clinard, 1978; Downes, 1982; Smith,

1983; Salas, 1979). Moreover, although many other industrial societies did suffer rising levels of crime in the 1960s and 1970s, the rises were in property and drug offences, not in violent crimes like homicide. (Throughout this chapter, I will observe the standard American practice of defining homicide, forcible rape, robbery and theft with at least the threat of force – and assault as violent crimes. *Property* crimes include burglary and other forms of theft *not* involving force.) In the mid-1970s – just as Wilson was portraying every country as racked by rapidly rising crime – it was still possible for two respected Scandinavian criminologists to conclude that the risks of victimization by criminal violence remained quite low in Denmark and Norway; indeed, the Danish and Norwegian homicide rates had been "fairly constant" for 40 or 50 years.

An even more important difficulty with the Wilson argument is that the industrial countries whose rates of criminal violence did rise in the 1960s and 1970s usually began (and ended) at such low levels that to emphasize the similarities between those countries and the United States obscured the much more compelling and dramatic point – the scale of the differences. After what Wilson and others described as nearly two decades of unremitting increases in crime 'throughout the world', by the late 1970s (in per capita terms) about 10 American men died by criminal violence for every Japanese, Austrian, West German, or Swedish man; about 15 American men died for every Swiss or Englishman; and over 20 for every Dane. During the 1960s and 1970s, murder rates increased in some of those countries and didn't in others – but in none of them, when Wilson wrote, did they begin to approach those of the United States; nor do they today; nor are they likely to in the foreseeable future.

Obviously, this stubborn reality causes tough problems for a criminology that blames crime on a vaguely defined and immutable 'human nature'. Consider Wilson's remarks on the prospect for reducing robbery rates. 'A sober view of man', he wrote in 1975, 'requires a modest definition of progress. A 20 percent reduction in robbery would still leave us with the highest robbery rate of almost any Western nation but would prevent about 60,000 robberies' (Wilson, 1975: 223). The internal contradiction in Wilson's reasoning is painfully clear. The wide cross-national variations in crime to which he alludes completely undercut the explanatory power of a 'sober view of man' – for 'man' is presumably no worse in the United States than in Denmark or Switzerland. But the differences in robbery rates between these places are staggering.

In his more recent work, Wilson acknowledges that several factors – the effects of 'real and imagined' racism, the 'sharpening of consumer instincts through the mass media', the increased availability of handguns, and the abandonment of the inner city by 'persons with a stake in impulse control', among others – may have a special impact on crime in the USA. Nonetheless, Wilson continues to insist on the curious argument that since the recent increase in crime 'is not a peculiarly American phenomenon, but a feature of virtually every industrialized society', a 'true understanding of crime depends on what these nations have in common, not what differentiates them'. This remarkable conclusion allows Wilson to retain intact what turns out to be his central premise: that an 'ethos of self-expression' common to most modern societies is the fundamental cause of the industrial world's crime problem (Wilson, 1983b: 28–9). In the process, the uniqueness of the American situation simply drops out of sight.

The argument from human nature, then, is really too general to be of much help. A similar, unhelpful abstraction lies at the heart of the most systematic conservative theory of the causes of crime – something called, I think misleadingly the *economic model* of crime. There could, of course, be as many economic models of crime as there are economic theories, but in fact the conservative model is based on just one: the brand of neoclassical economics developed by the Chicago School. In this model, whether a potential offender commits a crime or not is determined by calculated choice based on a rational weighing of the relative costs and benefits (or *utilities*) of committing the crime versus not doing so. In an often-quoted formulation, the University of Chicago economist Gary Becker argued that someone commits a crime 'if the expected utility to him exceeds the utility he could get by using his time and other resources at other activities. Some persons become "criminals," therefore, not because their basic motivation differs from that of other persons, but because their benefits and costs differ' (Becker, cited in Thompson et al., 1981: 31–2).

Similarly, the conservative economist Gordon Tullock (1974: 105) wrote some years later, 'If you increase the cost of committing a crime, there will be fewer crimes'. Still more recently, the philosopher Ernest van den Haag put the same argument in terms of the 'comparative net advantage' of crime over other activities:

> The number of persons engaged in any activity, lawful or not, depends on the comparative net advantage they expect. . . . Thus the number of practicing dentists, grocers, drug dealers, or burglars depends on the net advantage which these practitioners expect their occupations to yield compared to other occupations available to them. (van den Haag, 1982: 1025, 1035)

Human behaviour, criminal or otherwise, is assumed to be like any other exchange in the marketplace. Armed with this conveniently simplified view of human motivation, conservatives have generally blamed the crime rate on the lack of punishment – crime is common because it's 'cheap' – although they could just as plausibly argue that where crime rates are especially high, the 'comparative net advantage' of lawful behaviour must be particularly low. In practice, conservative criminology has concentrated on increasing the 'cost' of crime; increasing the relative 'benefits' of lawful activity has taken a distinctly subordinate place. . . .

This choice of strategy rests, in part, on a set of arguments about the inability of social policy to do much to boost the 'benefit' side of the ledger. I'll come back to those arguments later. For the moment, though, we can focus on the merits of the 'cost' argument itself. On the most abstract level, it certainly isn't unreasonable to believe that perceptions of 'cost' have some weight in determining the course of individuals' behaviour. But to make the basic argument stick as an explanation of *variations* in crime rates – why a particular country or period has more crime than others – it is necessary to go further: to show that the 'costs' of crime are, in those instances, actually lower than in other times or places with less crime. To the extent that the criminolgical right offers an explanation of American crime patterns vis-à-vis those of other countries (or other periods in our own history), it is that the costs of crime are peculiarly low in the US and, at least by implication, lower than they were in the past.

There is a fundamental difficulty for the conservative argument: it is hard to maintain that our high rates of crime are caused by insufficient punishment when our penal system is one of the most punitive in the developed world. We lock up offenders at a far greater rate than any other advanced society (except the Soviet Union and South Africa – where the comparison is not wholly appropriate, since many prisoners are political, not 'street' criminals). At the beginning of the 1980s, the incarceration rate in the United States was about 217 per 100,000. (The rate is higher now, but I'll use the earlier figure to make comparison with other countries possible.) At the opposite extreme, the Dutch rate was about 21 per 100,000. In between lay most of the rest of the world's industrial societies, many clustered toward the lower end of the scale: Japan's rate was 44 per 100,000, Norway's 45, Sweden's 55, West Germany's 60, Denmark's 63, France's 67, Great Britain's a relatively high 80 per 100,000 (Doleschal and Newton, 1981).

In part, these low rates reflect some countries' use of prison only as a last resort, for the most dangerous offenders; in part they reflect a common practice of incarcerating criminals for relatively short periods. The latter is especially true in Holland, where the average time served in the late 1970s was an astonishing 1.3 months, versus about 5 months in Britain and about 16 in the United States. The shorter sentences are not simply a reflection of the less serious range of offences in Holland; average sentences handed down for a given *class* of offences also differ greatly. Thus the average maximum sentence for robbery was 150 months in the US federal prisons and 68 months in the state prisons; in the Dutch prisons, it was 19 months (Downes, 1982; Steenhuis et al., 1983; US Bureau of Justice Statistics, 1984).

Moreover, many West European countries deliberately decreased their use of imprisonment during the 1960s and 1970s, while beginning in the 1970s the USA moved relentlessly in the other direction. The average Dutch robbery sentence fell to 19 months in 1981 from 32 months in 1950; between 1951 and 1975, the Dutch prison population as a whole dropped by *half.*

Given these huge and growing disparities between our rates of imprisonment and those of otherwise comparable societies, how can one argue that our crime rate (as the *Wall Street Journal's* editors recently put it) 'has undoubtedly resulted from the absence of punishment'? One attempt to maintain the argument is to turn it on its head and claim that, given the severity of the American crime problem, we make relatively limited use of incarceration – so that the likelihood of punishment for convicted offenders is actually smaller here. Wilson, for example, draws an analogy with medical care; to claim that we 'overimprison' people in the United States, he writes, 'is like disproving the need for hospitals by saying that the United States already hospitalizes a larger fraction of its population than any other nation', for it 'implies that we are sending people to prison without any regard to the number of crimes committed (or sending them to hospitals without regard to whether they are sick)'. The 'proper question', Wilson insists, is 'whether we imprison a higher fraction of those arrested, prosecuted, and convicted than do other nations.' His answer is that we do not (Wilson, 1982: 68).

There are two things wrong with Wilson's argument. To begin with, it is not at all clear why this is the 'proper question'. Certainly, it doesn't help us understand the relationship between levels of crime and levels of punishment. For if it is offered as an explanation of high crime rates in America, the argument is perilously close to circular, since it does not tell us why so many crimes are committed here in the first place. A closer look at the medical analogy reveals the logical problem. If one country already possess more hospitals per capita than any other but still produces more sickness, it is implausible to blame its comparative ill-health on the relative lack of hospitals. To be sure, a country with a lot of illness will 'need' many hospitals, just as a country with a lot of crime will 'need' many prisons. But if we want to understand either why so many people are ill to begin with or how we could prevent these excessive levels of illness in the future, we will need to look at other aspects of the country – sanitation, nutrition, environmental hazards, perhaps even cultural values – or we will be fruitlessly building hospitals forever to accommodate the ever-increasing flow of the sick.

The same logic ought to apply in the case of criminal justice. If we already imprison people at a higher rate than other countries, we cannot blame our own uniquely high crime rate on the under-use of imprisonment, without reasoning in a circle. It we want to understand why so many people here have become criminals, we will need to look at other factors that distinguish us from more fortunate countries.

But there is an even more immediate difficulty with Wilson's argument – its facts are wrong. Wilson's only source of evidence for his contention that the United States is relatively sparing in its use of prison is a 1978 study by the Yale economist Kenneth I. Wolpin. This analysis showed that in the 1960s – when American incarceration rates were much lower than they are today – the chance of imprisonment for convicted robbers was higher in England than in the United States (although the American sentences were more severe): between 1961 and 1967, a convicted robber's chance of going behind bars was 48 percent in England and 31 percent in the United States (for an average sentence of 2.9 years in England, 3.5 years in America) (Wolpin, 1975).

On the surface, these figures lent some credence to the notion that the British might be 'tougher' on robbers, if only in the sense of greater consistency, not severity, of punishment. The trouble is that Wolpin's analysis – as he pointed out himself in a later study – neglected to include in its estimates of incarceration rates the great numbers of convicted offenders sent to *local jails* in the United States – a crucial omission indeed, since including them in the calculations completely reversed the outcome.

Wolpin's later, more inclusive, study compared robbery in the United States (specifically in California), to England and Japan. This time he found that convicted robbers were considerably *more* likely to go to prison or jail in the United States than in either England or Japan. Wolpin's study covered the years from 1955 to 1971 – well before the prison 'boom' of the 1970s that doubled the American incarceration rate. But even then, a convicted robber had a 63 percent chance of going behind bars in California, versus 48 percent in England and 46 percent in Japan. England's robbers, furthermore, spent only about half as much time behind bars as those in Japan or in California. Meanwhile, according to official statistics, California's robbery rate averaged over 17 times the British rate and over 28 times the Japanese.

Developments over time are also revealing. In all three countries, as Wolpin's later study showed, convicted robbers were *less* likely to go to prison at the end of the period than at the beginning. But this consistent decline in the 'costs' of robbery had completely contradictory effects on robbery rates in the different countries: robbery increased in California and still more in England, but declined rather dramatically in Japan (Wolpin, 1980).

In short, contrary to Wilson's claims, we do indeed incarcerate more of those arrested and convicted than do the English and Japanese – who, in turn, use incarceration more readily than, for example, the Swiss or the Dutch. Wolpin's studies do bring up an important distinction: the Japanese and the British *catch* criminals more often than we do, and generally convict them more frequently once caught. Why this should be so is a difficult and unresolved question. Suffice it to say that the difficulty in apprehending criminals has little to do with the *leniency* of American justice. And while the difficulty in convicting them once caught may have some relation to American court practices, the evidence indicates that any effects of this on the crime rate are quite small. The fundamental point at issue here remains: the United States is indeed the most punitive of advanced Western industrial societies towards those offenders who are brought to the stage of sentencing.

Moreover, we have become dramatically more punitive over time. If there ever were 'years of neglect' in the punishment of criminals in America, they are long past. In the 1960s, those who believed that the 'softness' of American justice was responsible for our crime rate had a more plausible case. In some places, at least we made less use of imprisonment than we had some years before. Our incarceration rates fell for several years, and didn't rise even as the crime rate began to do so in the 1960s. In this context it was at least possible to argue that crime might be rising because criminals had it easier than before. But we have been steadily and massively increasing the 'costs' of crime for many years.

The simplest way to measure these changes is to look at the national incarceration rate. In 1970 there were fewer than 200,000 inmates of state and federal prisons in the United States: by mid-1984, more than 450,000. Because the country's population grew during the same years, the change in the *rate* of incarceration is slightly smaller, but not much: about 96 of every 100,000 Americans were in a state or federal prison in 1970; in 1984, about 195 of every 100,000. (Note that these figures do not include the rising population in local jails. And in some states, the rise was even more rapid – South Carolina went from 105 per 100,000 in 1970 to 268 in 1982.)

It might be argued that these huge increases only reflected a desperate race to keep up with the crime rate – or to cope with a much more serious mix of criminals coming before the courts. But this is not the case. The rate of imprisonment was rising much faster than the crime rate; yet not only did the crime rate refuse to fall in some reasonably corresponding fashion, but at the end of the 1970s it surged sharply – and by the logic of the conservative model, incomprehensibly – upward.

Some conservatives have come to recognize the inadequacy of the declining-cost argument, especially given the depressing results of a decade of getting tough with criminals. Yet this experience has not generally altered the underlying premises of the conservative argument – only shifted its ground. For most conservative writers, crime still represents a weakening of controls over what is solemnly regarded as an obdurate and fundamentally wicked human nature. The finger of blame points more often these days to a range of institutions outside the criminal justice system – the schools, the family, and American culture as a whole, along with a wide gamut of 'misguided' liberal social policies and the malignant influence of 'government'. The central theme is still that our society is insufficiently punitive and controlling, especially of children and youth; that we allow too much easy gratification of the darker impulses and actively encourage a destructive 'self-expression', instead of the virtues of sobriety, self-restraint, and the curbing of appetites. The institutions that ought to keep wayward impulses in line – and, according to this argument, once did – have lately lost much of their influence. This is usually blamed either on long-term shifts in the norms and values common to 'modern' societies or on the naivety (or malevolence) of the liberal shapers of contemporary opinion.

The evolution of James Q. Wilson's views reflects this change of emphasis. His *Thinking about Crime* was a fairly conventional mid-1970s statement of the economic model of crime. We had 'trifled with the wicked', Wilson thundered, and 'encouraged the calculators'. Even then, Wilson – unlike some of his less restrained colleagues – did not argue that we could expect *great* reductions in crime through increasing its 'costs', but this was still the main policy recommendation in what was generally an admonition that we would have to 'learn to live with crime' (Wilson, 1975: 236).

In his recent revision of the book, Wilson still insists that 'deterrence works', but he has moved further away from believing that *much* can be accomplished by increasing penalties – and even less by improving 'benefits'. The deeper, more intractable sources of crime, Wilson now insists, are the effects of 'discordant homes, secularized churches, intimidated schools, and an ethos of self-expression'. What has ultimately corroded social life in the United States during the twentieth century is the triumph of 'self-expression over self-control as a core human value': we have learned to 'exalt rights over duties, spontaneity over loyalty, tolerance over conformity, and authenticity over convention' (Wilson, 1983a: 88).

This is little more than the stock theme of insidious moral decline that has predictably been invoked to explain not just crime and delinquency but nearly everything the contemporary conservative finds wrong with US society – from the divorce rate and the decline in the growth of productivity to the much-lamented weakening of America's will to impose military solutions on a recalcitrant world. What should we make of it as an explanation for US crime rates?

Not much. The links between these broad cultural shifts and crime – particularly serious, violent street crime – are not at all evident, even if we accept Wilson's assessment of our recent moral decline. For one thing, as he himself makes clear, the moral and cultural changes that he says explain America's *current* crime problem started decades before our recent rises in crime; furthermore, they don't correlate even remotely with the trends of serious criminality in American history.

For Wilson, America's moral downfall can be traced back to the 1920s, when 'we see the educated classes repudiating moral uplift as it had been practiced for the preceding century.' (The next few paragraphs are based on Wilson (1983b).) A pervasive and, Wilson believes, largely effective nineteenth-century effort to control 'self-indulgent impulses' was increasingly derided by the 'educated elite' as narrow-minded, fundamentalist and provincial, and replaced by the 'self-expression ethic'. This transformation was facilitated by an imposing, if unusual, array of villains, including Freudian psychology, cultural anthropology and women's magazines. Popular versions of Freudian theory (Wilson acknowledges they may be distorted) proclaimed that 'repressing one's instincts was bad, not good'. Cultural anthropology further undermined the moral order of American society by promoting the view that 'this culture was wrong, or at the very least no better than several competing cultural forms'. Margaret Mead comes in for a special drubbing for having claimed that 'the greater happiness of Samoans arose from their being granted greater sexual freedom and from being raised in more nurturant, less repressive families'.

Granted, these changes are real, and Wilson is entitled to his jaundiced view of them. But what do they have to do with crime? Wilson himself vacillates between acknowledging that he isn't sure they have anything at all to do with it, and speculating that these cultural and intellectual shifts somehow created a moral climate that must be held responsible, albeit 40 years later, for the crime rates of the late 1960s. One way in which they could have influenced crime, he suggests, is by prompting changes in child-rearing, which might 'alter the behavior of the young by making them more daring and more impatient of restraints'. Possibly. But, as Wilson admits, 'it is quite difficult to say much about the changes in child-rearing that occurred, and it is almost impossible to say anything about how these changes might have affected the behavior of the young'.

Then why should we continue this unpromising line of investigation? Because, Wilson insists, despite our lack of evidence, we can still say 'something about' how elites *advised* mothers to bring up their children: and since the advice appeared in popular magazines, it reached a wide audience, whether in fact it influenced anyone or not. This advice shifted the aims of child-rearing away from the nineteenth-century emphasis on guarding the child from 'evil within and evil without' – that is, from a view of the child as 'endowed by nature with dangerous impulses that must be curbed' – to one in which the child was seen as equipped with 'harmless instincts that ought to be developed'.

Wilson's description of this literature is something of a caricature; in fact, it is hard to find any child-rearing literature in this period that totally ignores discipline and supervision in the name of developing 'harmless instincts'. More crucially, it is difficult to detect any convincing chronological relationship between the cultural changes that did take place in the 1920s and the course of serious crime over the next 60 years. Wilson does not claim that the rise of an ethos of 'self-expression' had any observable, direct connection with crime rates. Indeed, he concedes that 'it is not clear that this shift in the dominant ethos of the social and intellectual elites had immediate and important practical consequences'. After all, in the 1920s and the early 1930s criminal violence was high (a phenomenon often considered an unfortunate side-effect of Prohibition, a programme of 'moral uplift' that Wilson apparently admires), but it was lower thereafter until its rise during the 1960s. How then can we argue that the two are strongly and closely related – or explain why the new ethos skipped a generation before causing the crime rates of the 1960s and 1970s?

Wilson's answer has two parts. First, the deadly suffusion of the ethos of self-expression was 'cut short' by the Great Depression. Youths in particular were forced by grim economic reality into hard work and 'traditional' attitudes, and the crime rate went down. Though this is a vastly oversimplified rendering of what the evidence says about crime in the Depression, it isn't altogether far-fetched. But it wasn't grim economic reality that kept the crime rates low in the prosperous post-war period – precisely the years that witnessed both the emergence of the 'youth culture' Wilson deplores and the spread of the child-centred approach to upbringing whose pernicious impact Wilson singles out for blame. An 'explanation' contending that both good times and bad had similar restraining effects on the movement towards 'self-expression' is not easily grasped. Indeed, Wilson barely tries to make its logic clear to us.

The second half of the explanation for the delay of more than four decades between the onset of the disease of self-expression and the sudden, explosive manifestation of its symptom of criminal violence is that – as Wilson puts it – in the early years these cultural shifts affected only 'elite', rather than 'mass', attitudes. The hint here, never fully articulated, is that at some point, by some mechanism, destructive ideas about authenticity and self-expression filtered down from the avant-garde to a wider audience. In the 1960s, apparently, this resulted from a 'celebration of the youth culture in the marketplace, in the churches, and among adults'. This 'institutionalization in all parts of society of the natural desire of youth for greater freedom', Wilson suggests, 'may well have given legitimacy to all forms of self-expression – including, alas, those forms that involve crime and violence'.

Once again, this line of argument combines a blend of truisms with dizzying leaps of inference that, on close inspection, lack support. Wilson merges a common critique of the 1960s youth-culture shenanigans with another matter altogether: the serious criminality that racked the United States in the late 1960s and the 1970s. Certainly, some of what went on in the name of self-expression and liberation was at best silly and at worst destructive and inhumane. No doubt, there was a connection between these attitudes and a wide range of youthful behaviour that violated the law, especially with regard to drugs and sex. But that isn't the issue. The crucial question is whether the ethos of 'rights, not duties', a preference for 'spontaneity over loyalty, conscience over honor, tolerance over conformity, self-expression over self-restraint', which animated the salons of the 1920s and the campuses of the 1960s, also accounts for the brutal violence in the streets and homes of the 1960s, 1970s and 1980s. And here the argument collapses.

It collapses partly because it makes the wrong prediction about where serious criminal violence takes place. 'Elite' and intellectual communities are not where violent crime is common; in fact, they are usually remarkably free of it. Places like Madison or Ann Arbor, which led the campus counterculture in the 1960s, maintained the low rates of serious crime that we rightly associate with communities of fairly affluent young people and professionals. The same is true of the urban and suburban concentrations of the 'new class' that Wilson holds responsible for many of the social problems of the past 20 years. His position seems to be that the real problem isn't that 'elite' values led to violence among the elite themselves, but that, in a wonderful parallel with supply-side economics, they 'trickle down' to the lower orders, who promptly go out and put guns to people's heads.

I am not suggesting that cultural changes had nothing to do with the rising crime rates of the 1960s. One such change – the weakening of longstanding social norms justifying racial inequality – probably had an important influence. Although we have no hard quantitative measures, many careful observers at the time were convinced that this momentous change helped turn minority anger fuelled by decades of injustice and deprivation outward against whites and their institutions. Some of that anger was expressed in formal protest, some in rebellion, and some in street crime – which may help explain the rising incidence of inter-racial robbery and of 'stranger-to-stranger' crime generally in the 60s. But this is not the same as the vague argument that the values of 'tolerance' and 'authenticity' were what motivated the youth of the New Orleans or Detroit ghettos to inaugurate the rising curve of urban violence in the late 1960s.

In fact, everything we know from social research about the values usually found in the social strata that produce most severely violent criminals tells us something very different. There, tolerance and individual expression in child-rearing practices are not encouraged; but more often, their opposite – conformity, constraint and un-questioning obedience, sometimes enforced by violence. Obviously, parents' efforts to instil these values often fail. But that is very different from saying that young people from the ghettos and barrios of America's inner cities go astray because their parents have taught them bohemian values learned, at some distance removed, from the writings of elite, liberal intellectuals.

The overemphasis on control to the exclusion of other issues appears even in some more thoughtful writers who have moved beyond this simplistic reliance on 'permissiveness' as an explanation of America's unusually high crime rates....

David Bayley's analysis of the causes for Japan's low, relatively stable (and at some points declining) crime rate in recent years leads to a fashionably pessimistic conclusion:

> The levels of criminal behavior that Americans find so disturbing may be the inevitable consequence of aspects of national life that Americans prize – individualism, mobility, privacy, autonomy, suspicion of authority, and separation between public and private roles, between government and community. The United States may have relatively high levels of criminality because it is inhabited by Americans. (Bayley, 1976: 68)

This argument does point to something important about the American experience – but in this form it obscures more than it illuminates. By shifting the explanation of the causes of crime on to an amorphous, ill-defined realm of culture or values detached from the social and economic context that nourishes or undermines them, such reasoning conveys a vague sense – more a mood than an argument – that the roots of crime are beyond human control, thus encouraging inaction and passivity. If we have a lot of crime in America *because* we're Americans, there isn't much we can do about it. But the argument fits uneasily with the facts. If 'individualism' and a cultural penchant for 'autonomy' are indeed the problem, why do the notoriously individualistic Yankees of New Hampshire ('Live Free or Die') or the ruggedly individualistic

Scandinavians of Minnesota have rates of serious criminal violence that compare well with those of Western Europe, or of Japan? Why do black Americans, who presumably do not value 'individualism' any more than white Americans (or Hispanic Americans, who may value it less), have rates that are so much higher?

It is important to acknowledge that even with all its rhetorical excesses, the conservative argument about the links between crime and culture raises important questions – questions that liberal criminology has sometimes side-stepped. The criminology of the 1960s too often focused on the simpler malfunctions of what was viewed as an otherwise smoothly functioning social and moral order: it implied that a little income support here, a summer-job programme there would, by themselves, stop crime. The conservative argument, at its most suggestive part, points beyond to what Peter Steinfels, in *The Neoconservatives*, aptly calls the 'murkier and more trying questions of culture and spirit' – and, I would add, of family and community (Steinfels, 1980: 92, 246). These are difficult issues to grasp, and especially hard to frame in the manageable terms of quantitative social science, but I do not think we will really understand crime without paying them respectful attention.

In the hands of conservative writers, however, these issues have usually been raised in terms so mired in ideology and so beholden to political agendas as to obscure the questions they suggest. Conservative analysis has steadfastly shied away from confronting – or even naming – the underlying forces that shape cultural, communal and family life. As Steinfels has also noted, this stance fixes our attention on a 'realm of ideas and ethos' that seems to float free of its moorings in the economic and social changes that have transformed American society, and as a result obscures the interconnection between them.

Conservative writing on crime, for example, has often focused on the spread of an ethos of 'immediate gratification', a concern voiced even in the pages of the report of the Reagan administration's Task Force on Violent Crime. There is reason for this concern; some kinds of crime are almost by definition the expression of a search for immediate gratification. Yet – aside from the incessant references to the noxious influence of liberal permissiveness – conservative writers don't identify the forces that might foster such an 'ethos'. This is surely a remarkable omission in a society where, more than in any other, an ethos of ever-increasing consumption for the sake of impulse gratification has become indispensable to our economy and has penetrated almost every corner of our life; where the world's most sophisticated advertising industry devotes itself day in, day out, to promoting just that ethos; and where, in contrast to many other advanced industrial societies, the search for the highest and fastest short-term profit at the expense of longer-term economic stability – the corporate version of instant gratification – is enshrined as the overarching principle of economic life.

I've argued that, from an international perspective, America cannot plausibly be considered a 'tolerant' or lenient society; it is, however, an acquisitive and hedonistic one. These cultural attitudes surely have some relationship to the severity of our crime problem. But we must understand that they are indissolubly linked to an economy dependent on the incessant stimulation of mass consumption. As Daniel Bell writes in *The Cultural Contradictions of Capitalism*, 'the one thing that would utterly destroy the "new capitalism" is the serious practice of "deferred gratification" ' (Bell, 1971). If we have moved away from a less grasping, more co-operative culture in recent years – and I believe we have – we must look, as Bell does, to the social and economic forces that have brought about this shift.

In the absence of that sort of analysis, the conservative emphasis on culture, values and tradition degenerates into wistful nostalgia or, worse, into a self-righteous, punitive demand for more corporal punishment, harsher discipline in the family and the schools, and the indiscriminate use of the prisons as holding pens for an urban under-class we have decided 'to give up on'.

The conservative model turns out to be shot through with contra-dictions. In a world of dramatic national variations in criminal violence, it blames crime on an invariant human nature. In a society that ranks among the most punitive in the developed world, it blames crime on the leniency of the justice system. In a country noted for its harsh response to social deviation, it blames crime on attitudes of tolerance run wild. If we want to understand the American experience of criminal violence, we must look elsewhere for the elements of an explanation, particularly to those features of our social life that distinguish us – in fact rather than in fantasy – from more fortunate societies.

JAMES Q. WILSON

On Crime and the Liberals

Elliott Currie criticizes conservatives, of which he takes me to be a leading representative, for their views on crime. Since I have not yet seen Mr Currie's book, I do not know what his views are, but some of them can, perhaps, be inferred from how he criticizes mine. If my inferences are correct, and if Mr Currie is to be taken as a representative of liberal or socialist thought, then the liberal or socialist position on crime has some serious problems of its own.

He makes essentially four arguments. First, that conservatives refuse to deal seriously with the root causes of crime; secondly, that conservatives fail to explain why the rate of crime, especially violent crime, should be so much higher in the United States than in other nations; thirdly, that the favourite conservative remedy for crime – more imprisonment – has been tried and found wanting; and fourthly, that cultural explanations for the growth of crime in America are false and, worse, misleading, for they justify inaction (presumably inaction with respect to economic and other material matters).

When I published the first edition of *Thinking about Crime* in 1973, I wanted, among other things, to persuade readers that *both* the liberal *and* the conservative positions of the time were in error. The view of many liberals (perhaps best expressed in writing of Ramsey Clark) was that the cure for crime lay in an assault on its root causes, which were assumed, on the basis of the shakiest evidence, to lie in material deprivation; failing that, criminals should be rehabilitated. The argument of many conservatives (exemplified by the campaign rhetoric of Richard Nixon) was that the proper approach to crime was to take the 'handcuffs' off the police (by repealing court-ordered exclusionary rules), restore the death penalty, increase the severity of penalties for crimes, and appoint a 'get-tough' attorney general.

I believed that both positions were wrong. It was not hard to show the weaknesses in the conservative position. The attorney general, and the federal government as a whole, had little to do with crime control, which was essentially a local responsibility. Within those localities, the conventional policies – increased police patrols, hiring more detectives, loosening the restrictions on police – seemed to have little measurable or lasting influence on crime rates. There were clues that new forms of police deployment, such as reintegrating the police into the community and developing specialized squads that would target high-rate offenders, might make a difference, but the evidence was still fragmentary. (It has since become much stronger.) There was little evidence that the severity of penalties (as opposed to their certainty) had an effect on crime rates. Since much in the conservative position was based on the assumption that there was a technological quick fix for crime, studies showing that the technologies did not work as hoped were sufficient to rebut the assumption.

The liberal position was a more difficult issue. It was based less on faith in technology than on what I took to be a false view of human nature. That view was that man was wholly the product of his environment and that by making marginal alterations in that environment one could alter human behaviour in predictable and desirable ways. I did not believe there was any evidence to support such a view; moreover, even if altering the social context of crime would reduce criminality, it would take decades – perhaps generations – of effort for such efforts to have a significant effect. I worried that the pursuit of a distant hope was tantamount to condemning people to be victims of crimes, some of which could be avoided by different, less ambitious policies. Moreover, I suspected that some advocates of reducing crime by eliminating its causes knew full well that such methods would not work in a timely manner and were not in the least troubled by that fact, for their real agenda was not to reduce crime but to remake society. This suspicion was heightened by the number of liberals who, when asked what they proposed to do about street crime, would immediately change the subject and rail against corporate crime, as if it was ITT, not the neighbourhood mugger, who was terrorizing the people – especially the poor people – in our cities.

It was in this context that I began my book with the sentence Mr Currie attacks: 'I have yet to see a root cause or to encounter a government program that has successfully attacked it, at least with respect to those social problems that arise out of human volition rather than technological malfunction.' I grant you that was a rather testy way of phrasing the matter (I said as much at the time), but bear in mind what Mr Currie forgets – it was true, literally true. The Great Society had been put in place almost ten years earlier, and all that we had learned so far was that federal aid to education was not improving school achievement, Project Head Start did not seem to be working, community-action programmes were not reducing crime, job-training programmes were not reducing hard-core unemployment, and drug-treatment programmes were having, at best, an uncertain effect on heroin addiction.

Efforts to rehabilitate criminals had been under way for decades, and the clear lesson from the research was that we had not yet learned of any programmes that made much of a difference. The inference I drew from this was also true: the search for ways to cure the root causes, given the knowledge we had at the time, reflected a 'cast of mind that inevitably detracts attention from those few things that government can do reasonably well and draws attention toward those many things it cannot do at all'.

At the time, some liberals protested that the Great Society programmes were not a fair test of what could be accomplished by social melioration. If only more money had been spent, if only it had been spent more wisely, if only the spending had gone on longer.... What sustained such protests, in absence of any evidence of any gains? Hope, I suppose, or ideology, or both. I was not opposed to the hope, and said as much ('reducing poverty and breaking up the ghettoes are desirable policies in their own right, whatever their effects on crime'). What I did oppose were untested hopes, and the ideology that sustained them: with social policies as with police tactics, I wanted experiments conducted that would find out what works. I'm certain Mr Currie views me as an ideologue, loving to punish and hating to help, but he is wrong; I am, or try to be, a pragmatist. Given that everybody wants less crime, how do we find out what policies will make a significant difference at a reasonable cost? 'Above all', I wrote, 'we can try to learn more about what works, and in the process abandon our ideological preconceptions about what *ought* to work'. I can assure Mr Currie that this message was as strongly resisted among certain elements in the police world as it was among the enthusiasts of social spending.

Given what we knew, I argued that society should try to manage conduct by altering the rewards and penalties consequent on that conduct. Punishing crime was no more illiberal than rewarding virtue, and punishing criminals was no less likely to work than providing jobs to would-be criminals. Mr Currie takes me to task for embracing, without evidence, a theory of human nature that assumes that people choose a course of action based on its likely consequences, consequences evaluated in terms of learned rules of conduct that moderate their natural desire for self-gratification. In *Thinking about Crime* I did make that assumption but not, I think, unreasonably; not only does it accord with everyday experience and the teachings of psychology, it is also consistent with such evidence as we have on the responsiveness of criminal behaviour to the probability of it being punished.

The studies of deterrence that were available in the mid-1970s, almost without exception, supported such a theory. We now know more than we knew then. We know in particular that some of the older aggregate statistical studies of deterrence were flawed, but we also know that newer statistical studies have corrected many of these flaws while coming to essentially the same conclusions and that experimental evidence (such as the Minneapolis spouse-assault project) gives dramatic proof of the capacity of even relatively minor sanctions to reduce criminality. I review these studies at length in the revised edition of *Thinking about Crime* (1983); I will not repeat the review here.

Moreover, Richard J. Herrnstein and I have discussed at length the development of criminality among young persons in *Crime and Human Nature* (1985). The evidence from biology, child development, the sociology of the family, and research on schooling shows quite clearly how early childhood experiences, interacting with individual predispositions, affect the extent to which people take into account the distant consequences of their actions and the feelings and interests of others. One must be impressed with the vast accumulation of evidence pointing to the importance of these very early experiences –

experiences occurring long before the child can have much contact with the labour market – in producing the high-rate offender. *Crime and Human Nature* amply supports the view, earlier suggested in *Thinking about Crime*, that the root causes of crime among the career criminals tend to be found in intimate settings that policy makers will find difficult to reach, much less to change.

Difficult, but not impossible. Of late, some experimental evidence has been gathered indicating that parent-training programmes can improve the ability of parents to cope with difficult children in ways that improve school performance and reduce misconduct, and that certain kinds of preschool education programmes can produce significant reductions in later delinquency. These experimental results, unavailable five years ago, offer real glimmers of hope and deserve the most careful exploration. I am now engaged, with others, in summarizing the more promising leads and trying to persuade policy makers to invest substantially in replicating and enlarging these experiments. Many questions remain unanswered: can the gains produced by a small number of gifted therapists and educators be reproduced by a larger number of (inevitably) less gifted or motivated workers? Will the gains observed in certain groups of youngsters be found in other kinds as well?

More leads may emerge in the future. We are beginning to learn how schools that achieve an orderly environment for learning differ from those that can barely cope with riotous misconduct. We may learn whether the more effective schools produce lasting or only temporary reductions in delinquency. Efforts to reduce crime by giving jobs and job-training to ex-convicts and delinquent high-school dropouts have not yet been very successful, but it is conceivable that by focusing attention on younger children who have not yet found crime rewarding, more can be achieved.

In the meantime, justice alone, to say nothing of a desire to reduce crime, requires that the guilty be punished. Wicked people *do* exist, and a just society cannot treat them with the leniency advocated by the dwindling but still ardent band of prison opponents. Of course, prison is not the proper sentence for every offender. We are now beginning to gain experience – again, unavailable five years ago – with alternatives to prison such as community service, house arrest and intensive probation, experience that may make it possible to satisfy society's legitimate demand for justice and protection and at the same time minimize the human and financial costs of full-time incarceration, at least for non-violent, relatively low-rate offenders. But 'alternatives to prison' has been for many years a slogan around which all right-thinking progressives can rally rather than a tested policy that prudent people can endorse. We still await substantial empirical evidence that a given alternative will work as well as (if not better than) jails or prisons for a given kind of offender. But if the matter is approached as a question of strategy rather than ideology, that evidence may well be forthcoming and I, for one, would welcome it.

Let me now turn to the specific issues Mr Currie has raised. Why does the United States have so much higher a rate of violent crime than other industrialized democracies? I do not know. I hope Mr Currie will enlighten me. In *Crime and Human Nature* Herrnstein and I summarize such evidence as we can find on the matter, but it is inconclusive, especially with respect to such dramatic exceptions as Japan. It probably has to do with the complex, poorly understood interaction among individual temperaments, familial processes, criminal opportunities, law-enforcement practices, and national culture – which all vary, to some degree, from one society to another. There are some hypotheses worth considering, and a few scraps of evidence, but not much else.

But the existence of different levels of crime across nations (or cities, or states, or individuals) does not, as Mr Currie seems to think, disprove any particular theory of human nature or discredit any particular public policy. To use national (or city, or state) differences in crime rates as a test of some theory, one must fully state the theory and then hold constant those variables that are not of interest while examining the independent effect on crime of the variable that is of interest. This is so elementary a methodological point that I am embarrassed to mention it, but Mr Currie seems not to understand it. To him, the fact that incarceration rates and crime rates differ, without obvious pattern, across nations is ipso facto evidence that there can be no connection between the two.

Imagine what a reader's reaction would be if I asserted that Anglos are less criminal than Hispanics because crime rates are always higher wherever Hispanics are especially numerous. The reader would immediately, indignantly, and rightly demand that I take into account differences in earnings, employment rates, age structures, degrees of urbanization and police practices, among other things, before entertaining such a conclusion. Or suppose I were to state that unemployment rates had no effect on crime because England, Italy, and the United States all had comparable unemployment rates but very different crime rates. Again, the reader would want to know what effect unemployment had after controlling on the age structure, ethnic composition, labour-force participation rates, and so on, of the various nations.

But we need not let the matter rest on what some readers may (erroneously) regard as a methodological quibble. We can consult Mr Currie's own evidence, the cross-national study by Kenneth I. Wolpin of Yale. Wolpin is one of the very few scholars who have compared crime rates across nations in the context of a well-defined theory of criminal behaviour. (Dane Archer and Rosemary Gartner have also made useful international comparisons of homicide rates.) Mr Currie claims that Professor Wolpin's data show that California is much more likely to send a robber to prison than England or Japan, yet California has a robbery rate that is many multiples of England's or Japan's. Mr Currie's inference – that greater punitiveness is associated with higher crime rates – is wrong. The data from Professor Wolpin he cites refer only to the probability of going to prison if convicted. The true risk of prison, given the commission of a crime, is the product of three probabilities – the chances of the crime being cleared up (solved) by the police, the chances of the arrested criminal being convicted, and the chances of the convicted criminal being imprisoned. This combined conditional probability is easily calculated from the data in Professor Wolpin's article. The odds of a given robbery resulting in the imprisonment of the robber are as follows: California, 0.040; England, 0.161; Japan, 0.233. In short, a given robbery is *four times* as likely to result in incarceration in England, and nearly *six times* as likely to result in incarceration in Japan, as in California.

Far from thinking that sanctions have no effect on crime, Professor Wolpin concludes that they have a very large effect. In his words: 'It is apparent that increased crime control either through greater certainty of capture or conviction given capture, or through increased severity of punishment given conviction, is related to the reduced level of robberies.' He also observes that the more youthful the population and the higher the unemployment rate, the greater the criminality. Professor Wolpin properly and carefully notes the limitations of his findings and the large effect that is played by culture or other hard-to-measure factors. Nonetheless, his findings lead him to precisely the opposite conclusion than the one Mr Currie draws from them.

Finally, Mr Currie dismisses my view that cultural factors play a large role in determining the major increases and decreases in crime in US history; presumably, he would also dismiss the role of culture in explaining differences in crime rates between, say, Japan and the United States. Since virtually every serious historian of nineteenth-century crime rates in the US (I refer to Eric Monkkonen, Roger Lane, and Ted Gurr) believe that culture plays some significant role, and since virtually every serious observer of crime in Japan (I think of Ezra Vogel and David Bayley) assigns a very large role to culture, I am at a loss to understand why Mr Currie rejects the argument.

One reason may be that he thinks a cultural argument is inherently conservative. He refers to the 'stock theme of insidious moral decline' that is invoked to explain 'nearly everything the contemporary conservative finds wrong with American society'. Later, he backs up a bit and admits that 'the weakening of longstanding norms of racial inequality' probably had 'an important influence'. Of course, he cannot prove that, any more than I (or Monkonnen, or Lane, or Gurr, or Bayley, or Vogel) can prove that other cultural factors may also be at work. Proving, by the standards of modern social science, the power of any cultural factor is notoriously difficult. But if Mr Currie wishes to advance his favourite cultural explanation, is it wrong for me to adance others? And if neither kind can be proved, is it irrelevant that I try to show that it is consistent with a large body of historical information? And if not, why dismiss plausible, but inherently unprovable, cultural arguments with a sneer? I do not reject the possibility that changing racial norms or unleashed black rage may contribute to changing crime rates; indeed, Herrnstein and I devote a large part of one chapter to considering just such a possibility. I certainly do not label that theory the 'stock theme of insidious moral rage' used to explain 'nearly everything the contemporary liberal finds wrong with American society'.

I look forward to Mr Currie's book because I want to know, given his impatience (and sleight of hand) with any arguments based on cultural factors or criminal justice, how he proposes to explain and cope with criminality. I hope in that book he uses evidence in a more sensible way than he uses it here and that he addresses, seriously, the very limited choices a free society faces in trying to deal with crime. Otherwise, he will once again make liberalism (if, in fact, he is a liberal) what it was in the mid-1960s – a victim of crime in the streets.

ELLIOTT CURRIE REPLIES

I was happy to learn that James Q. Wilson planned a response to my critique of his (and others') work. I was less happy upon actually reading it. I'd hoped that Wilson's response might help stimulate a healthy debate on the issues I raised. But to my considerable disappointment I think it mainly sidesteps them. That's too bad, because a more straightforward confrontation might have advanced the discussion of crime in America considerably.

Wilson's response muddies the waters in two ways. First, he largely skirts the *specific* criticisms I made of the conservative view in the original article – notably its emphasis on judicial leniency as a central cause of America's high crime rate and the similar, but broader, assault on the laxity or 'permissiveness' of American culture and institutions generally. Secondly, his long, more general critique of the liberal and left position on crime – past and present – misrepresents the views of his opponents, overstates the evidence against those views, and exaggerates the evidence in support of his own. The liberal position is reduced to an easily deflated caricature, a strategy that makes Wilson's own views seem by comparison most sophisticated indeed; but in the process, most of the really tough issues about crime and what we might do about it get lost.

Let's begin with the first problem – Wilson's treatment of those issues of culture and criminal-justice policy that my article most directly addressed. I took issue with conservative criminologists for their insistence that the leniency or 'tolerance' or 'permissiveness' of American culture in general and American justice in particular was to blame for our disastrous rates of criminal violence. I argued that as an explanation for American crime rates this simply didn't stand up to the evidence. Our criminal justice system, while not overwhelmingly efficient in putting away dangerous offenders, was nevertheless unusually punitive with those it was able to catch and convict – in comparison with other countries which still managed to maintain far lower rates of crime. Moreover, we had become much *more* punitive in recent years without witnessing a corresponding reduction in crime. Similarly, we were, again by comparison with many other advanced industrial countries, extraordinarily punitive in many of our cultural values and institutional practices – as evidenced by such things as our continued support for the death penalty and for corporal punishment of the young.

Wilson in turn takes me to task on these issues, but in ways that convince me, if I needed convincing, that my original criticisms were on target. Consider first the argument about judicial leniency. He simply avoids my central point – that our courts are not notably lenient with most serious convicted offenders – and instead shifts the terrain altogether, suggesting that I believe that 'sanctions have no effect on crime'. But that's not what I said, nor what I believe. 'It certainly isn't unreasonable', I wrote, 'to believe that perceptions of "cost" have some weight in determining individuals' behavior.' What I did say was that such abstractions, by themselves, are of little use in helping us understand variations in crime rates, or in devising specific policies that might realistically reduce crime. In practice, I argued, the conservative argument has usually been more specific – that the courts are soft on offenders, and – at least by implication – that they are softer here than elsewhere, softer now than in the past; hence getting 'tougher' with offenders in the courts would substantially reduce crime. I argued that none of this was in fact true; nothing in Wilson's response convinces me otherwise.

All of the data we have, in fact, support the contention that we are more punitive with offenders who have been caught and convicted than most other developed countries. Wilson accuses me of a little sleight of hand in my use of data from a study by Kenneth Wolpin to bolster my point. Well, the sleight of hand is there, all right; but I'm afraid it's his, not mine. Let's look closely at the original argument. I used Wolpin's data to show that, even *before* our massive 'get-tough' efforts of the 1970s and 1980s, the United States incarcerated more of those robbers we had managed to catch and convict than did the British or the Japanese. I made that point in response to a direct quote from a recent article by Wilson that asserted the contrary – that we do *not* 'imprison a higher fraction of those arrested, prosecuted, and convicted than do other nations'. I pointed out that Wilson had based this argument wholly on an earlier study by Wolpin which, as Wolpin himself later acknowledged, failed to count Americans sentenced to local jails. When they are added in, the picture changes altogether, as Wolpin's later research shows. We do indeed put more convicted robbers behind bars than other countries. Hence Wilson's earlier statement was simply wrong – wrong even for the period before the 'get-tough' 1970s, even more so now.

Wilson, however, seems unable to acknowledge this. Instead, he argues that since the chances of being caught and convicted are higher in Japan (according to the Wolpin study), the overall chances of incarceration are higher there. That's true, but it's also not the issue; I pointed it out myself, after all, in the same article. The question is what we make of this for purposes of intelligent social policy – or for understanding the causes of crime. To me, what this evidence tells us is that blaming judicial leniency for America's crime rate is easy but fruitless, since the problem lies primarily in the difficulty of *catching* criminals – not in our failure to get 'tough' with them once caught. And since no one has ever shown that it is 'leniency' that keeps us from catching criminals at the rate the Japanese do, we need to look elsewhere both to understand why our crime rates are so high and to develop realistic ways of doing something about them. Wilson has done some creditable writing on the police, and I suspect he understands this dilemma as well as I do. Why doesn't he simply acknowledge that his original statement was incorrect?

Something similar happens in his objection to my treatment of his argument about the links between crime and American culture. Nowhere does he respond to the substance of my criticism – that blaming America's crime rate on 'tolerance' or an 'ethos of self-expression' simply doesn't fit the evidence, either from our own experience or that of other countries. I argued that by international standards we are not a particularly tolerant society; nor are the social strata from which most violent criminals come noted for their encouragement of tolerance or self-expression. Wilson sidesteps those points, instead chiding me for rejecting cultural explanations of crime altogether. But did I really do that? On the contrary, I *commended* the conservatives for raising cultural issues. I said that 'with all its rhetorical excesses', the conservative argument about the links between crime and culture 'raises important questions' – ones that 'liberal criminology has sometimes sidestepped'. My beef with Wilson's specific argument wasn't that it was 'cultural', but that it was wrong. Once again, since he makes no effort to challenge – or even acknowledge – the specifics of my argument, I see no reason to modify that judgement.

I *did* say that explanations of crime that detach cultural from other social and economic forces are likely to be misleading; and I did say that they are also often used to justify a certain ideological passivity, an antipathy towards attacking the roots of crime through conscious social action. I still think so. Wilson's comments on Japan in his response simply add to that conviction. In his list of the things that might influence Japan's low crime rate, he includes just one – police practices – that has anything to do with public policy. But the Japanese do many things differently than we do when it comes to organizing their economic and social lives. And much evidence suggests that some of them may help us understand the difference between their crime rates and ours. Are we really to believe that such things as an effective employment policy – to take just the most obvious example – or a narrower spread of economic inequality don't even rate a place on the list of *possible* factors that might help explain those differences?

Much of the rest of Wilson's response amounts to a wide-ranging defence of the whole gamut of his views on crime; it would take a book to respond thoroughly to all the points he raises. Since I've already done that, let me just note a few of the more obvious and distressing ways in which his remarks misrepresent or oversimplify the evidence.

First, there were many things wrong with the liberal position on crime in the 1960s, as I've argued at some length in *Confronting Crime*. But Wilson consistently caricatures that position and exaggerates the evidence against it. The caricature begins with the statement that the liberal view rested on the (hardly credible) belief that 'man was wholly the product of his environment'. I don't know anyone who believed that, and I know a great many liberal criminologists; indeed, I *was* one, and I certainly never believed it. What liberals – and those to their left – *did* believe was that certain aspects of the socioeconomic environment had a profound effect on the crime rate – extremes of economic and racial inequality, blocked opportunities to achieve the economic and social rewards others could expect, intermittent or inadequate employment. Wilson says that no evidence supports this view, but I'm afraid that tells us more about his own lack of familiarity with the criminological literature of the time than it does about the actual state of the evidence. For there was considerable evidence even by the late 1960s (much of it summarized in such compendia as the report of the Task Force on Violent Crimes of the National Commission on the Causes and Prevention of Violence) – and there is much more today. On the other hand, there was not then, nor is there now, a shred of evidence to support Wilson's sweeping claim that 'altering the social context of crime' would take decades or 'generations' to have an effect, if it had any at all. How would he know? What studies have tested and supported that astonishing proposition?

Wilson is on stronger ground in arguing that the early literature on the effects of social programmes on crime wasn't very encouraging (it is far more so today). But his insistence that this disproved his opponents' position is unconvincing. Wilson argues that all that sustained the liberal (and left) position in the face of the 'failure' of some Great Society programmes was 'hope or ideology or both'. But what really sustained it was simple common sense. For the objection that the programmes weren't adequate to the problems was basically correct. Take employment policy. Liberals and socialists had long argued, with considerable evidence, that poor jobs bred crime. They also knew that the United States was unique among the advanced industrial societies in having developed no effective or comprehensive post-war employment policy. They knew, too, that this default was especially critical because of the massive migration of jobless people to the cities following the mechanization of agriculture and the consequent elimination of rural livelihoods. This understanding called for serious intervention in the labour market in the form of substantial training and job-creation efforts. But that isn't what we got. Indeed, that sort of effort was deliberately shot down in Congress three times after the Second World War – in the Employment Act of 1946, the manpower legislation of the 1960s, and the revised Humphrey-Hawkins bill of the mid-1970s. Instead, Congress created a welter of scattered programmes that by anyone's accounting – and especially by comparison with what went on in many other countries – were grudging and minimalist responses to a problem that demanded massive intervention. Wilson implies that developing an effective employment policy is one of those things 'government' 'cannot do at all'; but other governments *did*. The problem in America was not that government *could* not, but that it *would* not, take on the task.

Secondly, Wilson similarly misrepresents the strength of the evidence on deterrence, in order to support the uncontroversial – but also unhelpful – platitude that people 'often choose a course of action based on its likely consequences'. First, the early evidence – as the National Academy of Sciences pointed out in its exhaustive 1978 review of the issue – simply wasn't strong enough or clear enough to be of much use in informing social policy. It is true that most criminologists believed, in general, in the existence of some deterrent effect of punishment. But how well it worked, compared to what alternatives, for which offenders, and how to better accomplish it within the confines of the criminal justice system – the early evidence couldn't say. Today we know more. But what we know is not especially encouraging.

It seems clear that in the case of certain specific crimes – like domestic violence, the example Wilson uses – tougher sanctions against offenders can make a difference. But that's because sanctions of *any* kind are now so rarely enforced; the same may hold for drunken driving, another crime for which the evidence of a deterrent effect of getting tough is fairly persúasive. But this doesn't apply to other violent crimes where the probability of punishment is already high, such as murder or armed robbery. The record of efforts to get still 'tougher' on such crimes, especially through mandatory sentences, is not compelling. Wilson and I would probably agree that a tougher approach to wife-batterers would be a good thing; had he in fact read my book, he would have known that. But he ducks the central issue: that years of getting 'tougher' on most other serious violent crimes have brought disappointing results, not necessarily because people don't respond to punishment but because devising realistic ways to increase the *certainty* of punishment for most violent crimes has proven difficult indeed. (Wilson also chooses to ignore the evidence – dramatically accumulating in recent years – that the deterrent effect backfires for some offenders, that the experience of incarceration makes them *worse* – a good liberal argument that turns out to have been correct.)

Thirdly, Wilson argues that the root causes of crime lie in 'intimate settings' – notably early childhood expeiences – that are inherently 'difficult to reach, much less to change', through social policy. He has been advancing this argument for many years, and I confess I still don't know what to make of it. I tend to agree that, especially when it comes to serious violent crime, much of what goes wrong goes wrong at an early age. What I cannot fathom is why Wilson seems unable to comprehend that what goes on in the intimate settings of early childhood is profoundly influenced by forces *outside* those settings – forces which are indeed often amenable to conscious intervention. In my book I call this the 'fallacy of autonomy' – the belief that what goes on inside the family can be separated from what goes on outside it. Consider Wilson's curious example: since these early experiences happen 'long before the child can have much contact with the labour market', the labour market is irrelevant to understanding the child's early experiences! But can Wilson really believe that what happens to *parents* in the labour market has nothing to do with how they bring up their children, or the quality of the resources they're able to bring to that task?

Wilson suggests that I must regard him as one who 'loves to punish and hates to help'. He's wrong. I do not know Professor Wilson, have never met him, and have no idea what his personal feelings are on these matters. I have no doubt they're much more humane than that. However, he's certainly no 'pragmatist', as he claims, but an ardent and influential advocate of a view of crime that rests on certain important political assumptions – particularly the common conservative insistence on the limits of 'government'. Wilson is surely as entitled to these views as I am to mine, but it isn't helpful – or fair – to declare oneself above the political fray while dismissing one's opponents uniformly as ideologues. Wilson's writings have in fact been among the most important intellectual underpinnings of an approach to crime that has stressed incarceration at the expense of more constructive or preventive social action. That choice is not pragmatic, but political. Moreover, it is a choice whose results have been meagre and disappointing in the very terms Wilson claims to care most about: the risks of victimization by crime. Those who cling to this strategy in the face of the mounting evidence that it has been a costly failure typically claim – as Wilson does – to be on the side of crime's victims. But their often slipshod and cavalier rejection of more constructive alternatives actually condemns hundreds of thousands of Americans to brutalization and fear every year. If conservatives wish to defend that strategy with any credibility in the future, they'll have to do a much better job than Wilson has here.

References

Bayley, D.H. (1976) 'Learning about crime: the Japanese experience', *Public Interest*, Summer.
Bell, D. (1971) 'The cultural contradictions of capitalism', in D. Bell and I. Kristol (eds), *Capitalism Today*. New York: New American Library.
Clinard, M.B. (1978) *Cities with Little Crime*. Cambridge: Cambridge University Press.
Doleschal, E. and Newton, A. (1981) *International Rates of Imprisonment*. Hackensack, NJ: National Council on Crime and Delinquency.
Downes, D. (1982) 'The origins and consequences of Dutch penal policy since 1945', *British Journal of Criminology*, 22 (4).
van den Haag, E. (1982) 'Could successful rehabilitation reduce the crime rate?' *Journal of Criminal Law and Criminology*, 73.
Salas, L. (1979) *Social Control and Deviance in Cuba*. New York: Praeger.
Smith, R.J. (1983) *Japanese Society: Tradition, Self, and the Social Order*. Cambridge: Cambridge University Press.
Steenhuis, D.W. et al. (1983) 'The penal climate in the Netherlands: sunny or cloudy?', *British Journal of Criminology*, 23 (1).

Steinfels, P. (1980) *The Neoconservatives*, New York: Simon & Schuster.

Thompson, J. et al. (1981) *Employment and Crime: A Review of Theories and Research.* Washington, DC: National Institute of Justice.

Tullock, G. (1974) 'Does punishment deter crime?', *Public Interest*, Summer.

US Bureau of Justice Statistics (1984) *Prison Admissions and Release, 1981.* Washington, DC: Department of Justice.

Wilson, J.Q. (1975) *Thinking about Crime.* New York: Random House.

Wilson, J.Q. (1982) 'Dealing with the high-rate offender', *Public Interest*, Fall.

Wilson, J.Q. (1983a) *Thinking about Crime.* New York: Basic Books.

Wilson, J.Q. (1983b) 'Crime and American culture', *Public Interest*, Winter.

Wilson, J.Q. and Herrnstein, R.J. (1985) *Crime and Human Nature.* New York: Simon and Schuster.

Wolpin, K.I. (1975) 'An economic analysis of crime and punishment in England and Wales, 1894–1967', *Journal of Political Economy*, 86 (5).

Wolpin, K.I. (1980) 'A time-series cross-sectional analysis of international variations in crime and punishment', *Review of Economics and Statistics*, 62 (3).

3

Crime Prevention: the British Experience

John Bright

This chapter will examine the perspectives which lies behind crime prevention policy in the UK, describe the development of that policy and consider the various crime prevention programmes and activities that have been undertaken or sponsored as a result by central and local government, the police and the voluntary sector. It will conclude with a critique of current UK policy and suggest a way forward that may lead to more sustained and longer-term success.

Although it will concern itself mainly with the UK, occasional references will be made to ideas and developments in the USA. The significant differences in the scale and nature of the crime problem in the two countries should not be allowed to obscure the fact that arguments about its resolution have much in common. For example, on both sides of the Atlantic, those who promote the law enforcement (or criminal justice) approach to crime control are in vigorous debate with others who advocate approaches based on social development, youth investment and community reconstruction.

Crime prevention perspectives

There are three principal perspectives in the current crime prevention debate: a belief in the preventive effect of law enforcement and the criminal justice agencies; situational crime prevention in which opportunities for committing crime are reduced by modifying the design or management of the situation in which crime is known to occur; and social crime prevention, which aims to prevent people drifting into crime by improving social conditions, strengthening community institutions and enhancing recreational, educational and employment opportunities. It is fair to say that the law enforcement perspective dominates in the USA and still exerts a powerful influence in the UK.

In the USA, conservatives continue to argue for tougher legal sanctions, believing that to increase the 'cost of crime' to offenders will reduce its incidence (Wilson, 1975: xv). Indeed, it is reasonable to assume that perceptions of cost might have some weight in influencing people's behaviour. Tougher sanctions for some crimes (for example, domestic violence and driving while drunk) can reduce their incidence

(Currie, 1985). Incorporating sanctions for misconduct in community-based programmes for young offenders can reduce levels of reoffending (Krisberg, 1987). But generally, the evidence that deterrent custodial sentences prevent crime or reduce reoffending is not strong. Moreover, it is particularly difficult to maintain that high national crime rates are caused by insufficient punishment in a country whose exceptionally punitive penal system incarcerates one million people (four times the UK rate and more than any other industrialized country apart from South Africa). Nor is it easy to argue that crime will be better controlled by increased investment in the law enforcement agencies which already consume up to 25 percent of some city budgets. In spite of increased use of custody and increased expenditure on law enforcement during the 1970s and 1980s, the USA has the highest rate of crime and violence in the developed world (Curtis, 1990: 6). As the Federal judge who was chairman of the 1986 President's Commission on Organized Crime remarked, 'Law enforcement has been tested to the utmost, but let's face it, it just hasn't worked' (Eisenhower Foundation, 1989: 6).

In the UK, it is generally believed that the criminal justice agencies have a significant crime prevention effect, that if the police detect crime, the courts sentence offenders and the prisons and probation service discharge those sentences, crime will be prevented. Again, this view is not supported by the evidence. Since 1945, substantial increases in expenditure on the criminal justice agencies have been rewarded by an average rise in recorded crime of 5–7 percent per year (Home Office Criminal Statistics) and by high rates of reoffending by those given custodial sentences (Home Office Prison Statistics). We cannot of course measure the crime that has been *prevented* by the operation of the criminal justice agencies, but they do not appear to offer very good value for money in prevention terms. Although the law enforcement perspective prevails either as part of a theory of deterrence to which many politicians, right of centre newspapers and the judiciary subscribe or as an almost visceral response to crime from the 'average person in the street', it is less dominant than it was. Surveys in both the UK and the USA suggest that the public may be less punitive in their attitudes towards offenders than is commonly thought (Schwartz, 1990; Crime Concern, 1989).

The second perspective, situational crime prevention, is regarded by Home Office policy makers as having the greatest potential to make an impact on crime. Careful assessment of specific crime problems leads to changes to the design or management of criminogenic situations which are relatively easy to implement, monitor and evaluate. The theory and limitations of situational crime prevention are discussed in more detail in the next section.

Of the three perspectives, least attention has been given to social crime prevention, which aims to strengthen socialization agencies and community institutions in order to influence those groups that are most at risk of offending. This can be achieved by incorporating social crime prevention considerations into a wide range of social policies, most importantly planning, housing, employment, education, family, youth and health.

Conservative critics in the USA point to the difficulties of changing those social conditions which are associated with offending, compared with the greater possibilities to be gained by deploying legal sanctions (Wilson, in Hope and Shaw, 1988: 9). Clarke and Cornish in the UK add that 'there is little evidence to date that youth work, voluntary welfare, school liaison work by the police, community self-help groups, or tenants' associations have any effect on levels of crime' (Hope and Shaw, 1988: 9).

However, most social crime prevention programmes in the UK have been poorly resourced and rarely evaluated. In addition, much crime, especially violent crime, is not susceptible to situational approaches, and more research is necessary to identify the potential of social crime prevention. Many small-scale initiatives in both the USA and UK suggest that root causes can be addressed, the offending of high-risk groups reduced and the problems of high crime areas tackled successfully, although few have been carefully evaluated (Eisenhower Foundation, 1989; NACRO, 1987; Husain and Bright, 1990; Findlay et al., 1990).

Home Office policy makers are concerned about the enormous cost and limited effectiveness of the criminal justice system. At the same time, they are fairly suspicious of social crime prevention, believing that it is not rigorously conceived and is difficult and expensive to implement and evaluate. Also, there is probably some scepticism about the power of liberal democratic governments to change attitudes and behaviour, particularly when their efforts have to be mediated through tiers of local government, other local institutions and the media. As we will see, this has led to continued and substantial investment in the criminal justice agencies, lip-service to social crime prevention and a heavy emphasis on situational crime prevention.

The development of Home Office crime prevention policy

Let us now look briefly at the evolution of Home Office crime prevention policy and the views of its critics on both the left and right.

Personal or individual theories of crime holding that crime is caused by constitutional factors or inadequate personal development requiring medical treatment or rehabilitation have, until recently, been out of favour. (However, during 1990, there has been a revival of interest in theories which suggest that crime is a result of individual choice, strongly influenced by biological make-up and family relationships which are considered to be largely unaffected by outside forces. This has led to a debate on whether there is a permanent underclass whose criminality is unlikely to be affected by social and economic reforms (Wilson and Herrnstein, 1985).) It is argued that because criminal behaviour is so widespread, it cannot be put down to disturbed personalities, because no measurable differences could be found between the personalities of offenders and others, and because treatment and rehabilitation seemed to make little difference and often made matters worse. Whatever custodial agencies did, a high proportion of offenders continued to offend.

By the 1960s, the qualified support of the public for the rule of law which characterized the period between 1890 and 1950 was beginning to break down and US theories linking crime with social disorganization and economic marginality seemed to have more validity in the UK than before (Reiner, 1985). Unfortunately, many of the structural explanations of criminal behaviour which located the causes of crime in the deprivation and social disorganization of inner urban communities and on the unequal distribution of opportunities did not offer governments politically achievable objectives. For example, the failure of the Community Development Projects (set up in the 1970s to develop models for regenerating disadvantaged communities) in the UK to confine themselves to specific and focused goals led to a disillusionment with any kind of social engineering. The alleged failure of penal policy, social intervention and social reform to prevent crime led to the 'nothing works' pessimism of the late 1970s, a shift in focus away from the offender to the victim and the development of 'situational' or 'opportunity reduction' theories of crime prevention (Mayhew et al., 1976).

These argued that crime had gone up in advanced industrial societies because opportunities for it had increased. For example, car crime had risen because there were many more poorly secured, valuable cars around than there were before the Second World War. Much crime was thought to be situationally determined. In some places and at some times it is temptingly easy to break the rules, to take goods without paying and to avoid fares. Some situations (such as fuel meters full of cash in otherwise poor housing) actually encouraged crime.

The genesis of the situational approach can be traced to the report of the Cornish Committee in 1965 (Cornish Report, 1965) but this was a period when reaction was still seen as the most effective answer to crime and the committee's findings did not command widespread attention. However, as crime figures continued to rise, it was clear that crime not could be controlled by increased detection, investigation and deterrence. By the early 1980s, research began to demonstrate that blocking opportunities for crime reduced crime itself (Heal, 1989). This led to an emphasis on the need for individuals and agencies to work together at a local level to prevent crime by target hardening and other situational measures.

The advantage of this approach is that it leads to practical action which can reduce the incidence of some crimes. Improving household security, redesigning the layout of shops, housing estates and car parks to enable easier surveillance and to reduce opportunities can bring obvious results. Manufacturers are now beginning to take account of security at the design stage of production, for example in the car and housebuilding industries.

But situational theory can never fully explain all crime. The obvious fact remains that most people do not steal cars or burgle houses. Environmental determinism is not a sufficient explanation of criminal behaviour, although it does help to explain why people with a propensity to offend commit particular crimes in particular places at particular times. While situational crime prevention, theoretically, can reduce the estimated 70 percent of recorded crime that is thought to be opportunistic, it is unable to prevent many violent crimes such as some categories of assault, domestic violence, child abuse and racially motivated crime.

In seeking a more complete explanation, what other clues are there? First, crime is not evenly spread across all areas. The *British Crime Survey* (Mayhew et al., 1988) showed that crime is concentrated in inner urban run-down areas and on council estates. Thirty-seven percent of burglaries and 33 percent of thefts from the person and robberies are concentrated in such areas, although they contain only 12 percent of households (Hough and Mayhew, 1985). Secondly, in low crime areas, informal social controls develop naturally and inhibit anti-social and criminal behaviour. In high crime areas, such controls are weak and need to be strengthened (Box et al., 1988). Thirdly, habitual offenders may come from a subculture where criminal behaviour enhances personal status. Many young male offenders have grown up on urban housing projects with a constantly shifting population, inadequate support from their families and limited access to educational and employment opportunities (Parliamentary All-party Penal Affairs Group, 1983).

From theory to policy

What policies follow from this analysis? As we have seen, the criminal justice system will never be sufficient in itself to prevent crime. Crime surveys have taught us that a high proportion of crimes are never reported to the police and, of those that are reported, a further proportion are 'decrimed' and not recorded. Only about one out of every four crimes that are committed is eventually represented in the official crime statistics (Mayhew et al., 1988). And only about 35 percent of recorded crimes are cleared up, less than 20 percent in the Metropolitan Police District (Home Office Criminal Statistics). It is clear then that only a small proportion of crime is dealt with by the criminal justice system, probably less than 10 percent. While the criminal justice agencies have some deterrent effect, their capacity to prevent crime is very much less than is generally believed.

This conclusion leads us to emphasize the crime prevention potential of agencies outside the criminal justice system, not only in terms of target hardening and situational crime prevention but also in terms of the extent to which they can encourage and promote community stability and cohesion. It is widely acknowledged that crime rarely occurs in communities where there is social cohesion and is common in anonymous urban areas where ties are weaker. Japan is the only advanced urban society with low crime rates and this is thought to be connected with the high social cohesion and tight informal controls of Japanese society. In Western society, mechanisms of social control are likely to be restored or strengthened by developing more stable patterns of housing, schooling and employment.

A third form of crime prevention is to find ways of preventing reoffending. The above argument suggests that it might be better achieved by encouraging offenders to join one of the primary social groups in the community. Custodial sentences transfer offenders from the normal community into criminal groups in custody, only to return them to the same unsocialized environment from which they came, with residual social ties and controlling influences even further weakened. It is not surprising therefore that so many reoffend after completing a custodial sentence. The appropriate treatment for most young offenders is to avoid premature custody and to try to strengthen their involvement with key community institutions. At present offenders leaving custody constitute the 5 percent who commit 70 percent of all offences traced to known offenders (Tarling, 1985).

There are therefore three different levels of crime prevention that government might pursue: (a) physical and environmental measures (situational crime prevention); (b) measures designed to strengthen community institutions and increase social cohesion (with the community as the focus of attention rather than the individual); (c) measures addressed to the offender (by both the criminal justice agencies and community institutions). The translation of this analysis into policy was to be influenced by the Conservative government's commitment to: (a) reduced involvement by local authorities in the delivery of social policy; (b) a reliance on the more efficient and effective use and co-ordination of existing resources by the police, probation service and local authorities; (c) encouragement of voluntary or citizen activity; (d) reduced use of custody for juveniles and the concept of 'punishment in the community'.

As a result, Home Office policy since the mid-1980s has been characterized by an emphasis on multi-agency co-operation, situational crime prevention and Neighbourhood Watch (the latter representing the embodiment of the citizen's contribution to local crime prevention activity), supported by high-profile crime prevention campaigns and the inclusion of crime prevention in the programmes of other departments participating in the government's Action for Cities initiative. The programmes and activities inspired by this policy are outlined below.

Critics on the Left argue that criminal behaviour is an attractive and sometimes inevitable option for those young people whose class position and relative disadvantage offers them few opportunities for status and material rewards. Crime policy must take into account the social and economic conditions which predispose people to offend. At a national level, this will involve tackling homelessness, unemployment and low income. At a local level it will involve addressing the design and management of the built environment and improving the level of services and opportunities offered to young people. The Action for Cities initiative consisting of small, fixed term interventions directly managed by central government and involving few, if any, new resources, is not, the Left would argue, a sufficient response.

In addition, crime surveys, undertaken by criminologists of the Left Realism school, have shown that government-sponsored national surveys have consistently underestimated the amount and severity of inner-city crime and its effect on city dwellers (chapter 7; Jones et al., 1986). By focusing on inner-city districts, these surveys showed that the impact of crime is relatively greater on the poor, its effect is compounded by the other problems they face, such as low income and poor housing, and it falls heavily on women, particularly when unrecorded domestic violence and sexual assault are taken into account. They also showed that racially motivated crime and harassment continue to damage the lives of Britain's ethnic minorities.

Right-wing criticisms come principally from those who feel that there is insufficient commitment to the law enforcement model. For them, crime results from inadequate socialization in both the home and the school, a situation to be rectified by more punishments to bring offenders in line with social norms and more pressure on parents and teachers to enforce law-abiding attitudes. They emphasize individual responsibility, and are unconvinced by sociological explanations of crime or social crime prevention.

It would be interesting to apply Elliott Currie's critique of American crime control policy to the UK situation (Currie, 1988). He identifies two phases of community crime prevention which rest on sharply differing conceptions of what a community is and what needs to be done to it to reduce crime. They also differ in the balance to be struck between public and private responsibility for crime prevention.

Phase 1 is typified by a victim-centred, defensive approach to crime prevention which emphasizes citizen action, opportunity reduction and the need to protect the community from offenders who are seen as outsiders. It focuses mainly on property theft, 'incivilities' and fear of crime, and tends not to address crimes such as domestic violence, child abuse and racial harassment. This contrasts with the structural or institutional concerns of phase 2 in which potential offenders' behaviour is seen to be influenced by wider forces and by the quality of the community institutions with which they come into contact. It accepts that offenders are likely to be part of the community and aims to tackle the processes which lead to criminal behaviour, by strengthening these institutions and increasing the range of opportunities available to potential offenders. For Currie,

> the biggest problem with the (phase 1) approach is that programmes based wholly on it do not seem to work well, and sometimes not at all, as the more serious evaluations of Neighbourhood Watch have shown. Moreover, to the extent that they work at all, they tend to work for communities with the least serious crime problems, the lowest risk. They work badly in resource-poor communities where victimization is more severe. (Currie, 1988)

Would Home Office policy work in such communities? Would it make an impact on the incidence of crime? Would it reassure the public who throughout the 1980s consistently registered crime as one of their top three concerns?

Crime prevention activity and programmes in the 1980s

We have looked at the development of government policy and considered the criticisms that have been levelled at it from both the Left and the Right. During the 1980s, a number of crime prevention programmes, projects and initiatives were sponsored by central and local government, the police and the non-statutory or 'not-for-profit' sector.

Activities of central government

In 1983, the Home Office Standing Conference on Crime Prevention (established following the recommendations of the Cornish Commitee) was strengthened by a Home Office minister taking the chair. In the same year the Home Office Crime Prevention Unit was set up. In 1984 an interdepartmental circular on crime prevention was issued by central government to all Chief Constables and local authority chief executives encouraging them to co-ordinate their resources in the fight against crime. This was a clear statement from government that crime would not be prevented or even reduced by the activities of the criminal justice agencies alone. It also represented an attempt to harness systematically the resources and energies of local agencies to the crime prevention effort. The circular was unquestionably successful in promoting the concept of multi-agency crime prevention. However, its guidance on leadership was weak (reflecting its unwillingness to confer a central role on local authorities) and it offered no extra resources. As a result, many of the multi-agency committees that were set up did not know what to do, those that did had no resources with which to do it and many crime prevention initiatives inspired by the circular probably had little effect.

In 1986, the profile of crime prevention was raised still higher by a special seminar chaired by the then Prime Minister which laid emphasis on the role of the business sector and led directly to the creation of the interdepartmental Ministerial Group on Crime Prevention. In the same year, the Home Office launched its Five Towns Initiative, a demonstration project to test the methodology advocated in the 1984 circular which involved the towns of Bolton, Croydon, North Tyneside, Swansea and Wellingborough. This was not as innovative as its publicity made out – the model on which it was based owed a lot to the estate improvement programmes which have been pioneered by NACRO and others since 1980. Crime patterns were analysed, multi-agency committees set up, residents consulted, action plans prepared and their implementation negotiated. Three of these projects led to modest reductions in crime and continued beyond the initial funding period (Home Office, 1989).

Although the 'Five Towns' were not strictly town-wide or strategic initiatives (most concentrated their efforts on one problematic area), they provided the impetus for the more ambitious Safer Cities Programme launched in 1987. This programme involves 20 high-crime English cities and is again managed directly by central government. Its full-time co-ordinators are seconded to the civil service and their salaries are paid by the Home Office. Each project has a budget of £¼m a year for three years. Among the crime prevention measures sponsored by the programme to date are home security schemes, design modifications, improvements to lighting, courses in personal safety, diversionary activities for young people, design and management measures to address city centre crime and nuisance, security improvements for small businesses and estate security programmes (Home Office, 1989).

The Safer Cities Programme has been criticized on three grounds. First, it is directly managed from Whitehall, local councillors were initially excluded from its local steering committees, and all spending decisions have to be sanctioned by the Home Office. Secondly, it is operating in 20 cities/boroughs although there are at least twice as many with crime problems deserving of extra resources. Finally, the £¼m p.a. for three years is an inadequate sum for cities the size of Liverpool or Birmingham. It remains to be seen whether permanent crime management arrangements are created (similar to the municipal crime prevention councils in France), or whether the schemes confine themselves to crime analysis and grant distribution.

The Home Office's activities have been supported by its policy and research units and by regular, high-profile media campaigns, informed by national crime surveys and complemented by the inclusion of crime prevention in the programmes of other departments involved in the government's Action for Cities initiative. For example, its 'Crack Crime' campaign in 1988 was well presented and an improvement on previous campaigns, although it focused principally on exhorting people to secure their property and take care of themselves. This is not a new message – advice on household security and personal safety is readily available. Crime prevention campaigns may raise awareness and reinforce normative standards but they are expensive and there is little evidence that on their own they influence behaviour, especially in the long term (Riley and Mayhew, 1980).

The three *British Crime Surveys* of 1982, 1984 and 1988 generated an enormous amount of information about the distribution and amount of crime, and such surveys are a more reliable guide to underlying trends than recorded crime figures. At the same time, these national sweeps have been criticized for underestimating the impact of crime on inner-city residents, especially women and members of ethnic minority groups (Jones et al., 1986).

Among the other government departments which have included crime prevention in their programmes are the Department of the Environment in its Estate Action Schemes, the Department of Trade and Industry through its Inner City Task Forces and City Action Teams and, more recently, the Department of Education and Science in its guidance to schools. Much of this effort has been concentrated in the areas where crime problems are known to be most serious, namely inner city and outer urban housing estates. Targeted investment in these areas might reasonably be expected to reduce crime rates.

Unfortunately, the level of input has not approached the scale of the problem. The Department of the Environment's Housing Investment

Programme and Estate Action Scheme allocations amounted to £2.2bn 1990/91, a limited contribution to the £19bn needed simply to repair housing stock and only a proportion of which was designated for crime prevention purposes (Department of the Environment, 1985, 1990).

The housing crisis in the capital is particularly severe. Apart from a worsening homelessness problem, 40–60 percent of the housing stock in some London boroughs is owned by local authorities and much of it is badly designed or in disrepair or both. Spending on council housing has declined dramatically throughout the 1980s. For every £1 spent in 1980, only 33p was spent in 1988 (*New Statesman and Society*, 1989). Added to this are the reductions in rate support grant (between 1979 and 1988) from central to local government. Of course, these losses to local government funds reflect the shift from public to private-sector-led inner-city policy and some will have been used to subsidize private sector initiatives such as development corporations and task forces whose success is intended to result in a 'trickle-down' of resources to the least well off. The mechanism by which this is expected to bring about improvements to the fabric of housing estates is unclear.

In 1988, the Home Office set up Crime Concern, an independent not-for-profit body, to stimulate more local crime prevention activity by acting as a catalyst, consultant, fundraiser and disseminator of good practice. It was also given the task of encouraging the private sector to address its own crime problems and to contribute to community crime prevention initiatives. Its work was to be undertaken in close co-operation with the police, local authorities and the private sector.

By the end of its first year, it had helped set up locally controlled, strategic crime reduction programmes in 15 towns, cities and boroughs, had published a handbook on youth crime prevention, was well on the way to developing a national strategy for supporting neighbourhood watch and crime prevention panels, was involved in a business and crime initiative and had raised £0.75m for local crime prevention activity.

It also discovered that while the private sector was keen to support crime prevention initiatives, it was unwilling to fund activity which it judged to be more properly the responsibility of government. Apart from relatively small charitable donations, most serious company giving is usually determined by an assessment of the community relations, or less frequently, marketing benefits, that might result from a proposal. This normally excludes long-term funding of 'problem-oriented' initiatives in high crime areas.

Finally in 1990, the government issued its circular *Partnerships in Prevention* which draws on the lessons learnt since 1984 and aims to spell out the essential elements of effective multi-agency crime prevention work (Home Office, 1990a). Sadly, it has failed in part to rectify some of the faults of the earlier circular by appearing to believe that strategic leadership, as with that for individual projects, is a matter that can be left to local preferences. In its wish to avoid prescription, it has left ill-defined the respective roles of the police, local government, other statutory bodies and the voluntary and private sectors, and failed to ascribe a strategic leadership role to local government. The response to the circular is being monitored. It will be interesting to see if an opportunity has been missed.

The police

Crime prevention is no longer the low-status police specialism that it used to be. Police crime prevention policy has moved on from a preoccupation with physical security and target hardening to a concern with the broader issues of community involvement, inter-agency work and environmental design and management. The police have supported Neighbourhood Watch and helped it to cover over four million households. Six forces have organized major youth activity programmes during the school holidays, some involving up to 20,000 young people. The police support adult and youth Crime Prevention Panels and most forces have developed school liaison schemes. Finally the police have initiated and participated in multi-agency crime reduction programmes with an enthusiasm not always matched by other agencies.

Although it is generally believed that the original role of the police was to prevent crime, and most people think that crime is prevented by police activity, as we have seen most police resources are devoted to responding to crime after it has occurred. Out of the 127,000 police officers, only about 1 percent are dedicated crime prevention officers. Many of these think that the proportion of police resources devoted to crime prevention is inadequate, and that the culture of the police is too heavily focused on maintaining public order and crime detection. Others argue equally forcefully that most police officers contribute to crime prevention in many different ways and that patrolling police (especially on foot) deter offenders and prevent them from committing further crime. The police generally feel that strong positive policing and stricter laws are more effective in reducing crime than 'soft' policing specialisms such as crime prevention and community liaison (*Police Magazine*, 1990).

Lack of clear guidance as to who should take the lead in crime prevention has led to a situation in which some local authorities and police forces think the police should lead, whereas others think the central strategic role should fall to local government. A compromise would be to propose that strategic programmes should be led jointly by both the police and local government, as is already happening in many areas. In due course it is probable that the principal strategic responsibility, in Metropolitan areas at least, will fall to local government. The debate about leadership often surprises those with more traditional views about crime and its prevention, and perhaps needs more explanation.

It is accepted that the police hold the information about crime and offenders, have much experience of situational crime prevention and are the only agency authorized and equipped to respond to most crime problems. Many community crime prevention initiatives are unlikely to work unless there is an appropriate police input, and in many areas this may be a precondition for community mobilization and activity by other agencies. A number of community policing initiatives have been demonstrably successful in reducing crime and there is a need for greater commitment to this area of work (NACRO, 1988). However, the police do not have the resources or authority to intervene in many of the circumstances which lead to crime being committed. They do not make decisions about the management and deployment of staff in housing estates, schools, youth centres and shopping centres (although they may be invited to advise). They are not responsible for street lighting or public transport or the design of new residential and commercial developments or planning applications. As one author has put it:

> The police are not, for the most part, the prime movers, the initiators of the social processes that control deviant behaviour. On the contrary, they work at the margins where the usual processes of control have broken down ... (they) act as a continuation of ... more general efforts by the mass of people and institutions to maintain order, control and coherence. In other words, they are a small but extremely important element within a much larger complex of inter-related systems of control. (Smith, 1983:10)

Local government

In the early 1980s, local government did not appear to accept that it had any responsibility for crime prevention. Conservative and some 'traditional' Labour councils thought it was entirely a matter for the police. In addition, members of some 'New Left' councils and many academic criminologists were suspicious of the concept. A few considered it to be a form of 'social control' and (with the important exceptions of racial and sexual offences) believed that crime was something that the working class were justified in committing against middle-class people (Kinsey and Young, 1983). These arguments prevailed in spite of the fact that local authorities owned and managed over five million properties, many of which were on estates disfigured by serious crime problems. They were gradually refuted by the findings of crime surveys which showed that the most frequent victims of crime were in fact the constituents of inner city councils. By the late 1980s, a number of Labour-controlled councils in the larger cities had included community safety within the remit of their police monitoring groups and many others were employing community safety officers or crime prevention co-ordinators or taking much greater note of crime prevention in the delivery of their services. ('Community safety' is a term sometimes used by local authorities to distinguish their contribution to reducing crime from that of the police, with whom the term 'crime prevention' is associated. 'Crime reduction' is sometimes used as an alternative to both.)

A small but increasing number of local authorities are now developing crime reduction strategies in which the crime prevention contribution of their various departments is identified, objectives and targets set and progress monitored (NACRO, 1989a, 1989c; Home Office, 1990a). During 1989, the Association of Metropolitan Authorities set up a working group on crime prevention to signal to its members – and to central government – the pivotal role that local government can play in crime prevention.

In this context, it is worth drawing attention to the range of powers and resources that local authorities can bring to this area. They can:

- Develop strategies across all departments to reduce the risk of crime by targeting high risk areas, incorporating crime prevention targets into departmental objectives, and by helping to bring their housing stock up to a minimum standard of security.
- Use their resources and expertise to strengthen communities by providing support for parents, activities for children and young people, youth crime prevention initiatives, education and training for the unemployed, and by supporting community organizations.
- Provide practical support for victims of crime by funding victim support schemes, tackling domestic violence and racially motivated crime, funding refuges and crisis centres and promoting insurance and compensation schemes.

In fact, the potential of local government is most likely to be realized by strengthening the crime prevention and community safety component of existing services such as housing, education, recreation, youth, planning and social services and then considering whether additional initiatives are necessary. Local crime prevention strategies depend on the efficient delivery of services by many departments. This can only be achieved by a high level of political commitment and a high standard of interdepartmental co-operation. Some local government associations have argued that local authorities should be given a statutory responsibility for crime prevention to encourage them to continue and extend what many are already doing, to prevent them from deferring their responsibilities to the police and to provide them with the powers to raise funds for crime prevention activity (AMA, 1990).

Crime prevention is clearly a natural function for local government, given its responsibilities for public administration, service provision and environmental management. However, if this function is to be discharged effectively, significant improvements to the way some local authorities deliver their basic services are required. For example, standards of housing management on many public housing estates are unsatisfactory for reasons that cannot be attributed entirely to resource limitations (Audit Commission, 1987). Yet such estates often experience high levels of crime and fear of crime on which good management might be expected to make an impact.

Activities of the voluntary independent or not-for-profit sector

Much of the pioneering community crime prevention work in the UK was undertaken by voluntary organizations such as NACRO (National Association for the Resettlement of Offenders) which in 1979 set up its Crime Prevention Unit (CPU) and in 1980 the Safe Neighbourhood Unit (SNU). Both units worked closely with local authorities, the police and local communities and concentrated their efforts on high crime housing estates.

The methods employed are now familiar; multi-agency steering committees were set up, consultations with residents and staff carried out and action plans drawn up, addressed mainly to the local council and the police. There was usually no prior commitment to funding recommended improvements but selection of the estate usually endowed it with a degree of priority and local resident/agency steering committees often acted as effective pressure groups. On a number of occasions, these estate-based schemes led to substantial improvements. More commonly, estates improved gradually over the ensuing 2 to 3 years. Sometimes not very much happened (Bright and Petterssen, 1984; NACRO SNU, 1987). However, three important lessons emerged from this experience.

First, it was clear that crime prevention projects on housing estates could not just be about crime prevention. The best were multi-focused projects tackling the multiple problems found in such areas. Estate design and management, play and youth provision, community facilities, policing, employment opportunities, all had to be addressed and many projects concentrated as much on estate management as they did on crime prevention. The focus of effort was determined by the local authority and the residents and invariably the key to perceived or real crime problems lay with improving the way the estates were managed and serviced. This was also the experience of the Priority Estates Project, which was set up by the Department of the Environment in 1979 to work with local authorities to improve the management of housing estates. For them, good, localized and locally accountable management is the key to safer estates (Power, 1986).

Secondly, it became clear that residents are more likely to become involved in community crime prevention programmes if the council and the police are seen to be tackling the problems which only they have the resources and authority to address. Without this input, efforts to mobilize the community will often be unsuccessful.

Thirdly, crime prevention in many high crime areas would not be achieved by relying on multi-agency co-operation and community participation alone. Resources are needed to support tenant management initiatives and to reorganize housing management, to rectify design faults, to improve poorly lit, vandalized environments, to make multi-storey blocks safe and secure and to provide facilities for children and young people. One additional consequence of reduced public spending during the 1980s has been the loss of the voluntary effort, in terms of participation in community organizations, youth facilities and Neighbourhood Watch, that would have been stimulated by a more generous allocation of resources.

A good deal of expertise in multi-agency work, youth work, neighbourhood policing, resident consultation, housing management and estate security emerged from the work initiated by these units, much of which has filtered through into mainstream professional practice. But they were small, poorly resourced, insecurely funded and their effectiveness often limited by the inertia of the bureaucracies which commissioned them. Their work was also affected by the political changes and financial constraints that impoverished and marginalized public sector housing during the 1980s. They demonstrated both the benefits and limitations of intervention by independent change agents who also found themselves acting as consultants, pressure groups and community workers.

Neighbourhood watch

Neighbourhood watch (NW) is often seen as a police initiative, yet its growth has taken the police by surprise and it has become by far the most popular voluntary crime prevention activity. There are now over 81,000 schemes in England and Wales covering 4 million households. For the last three years, the annual increase has been 15–20,000 schemes per year and there is no sign of this abating (Husain and Bright, 1990).

The usefulness of these figures has been questioned by many. Since there is no agreed definition of a scheme, the count is meaningless.

There is also a suspicion that many are no longer active or exist only on paper. There is some justification for these comments since inaccuracies in the way the Home Office compiled figures came to light in 1988. But despite these doubts, the figures are broadly corroborated by the findings of the 1988 *British Crime Survey* which found that only 4 percent of schemes could be classified as inactive, that 90 percent of the population had heard of NW and that two-thirds of non-members indicated interest in joining a scheme if one were to be set up in their area (Mayhew et al., 1988).

Two criticisms continue to be made of NW: that there is no evidence that it reduces crime; and that it only works in middle-class areas where crime rates are relatively low and thereby displaces police resources (essential for its maintenance) from high crime areas. (For a discussion of the displacement argument, see Barr and Pease (1990).) The research available on its effectiveness in reducing crime is inconclusive. However, it does not follow that support for NW is misplaced.

First, methodological problems make identification of a crime prevention effect very difficult. Secondly, the quality of schemes differs so enormously that contradictory conclusions are to be expected. Thirdly, many people involved with NW are convinced of its value and gain reassurance from its existence; and finally, Neighbourhood Watch may help to strengthen communities and lead to benefits that will only be apparent in the longer term.

The second criticism concerns the distribution of schemes. Research shows that the highest coverage is to be found in suburban owner-occupied housing and inner-city, high status neighbourhoods where membership levels of 12–24 percent are common. In contrast, NW has grown slowly in areas of public-sector housing, poorer quality older terraced housing, and in high crime multi-racial areas. This uneven distribution has been explained by the severity of the problems, low levels of community integration, distrust of the police, fear of victimization, apathy, cultural, religious and language barriers on the one hand and, on the other, by the greater motivation, resources and confidence of owner-occupiers (Husain and Bright, 1990).

Three questions face neighbourhood watch as it moves into its second decade:

1   What can be done to sustain the interest and involvement of scheme members?
2   How should it be managed and supported (given the demands it is placing on the police)?
3   How can its potential be developed in high crime areas?

Despite its popularity, the capacity of neighbourhood watch to reduce crime should not be exaggerated. In many areas, it is no substitute for good public services and home beat policing (although it may complement them) and it should not be seen as the central plank of a national crime prevention policy. However, because it is so popular, it could develop into a national network through which ideas can be put into practice. For example, schemes could also concern themselves with other matters which affect the quality of life and which touch on the problem of crime, such as poor lighting, dog nuisance, refuse, abandoned cars, vandalized parks and gardens and traffic and public transport problems, or with improving community facilities such as play and youth activities and provision for the elderly; or with arranging social and recreational activities for the benefit of all local residents. Many schemes have already started to diversify in this way. Such developments keep the membership active and can enhance the quality of life in the neighbourhood. The crime prevention function would also be strengthened because more people would be involved.

Under certain circumstances, neighbourhood watch can work in high crime areas and residents are often willing to join schemes. However, they must have confidence in their neighbours, they must feel that what is being proposed is likely to work, there must be consistent support from the police and other agencies, and related problems, such as poor housing or play provision, need to be addressed at the same time.

If some or all of these conditions are not present, it is unlikely that NW will develop successfully. Moreover, a more proactive approach by the police may be required. This does not mean imposing a scheme on neighbourhoods but encouraging key individuals and local organizations to adopt the idea and helping bring it to fruition, perhaps by including it as one element within a more broadly-based community crime prevention or neighbourhood improvement strategy. Building on existing community networks has often been the most successful route to achieving this.

Commentary
During the 1980s, crime prevention has been higher on the agenda of national concerns than ever before. There have been many innovative developments from central and local government, the police and the voluntary sector. There have been high profile publicity campaigns. Participation in local crime prevention activities has increased dramatically. The government has recently turned its attention to domestic violence, racial crime and drug-related crime and has targeted its Safer Cities resources in twenty areas with high crime rates.

Yet recorded crime continues to rise in many areas after a brief turndown in the late 1980s (Home Office, 1990b) and surveys confirm that crime continues to be one of the public's top three concerns. The reasons for this are complex and may be less to do with government crime prevention initiatives and more with the unintended criminogenic effects of some social and economic policies and with the failure to resource, strengthen and, where necessary, reform local government services. Addressing crime prevention at this level of policy development may be the key to achieving significant and sustained reductions.

Insufficient attention has been given to longer-term social strategies or to the question of resources for which there has been an over-reliance on the private sector and voluntary effort. There are also serious gaps in the distribution of crime prevention activity. Some urban areas (for example, some London boroughs) with the highest crime rates in the country, high levels of social disadvantage and local services close to collapse, have no crime prevention or community safety strategy, a situation for which government must share responsibility.

Possibly the most visible weakness of crime prevention policy in the UK has been the absence of a youth crime prevention strategy. This is surprising considering the very strong association between crime and the young. Much youth crime is non-violent, opportunistic and preventable. Unfortunately, the areas which are most at risk, namely inner urban areas and housing estates with high child populations, are usually the least well covered by existing youth services. Lack of suitable premises and a tendency for the most difficult young people to reject or be excluded from the existing provisions means that the youth service frequently has little impact.

We need to move beyond diversionary schemes. Initiatives in the UK, USA, Canada and France suggest that the best long-term prospects for preventing crime may lie with investing more in children and young people. This may be done by, for example, improving community and financial support for parents, increasing pre-school and nursery provision, substantially increasing the range of play and youth activities in residential areas, especially those with high child populations and high crime rates and developing high quality work training and employment opportunities.

There is also a need for more immediate and specific action in the form of local youth crime prevention programmes which are sharply focused and targeted on communities whose young people are most at risk. The best projects involve local residents as volunteers, include young people in managing their activities and aim to tackle the roots of crime. They do this by addressing all the problems faced by disadvantaged young people such as low self-esteem, lack of family support, poor education and limited employment opportunities (Eisenhower Foundation, 1989; NACRO, 1989b; Findlay et al., 1990).

Finally, well-managed and adequately resourced community-based programmes are necessary for those young people who have been convicted of non-violent offences.

Government is attempting to tackle a multi-billion pound problem with an under-resourced package of voluntary action, multi-agency co-operation and short-term, centrally controlled projects. Its own recent consultative circular is a shadow of the United Nation's resolution on crime prevention and urban safety to which it is also a signatory (United Nations, 1990). At a local level, 'bureaucratic drift' often inhibits the capacity of key public agencies, principally the police and local government, to respond adequately to public concerns about crime (Jones et al., 1986).

Much of what is described as crime prevention is in fact public relations. Campaigns, competitions school visits, conferences, seminars, slogans, mascots and multi-agency committees are only likely to contribute to a reduction in crime or fear of crime if they are part of a clearly conceived crime reduction strategy. Too often they are seen as ends in themselves.

Managing crime – the challenge for the 1990s

I have briefly considered the various perspectives which have underpinned crime prevention policy during the past three decades, outlined the development of that policy, described the main crime prevention programmes and activities that were developed in the UK during the 1980s and drawn attention to their limitations. We are probably witnessing a 'shift in paradigm' (Tuck, 1987) away from an emphasis on law enforcement and punishment as the main means of controlling crime towards a model which places less emphasis on the criminal justice agencies and rather more on the social development and environmental management functions of local government.

Yet there are difficulties here. Only a part of what we call social crime prevention involves policies which are exclusively and recognizably concerned with preventing crime. The essence of social crime prevention lies with the connections that must be made between crime and other areas of social policy. This has led some to warn of a danger in 'criminalizing' social policy, that is, endorsing a process whereby crime prevention becomes the justification for any social policy initiative which as a result becomes 'crime driven' (Smith, 1989). This has certainly occurred during the 1980s in response to a government with an ambivalent attitude to public services and a strong belief in law and order.

Similarly, although there are connections between crime and other social policies, crime prevention is not necessarily a priority for policy makers or service providers in these other areas. At a governmental level, crime prevention depends on a high level of interdepartmental co-ordination and agreement to ensure that its lessons inform all aspects of policy making. We know this is difficult to bring about, especially when there is a conflict of interest between departmental policy and crime prevention considerations. It also requires a similar level of co-ordinated action at a local level, not only between local authority departments but between different agencies and sectors. This too can be hard to achieve.

Social crime prevention is a second order policy area whose success depends on its advocates' ability to influence primary policy making. Although it may be undesirable for social policy to become 'crime driven', it is certainly desirable to take account of crime prevention in the formulation of 'mainstream' social policies. Nationally, this may be achieved by establishing an inter-ministerial group (as in the UK) or a crime prevention council (as in some European countries). At a local level, responsibility for crime prevention should lie with the local authority and strategic policies and programmes developed in partnership with the police, other statutory and voluntary agencies, community organizations and the private sector.

Such programmes can operate at a town, city or district level and would aim to build crime prevention into the day-to-day operations of public, private and voluntary organizations. As appropriate, they would promote 'multi-agency action' to replace the weaker concept of co-operation. The roles of participating agencies and community organizations would be clearly defined and the scope of the multi-agency project enhanced to address the social and physical symptoms of disorder as well as crime (Crawford et al., 1989; Skogan, 1990). The programmes would emphasize neighbourhood regeneration, support for parents and investment in young people, improved management of the environment and local services and youth crime prevention.

Neighbourhood regeneration, in order to improve the design and fabric of the built environment and to regenerate local economies. Financial and community support for parents and investment in young people, because parents play a major role in influencing the behaviour of their children and parental supervision needs to be assisted by that of others in the community. Improved management, because it is the key to reducing crime, disorder and fear of crime in many locations, notably housing estates, schools, town centres, hospitals, businesses and some public transport systems. Youth crime prevention, because mainstream activities for young people and youth crime prevention programmes, coupled with access to good quality training and employment opportunities, will divert many of the young people who currently commit 50 percent of all recorded crime. The costs of these measures need to be offset against the short-term savings and longer-term direct and indirect benefits to the economy that will accrue from less crime and disorder. It is estimated that crime currently costs £500 p.a. for every employed person, equivalent to the cost of the National Health Service hospitals.

No one measure on its own will necessarily be sufficient. The needs of communities need to be carefully assessed and a customized package of preventive measures prepared. Researchers often seem to be unaware of this. Many research designs aim to identify the causal significance of a single variable and do not always appreciate that a measure may only have a crime prevention effect in combination with others. In high crime areas, a range of measures may be needed and it is not always possible to disentangle the causal primacy of any one of them.

In the UK we are only beginning to understand what the potential for social crime prevention might be. A review of research into the links between parenting and delinquency concluded that more resources need to be diverted towards the early social prevention of crime. There are positive indications that parental training, family support and pre-school and supplementary education can improve educational performance, reduce the use of residential care and prevent delinquency. The review argues that resources should be targeted on disadvantaged communities with a high incidence of educational underachievement, receptions into care and delinquency, rather than on individual households (Graham, 1988). Continuing this theme, a report of the US Committee for Economic Development (composed of senior business executives) noted that:

> It would be hard to imagine a higher yield for a dollar of investment than that found in pre-school programmes for at risk children. Every dollar spent on early prevention and intervention can save $4.75 in the cost of remedial education, welfare and crime further down the road. (Curtis, 1990)

The approach to crime prevention advocated in this chapter is consistent with that being promoted by the European Forum on Urban Safety and Crime Prevention through its international conferences and worldwide network of town and cities engaged in crime prevention and community safety work (European and North American Conference on Urban Safety and Crime Prevention: Final Declaration, 1989). It also reflects the conclusions of a 1988 Home Office review of community crime prevention in the UK, Europe and North America which concluded that 'the most promising means of preventing crime and sustaining that reduction lie with strategies that strengthen community institutions' (Hope and Shaw, 1988:2).

Increasingly, many politicians and crime prevention professionals are coming round to the view that sustained reductions in crime may only be achieved by an approach which acknowledges the potential of social crime prevention, is prepared to invest in research and action and is willing to equip those agencies that are in a position to act with the guidance, encouragement, powers and resources necessary to make an impact. This is the challenge for the 1990s. It remains to be seen whether the UK and American governments are prepared to meet it.

I am grateful to Graeme Hart, Tony Holden and Nigel Whiskin for commenting on an earlier draft of this chapter. They bear no responsibility for its final form.

References

Association of Metropolitan Authorities (1990) *Crime Reduction – A Framework for the 1990s*. London: AMA.

Audit Commission (1987) *The Management of London Authorities: Preventing the Breakdown of Services*. London: HMSO.

Barr, R. and Pease, K. (1990) 'Crime placement, displacement and deflection', in M. Tonry and N. Morris (eds) *Crime and Justice: A Review of Research*. Vol. 12. Chicago: University of Chicago Press.

Box, S., Hale, C. and Andrews, G. (1988) 'Explaining fear of crime', *British Journal of Criminology*, 28 (3): 340–56.

Bright, J. and Petterssen, G. (1984) *Improving Council House Estates*. London: NACRO Safe Neighbourhood Unit.

Cornish Report (1965) *Report of the Committee on the Prevention and Detection of Crime*. London: Home Office.

Crawford, A., Jones, T., Woodhouse, T. and Young, J. (1989) *Second Islington Crime Survey*. London: Middlesex Polytechnic.

Crime Concern (1989) *Response to Questions in a Gallup Poll*. Swindon: Crime Concern.

Currie, E. (1985) *Confronting Crime – An American Challenge*. New York: Pantheon.

Currie, E. (1988) 'Two visions of community crime prevention' in Home Office (eds), *Communities and Crime Reduction*. London: HMSO. pp. 280–85.

Curtis, L. (1990) *The National Drug Control Strategy and Inner City Policy*. Washington: Eisenhower Foundation.

Department of the Environment (1985) *An Enquiry into the Condition of the Local Authority Housing Stock in England*. London: HMSO.

Department of the Environment (1990), press release.

Eisenhower Foundation (1989) *Youth Investment and Community Reconstruction*. Washington: Eisenhower Foundation.

European and North American Conference on Urban Safety and Crime Prevention (1989) *Final Declaration*. Communauté Urbaine de Montreal.

Findlay, J., Bright, J. and Gill, K. (1990) *Youth Crime Prevention: A Handbook of Good Practice*. Swindon: Crime Concern.

Graham, J. (1988) 'Families, parenting skills and delinquency', *Home Office Research Bulletin* No. 26. London: HMSO. pp. 17–21.

Heal, K. (1989) 'Crime prevention in the United Kingdom – from start to go' and 'In safer communities: A social strategy for Canada', (Special Issue) *Canadian Journal of Criminology*, 31 (4).

Home Office Criminal Statistics. Published Annually. London: HMSO.

Home Office (1983) *Prison Statistics England and Wales.* London: HMSO.

Home Office Statistical Bulletin 7/1985. London: HMSO.

Home Office (1988) *The Five Towns Initiative: A Community Response to Crime Prevention.* London: HMSO.

Home Office (1989) *Safer Cities Progress Report.* London: HMSO.

Home Office (1990a) *Partnership in Crime Prevention.* London: HMSO.

Home Office (1990b) *Statistical Bulletin 19/90.* London: HMSO.

Hope, T. and Shaw, M. (eds) (1988) *Communities and Crime Reduction.* London: HMSO.

Hough, M. and Mayhew, P. (1985) *Taking Account of Crime: Key Findings from the 1984 British Crime Survey.* Home Office Research Study No 85. London: HMSO.

Husain, S. and Bright, J. (eds) (1990) *Neighbourhood Watch and the Police.* Swindon: Crime Concern.

Jones, T., Maclean, B. and Young, J. (1986) *The Islington Crime Survey.* Aldershot: Gower.

Kinsey, R. and Young, J. (1983) 'Life and crimes', *New Statesman,* 7 October.

Krisberg, B. (1987) *Preventing and Controlling Violent Youth Crime: The State of the Art in Violent Youth Crime.* Centre for the Study of Youth Policy, University of Michigan.

Mayhew, P., Clarke, R.U.G., Sturman, A. and Hough, J.M. (1976) *Crime as Opportunity.* London: HMSO. Also cited in D. Smith (1989) 'Crime prevention: the past ten years'. Address to West Midlands Probation Service.

Mayhew, P., Elliot, D. and Dowds, L. (1988) *The 1988 British Crime Survey.* Home Office Research Study 111. London: HMSO.

NACRO Safe Neighbourhoods Unit (1987) *Report 1981–1986.* London: NACRO.

NACRO (1988) *Policing Housing Estates.* London: NACRO.

NACRO Safe Neighbourhoods Unit (1989a) *Crime Prevention and Community Safety: A Practical Guide for Local Authorities.* London: NACRO.

NACRO Safe Neighbourhoods Unit (1989b) *Growing Up on Housing Estates.* London: NACRO.

NACRO Safe Neighbourhoods Unit (1989c) *Safer Communities.* London: NACRO.

New Statesman and Society (1989) 'The forgotten army', 3 November.

Parliamentary All Party Penal Affairs Group (1983) *The Prevention of Crime among Young People.* London: Barry Rose.

Power, A. (1986) *The PEP Guide to Local Management* (3 vols). London: Priority Estates Project.

Police Magazine (1990) 'Survey of Police Officers', XXII (6): 22–6.

Reiner, R. (1985) 'The politics of the police', in T. Hope and M. Shaw (eds) (1988) *Community and Crime Reduction.* London: HMSO.

Riley, D. and Mayhew, P. (1980) *Crime Prevention Publicity and Assessment.* Home Office Research and Planning Unit Study No. 63. London: HMSO.

Schwartz, I. (1990) *Michigan Juvenile Crime Survey.* Ann Arbor: University of Michigan Centre for Study of Youth Policy.

Skogan, W. (1990) *Disorder and Decline, Crime and the Spiral of Decay in American Neighborhoods.* New York: Free Press.

Smith, D. (1989) 'Crime prevention: the past ten years'. Address to West Midlands Probation Service.

Smith, D.J. (1983) *Police and People in London.* London: PSI.

Tarling, R. (1985) *Criminal Careers of Those Born in 1953, 1958 and 1963.* London: HMSO.

Tuck, M. (1987) *Crime Prevention: A Shift in Concept.* Home Office Research and Planning Unit Research Bulletin No 25. London: Home Office.

United Nations Economic and Social Council Committee on Crime Prevention and

Control (1990) 11th session, Item 5, *Draft Resolution on the Prevention of Crime*. Vienna: United Nations.

Wilson, J.Q. (1975) *Thinking about Crime*. New York: Random House.

Wilson, J.Q. and Herrnstein, R. (1985) *Crime and Human Nature*. New York: Simon & Schuster.

4

The Political Construction of Crime Prevention: a Contrast between the French and British Experience

Michael King

The construction of crime as a major social problem demanding an immediate and effective government response has for at least the past 100 years allowed politicians in general, but the political party in power in particular, to define the problem, distil the issues and offer solutions which promote and sustain its particular collective vision of the ideal society and the ways of achieving that ideal. Far from embarrassing governments, 'the crime problem' permits them to reinforce with increased vigour and enthusiasm those policies which they believe will lead to the realization of that vision, while, at the same time, dismissing alternative interpretations of 'the causes of crime' or solutions to the 'crime problem'.

For reasons that will become apparent, we are not concerned in this chapter with a detailed evaluation of the likely effectiveness in reducing crime of the much-publicized government crime prevention programmes. Rather, we intend to apply to this major government initiative a theoretical perspective which will allow us to see crime prevention in the context of what has come to be known as Thatcherism (Ridell, 1984; Skidelsky, 1985; Hall, 1988). It will permit us to offer a reasoned explanation of why the British government chose to go down this particular path of social policy and to examine critically both the philosophy underpinning this policy and the mechanics of its implementation.

As has already been hinted at, this theoretical perspective sees the 'crime problem' as socially constructed and sustained largely by and for the benefit of certain interest groups which include politicians, journalists and specialist crime control and prevention agencies (Haines, 1979). Furthermore, it renounces any attempt to attribute in a positivistic way causes to specific types of crime or to crime in general, seeing the identification of causes as a political rather than a rational scientific exercise. Seeley, states, for example, '[T]hat the cause of delinquency, other things being equal, is any one or more of the following':

poor street lighting, alleys, immigration, paternal infidelity, differential association, neurotic acting out, broken homes, the American income distribution, lack of alternate meaningful activities, advertising and display, failure to nail down prized objects, the slum, the ecological organization of the American city, materialism, its opposite preoccupation with one's worth as a person, the law itself, the absurdity of society or the human condition; the want of religion, the nuclear family, the political system which needs crime as a training ground, prisons and reformatories; schools that engage few or no loyalties, the perversity of the individual delinquent, or his parents, or theirs; psychological ignorance, the unconscious wishes of those who deplore the activity or condemn the actors. 'Choose your pick', as they say. (1963: 60–61)

This does not mean to say that there are no causes, but rather that the reasons why an individual engages in a particular form of behaviour are so complex that explanations are necessarily constructed from selective and simplified accounts. What factors are selected from an almost endless list of possible influences on behaviour and the way they are simplified for public consumption depends upon essentially political decisions. Recent examples of this exercise are the identification by government spokespeople of alcohol, boredom and the influence of television as the main causes of offences committed by young people and the rejection by the same spokespeople of unemployment as a relevant factor (Patten, 1988).

Finally, our approach treats as suspect any claims that the effectiveness of crime prevention programmes upon individuals' behaviour may be adequately measured through official crime statistics and evaluated through positivistic methods (such as before/after or experimental group/control group). The reasons are: (a) it is almost impossible to isolate the specific effects of an intervention programme from everything else going on in the lives of those undertaking the programme, and (b) success or failure may depend more upon pre-existing attributes of programme participants, whether as 'interveners' or 'clients' than upon the 'treatment' imposed by the programme (Covington 1979: 18; Marshall, 1985: 141; Lotz and Regoli, 1985). This means in effect that, except in very constrained, closely defined situations, any claims relating the increase or reduction in crime statistics to specific causes should be treated with the utmost scepticism. Once again, in the face of such complexity, it is relatively easy for those having a stake in the continuation or cessation of specific programmes or projects to select certain factors for research or to highlight those aspects of research results which support their particular cause.

If we relate this theoretical perspective to crime prevention, it becomes clear that it is not only that the form and content of crime prevention programmes owe much to a governments' idiosyncratic view of the causes of crime and the ways to tackle those causes. It also means that, given the interpretative nature of any evaluations of the effectiveness of such government inspired intervention, whether through statistics or positivistic studies, they may well be framed in such a way as to legitimate and reinforce government policies. Crime prevention, like crime control, is seen here, therefore, as essentially political in nature and should be analysed as such and not as a rational, disinterested attempt to alter social behaviour in ways that are amenable to scientific evaluation.

This chapter sets out, then, to examine the present Conservative government's crime prevention policy, insofar as any consistent, readily identifiable policy actually exists. It argues that, far from being based on any coherent, independent account of the causes of socially disruptive behaviour, particularly among young people, or even upon some clear theoretical perspective that might identify such causes, the government, as in its economic policy, has chosen to accept and support only those policies which enhance its own narrow political ideology. Crime prevention, as a major government initiative, it is argued, contains all the main elements of the Thatcher vision, while systematically excluding any alternative view both as to how the 'crime problem' should be defined and solved and as to what sort of society the citizens of Britain might wish to create for themselves. Moreover, because of the anxieties and strong emotions of fear, pity and anger that crime evokes, crime prevention may also be seen as a powerful vehicle for disseminating this idiosyncratic vision.

La prévention in France

A useful comparison to the Conservative government's crime prevention strategy is the national crime prevention programme introduced by the French Socialist government in the early 1980s and continued when the right came to power in France in 1984 (King, 1987, 1988). Despite a professed admiration among British government ministers for the French experiment, and superficial similarities in crime prevention activities and strategies on either side of the Channel, there are fundamental differences in the political ideologies underpinning French and British approaches and, more specifically, in the attitudes and policies directed at promoting the social integration of young people.

Prior to 1981, France, like most other Western industrialized countries, experienced a sharp rise in reported crime and particularly in crime committed by young people. The catalyst for change came in the summer of 1981 when street violence broke out in parts of Lyon and Marseille. The new Socialist government's immediate response was to introduce a major programme of summer camps and activities. Its longer-term response was to set up an inter-ministerial commission to find solutions to the underlying problems of unemployment and social isolation among young people and also a committee of mayors from all major political parties under the chairmanship of Gilbert Bonnemaison, to report on ways of preventing crime (Bonnemaison, 1983).

The Bonnemaison Committee's report, *Face à la délinquance, prévention, repression, solidarité*, set out an extensive list of those factors which its members identified as the causes of crime. They included, 'living conditions, difficulties in social integration and employment problems, changes in the organization of family life, the absence of social controls in people's relationships with one another, poverty and exclusion from the mainstream of social life of certain categories of the population, aggravated by drugs, alcoholism, growth in disposable goods and the recent economic crisis' (Bonnemaison, 1983:31). What is interesting in this list is not so much what is included, but what is omitted. Those rhetorical accounts of crime causation, which in France, as in the United Kingdom, achieve popularity through dissemination in the popular press and mass media are nowhere to be found. The pragmatic, populist view of crime resulting from inherently evil men and women, irresponsible parenting, the corrupting influence of television and lack of discipline in schools and families, where they exist at all in the Bonnemaison discourse are seen not as causes but as effects of other, deeper and more complex social factors. On one level, the Bonnemaison report seeks in true Gallic tradition answers that go beyond the practical pragmatism that characterizes much of the Anglo-Saxon approach to crime, while, at the level of practical politics, the report represents a deliberate attempt not to point accusing fingers and not to alienate particular sectors of the community.

It should not be thought, however, that this deliberately uncontentious account of the causality of crime was politically neutral. Indeed, it sat very well both with the Socialists' highly interventionalist social policies, its decentralization strategy of devolving power to 'local communities' and with Mitterand's later attempt to unite the nation behind a government of national unity. It was part of the French government's strategy at the time to appear all things to all men, while pursuing essentially centre left policies. The adoption of the broad lines of the Bonnemaison report as official government policy and the subsequent setting up of local, départemental and national crime prevention councils allowed the government to influence directly many areas of social life – all under the widely accepted banner of crime prevention. Bonnemaison, therefore, provided the pole and the ropes which later enabled the French government to raise *la prévention* as a flag of convenience in all manner of social issues (Delatte and Dolé, 1987: ch. 1).

Although at the local level there are major differences in the political discourse supporting crime prevention programmes (Peyre, 1986), it is still possible to extract two consistent themes which characterize the general French approach. These are (a) solidarity and partnership, and (b) integration.

Solidarity and partnership
This idealized notion of the French as one homogeneous people working together to achieve nationally consensual goals is not merely a rhetorical cement holding together the various disparate elements, both social and political, in the French crime prevention programme (Delatte and Dolé, 1987). It serves also as a model for the organizational structures and financial arrangements designed to achieve these assumed goals through the setting up of projects, activities and services. In any one of the many cities in France to adopt the Socialist government's concept of a crime prevention council, for example, one finds on the *Conseils communaux de prévention de la délinquance*, representatives who display an enormously wide and varied range of political opinions, practical experience and expertise meeting together under the chairmanship of the mayor (elected by the local electorate) to co-ordinate fund raising and allocation to various local agencies and projects and to decide the general policies on crime prevention within the area.

It should be emphasized that none of this decision making was assigned to the traditional criminal justice agencies of police, judiciary or *éducation surveillée* (the specialist court social work agency). All three, of course, are represented on the crime prevention councils along with other agencies, but without being given a dominant voice in policy making. This was the result of a clear decision following the Bonnemaison Report's conclusion that, although repression and punishment through the criminal justice system was an essential element in crime control, it was not capable of tackling the underlying social problems which the committee saw as causing crime. The responsibility for solving these problems was deliberately to be given to a new administrative structure which had none of the authoritarian, repressive connotations associated with police and courts.

The financing of individual projects and indeed of the *conseils communaux* and their administration is undertaken through a number of 'partnerships', between central and local government, between the French equivalent of voluntary and statutory bodies, between the public and the private sector, although it should be emphasized that privately financed organizations, whether charities or businesses, provide only a very small proportion of funding for crime prevention. The partnership ideal means in practice that no one government ministry or local government department is exclusively responsible for funding any particular project. Many projects are funded from five or more sources. Accountability, therefore is not directly to the funding body, but to the crime prevention council or councils (national, départemental or local) which organized the funding and approved the project. These councils are not in any sense hierarchical, but operate independently (but often in co-operation with one another) at the local, county and city levels (King, 1988).

While the myths of social harmony and community based on geographical proximity doubtless conceal the many deep divisions in French society (as the recent success of Jean-Marie Le Pen in the presidential election demonstrates only too clearly) they have, when harnessed under the colours of crime prevention, made it possible for representatives from potentially conflicting social groups to sit around a table and reach decisions on criteria other than political allegiances or racial or class identity. Moreover, these myths do not exclude the explicit recognition of the disadvantages caused by the marginalization of certain categories of the population, including racial minorities and young, unqualified unemployed (Bonnemaison, 1983: 31). The existence of such groups in France is explained in the French crime prevention discourse by reference to the failure of the local community and French society in general to integrate them successfully.

Nor should it be forgotten that the new crime prevention policy in France has been superimposed upon rather than replacing the existing coercive and repressive tactics of *technoprévention*, as characterized by the water cannons and baton charges of the much-feared CRS. Yet an indication of the success of *la prévention* as a political strategy has been the continuation of the *conseils de prévention de la délinquance* unchanged when a right-wing government was elected to power under Jacques Chirac's premiership in 1984 and in the fact that government funding of crime prevention has not been substantially reduced. It was as if the political right also recognized the importance of preserving these myths, despite its strong anti-immigrant legislation and sweeping cut-backs in social services and social security spending – policies which would appear to fly in the face of the notion of one nation working together for the common good.

Integration

An important feature of the use by the French Socialist concept of 'community' has been in its potential as an integrating force (Bonnemaison, 1987). Local communities, if strong and healthy, are, according to this discourse, able to bring into their fold those marginal groups and individuals who hitherto have been excluded from the mainstream of French society.

The link between intervention and crime prevention came through the Bonnemaison Report which saw social isolation and feelings of exclusion and alienation as major causes of criminal and self-destructive behaviour. It followed, therefore, that the main thrust of any crime prevention programme should be directed towards the social integration of these two groups which were seen as presenting the greatest threat to the stability of French society, namely immigrants (coming mainly from North Africa) and unemployed, disaffected youth (Dubet, 1987, ch.8).

Important political initiatives accompanied specific crime prevention measures directed at these two groups. These included the creation of an inter-ministerial office for the vocational and social integration of young people in difficulty aimed particularly at assisting young people who had left school without formal qualifications (Schwartz, 1981). It was this office that was responsible for setting up the *missions locales* (youth bureaux) in most major French cities. Another, more controversial, political initiative was the proposal (never fully realized) for elected immigrant councils to represent the interests of all immigrants in local government issues, regardless of their citizenship status.

The specific crime prevention projects aimed at both young people and the immigrant population are too numerous and varied for detailed elaboration in an article focusing on ideology and policy. Suffice it to state that the political discourse of integration found expression, not only in individual projects, but also in the general policies, both local and national, which informed funding and organizational decisions. Perhaps the best example of this is the emergence of a new breed of professional youth organizers, called *animateurs*. They are drawn in the main from among young people of North African origin, being selected initially for their leadership qualities and the fact that they were held in high esteem by other youngsters. This was the result of a deliberate strategy aimed at 'penetrating' North African communities by eliciting the support and co-operation of the young, while at the same time providing paid employment for the most capable (and co-operative) of these young people, at first during the summer months and later on a full-time basis with the possibility of an eventual career in social work (King, 1988: 11).

The Conservative approach to crime control

A major problem for anyone seeking to comment on the British government's crime prevention policy is uncovering those theories of criminal causality on which the Home Office based its strategy. If one surveys the publicity literature disseminated by the Home Office and by Crime Concern, the overriding theoretical implication seems to be that most crime is a product of opportunity and the way to prevent crime is to reduce the opportunities. To quote from the Home Office publication, *Practical Ways to Crack Crime* (Home Office, 1988: 1),

> The first step towards preventing crime is understanding its nature. Most crime is against property and not people, and most is not carried out by professionals; nor is it carefully planned. Property crimes thrive on the easy opportunity. They are often committed by adolescents and young men, the majority of whom stop offending as they grow older...

In fact the government in its policy statements on crime prevention appeared to have turned its back on any form of theorizing concerning the motivation of offenders and ways of reducing their motivation through behaviour changes. The frequent use of the term 'criminals' in the official literature, even when referring to young people of 15 or less, is to apply a label which in effect rejects or regards as pointless any further analysis as to causality or motivation. Instead, the answer lies in the traditional pragmatism that has characterized successive British governments' responses to crime. In the case of the Tory government it took the form of 'practical' solutions.

Anyone who has followed the development of crime prevention in the United Kingdom over the past few years may have some sympathy with individual Home Office ministers in their efforts to devise a course of action which will win the approval of, or, at the very least, will not offend the Tory Party Conference, the right wing of the Parliamentary Party, and above all the Prime Minister. Any attempt to replicate the French Socialist Party's policies of social cohesion and integration through massive state intervention would clearly have posed serious problems for those in the party who have firmly set their mind against welfare intervention and consistently emphasized the importance of individual responsibility, initiative and self-discipline within the context of a free market economy as the only way of achieving 'the good life'.

Moreover, in view of the major cuts in public spending and the selective dismantling of the 'welfare state' undertaken by the Conservative government, it is not surprising that Home Office ministers should have wished to avoid any political discourse which raised the possibility that social factors, such as poor housing, unemployment, failure in the education system and financial insecurity might have had anything to do with the high rate of offending among young people. Indeed, these ministers went out of their way to throw cold water over any suggestion that crime might be causally related to poverty or unemployment, as John Patten, the Home Office Minister made abundantly clear in a recent article in *New Society* (Patten, 1988: 12):

> Setting aside the implicit insults to the poor and the unemployed contained

in that sort of gimcrack analysis, those who offered it have a lot of explaining to do. If it is poverty that causes crime, then why were crime rates lower in the 1930s when poverty, unemployment and inequality were all much greater?

Furthermore, the amount of attention given by government spokespeople in their speeches to crimes of violence committed by well-to-do, car-owning, credit card-holding young men in quiet market towns who go on drunken rampages to relieve their boredom (Patten, 1988) was quite out of proportion to the incidence of these events in the totality of reported crime. It is as if Home Office ministers had made a deliberate decision to replace in the public's eye the stereotype of 'the criminal' as poor, working-class and unemployed, once again weakening any causal connections that might be seen to exist between crime and social conditions.

Indeed, the only time that social environmental factors as a possible cause of crime were mentioned in the literature produced by the Home Office Crime Prevention Division was in the Home Office statement launching the Safer Cities Programme that '[I]n certain areas social and economic decline appears to be both a cause and effect of high crime rates'. However, in the Home Secretary's personal contribution to this document any causal link between living conditions and unlawful behaviour was studiously avoided. Douglas Hurd saw Safer Cities rather from the perspective of the victims of crime, be they individuals, businesses or general economic climates:

> ...a Safer Cities team will act as a catalyst, establishing and drawing the maximum effect from this local partnership, developing initiatives to address local crime problems, and creating a safer environment in which enterprise, community and personal responsibility can flourish. In this way the Safer Cities programme will make a powerful contribution to the economic and social regeneration of these areas. (7 March 1988)

As the party of 'law and order' the Conservatives found themselves wedded to a rhetoric which portrays all offenders as abnormal, different in fundamental ways from 'decent' citizens, and violent offenders as less than human and precludes any explanations which might detract from this classification of people into criminals and non-criminals. Political extremism of both left and right by necessity appears to breed its own reductionism and crude labelling. The Prime Minister's description of the violent football supporters as 'animals' and the Home Secretary's reference to young offenders who display 'a moral brutishness' (speech to the English Speaking Union, Oxford, July 1988) are only some examples from a long list of degrading epithets used by Tory politicians and the tabloid press to distinguish law-breakers from law-abiders. They include 'louts', 'thugs', 'brutes', 'hooligans', 'monsters'. This classification was not entirely abandoned in the government's crime prevention literature; it was merely modified. The quotation from *Practical Ways to Crack Crime* (Home Office, 1988) which we reproduced at the start of this section is followed, for example, by the following statements:

> This reliance by *criminals* on the easy opportunity is the key to much crime prevention...
>
> If opportunities like this did not exist, *criminals* would have a much harder time. (p. 1) (emphasis added)

The term 'criminals' is being used here to refer among others to those whom the authors of the booklet themselves describe as 'adolescents and young men, the majority of whom stop offending as they grow older' and for whom 'the peak age for offending is 15' (p. 1). Elsewhere in the document the same people are identified by the acts they commit – they are the 'burglars', 'thieves' and 'bullies' against whom we should be protecting our property and our children – or by the fact that they are 'strangers' and not part of our 'community'.

A more common rhetorical device in the crime prevention literature has simply been to disregard almost entirely those who commit the offences. Crimes are, therefore, portrayed as personal misfortunes, rather like accidents or illness, where the perpetrators are either invisible like microbes or viruses or remain shadowy, faceless and evil. Crime prevention in the British context has been presented by government spokespeople for the most part, not as tackling the causes of young people's anti-social behaviour, but as taking steps to guard against these personal misfortunes. We find the Home Secretary thus telling his audience at the launch of *Crime Concern*:

> ...we are present at the birth of something new and abundantly worthwhile. Crime and the fear of crime bear hard on our community. We must be increasingly imaginative in dealing with them. Crime is not something visited on us from another planet. It is not something over which we can have no influence...
>
> ...crime prevention should be an essential part of the daily routine for the whole community. By making it second nature to consider crime prevention possibilities and weaknesses the scope of the opportunistic, selfish and thoughtless petty offender can be drastically reduced. (Press release, 23/5/88)

This discourse has left the way clear for the 'target-hardening', 'fortress mentality' 'practical' version of crime prevention which has characterized the main thrust of the Conservative government's approach. Indeed, *Practical Ways to Crack Crime* resembles very closely a glossy publicity brochure for anti-crime devices. On one page, for example, there are large colour photos of screech alarms alongside a picture of a middle-aged woman walking along a deserted street at night and another of two younger women waiting by a bus stop (p. 5). Further on a bright crimson image of a house burglar alarm stands out from surrounding pictures of various forms of window and door locks. These pictorial images of technological anti-crime products are accompanied by copious and detailed advice in the text on how to 'protect yourself', 'protect your home' and 'protect your family' (p. 12). The pervading values are those of consumerism, individualism and self-reliance.

In the few places where children and young people receive any mention, it is as the potential victims of bullying and sexual attacks from strangers. The part to be played by schools in the 'Community Crime Prevention Programme' is 'to educate young people about crime prevention' and 'taking part in or organising crime prevention projects' (p. 27). Similarly, the Manpower Services Commission's contribution is to provide 'Community Programme Workers on crime prevention initiatives', including 'support for Neighbourhood Watch schemes' (p. 26).

Not only, therefore, has the British government's crime prevention initiative skilfully avoided any overt clash with traditional Tory law and order policies, but it also has powerful affinities with the social and economic 'revolution' promoted by 'Thatcherism' and the New Right.

Over and above the obvious emphasis placed on ownership, property and possessions in the crime prevention campaign, this compatibility with Tory policies has extended also to the very concepts of 'community' and 'neighbourhood' promoted in the government's crime prevention literature and in the establishment of neighbourhood watch and 'Homewatch' schemes. As we shall show, in the hands of the Conservatives, these are concepts which do not in any way clash with the ideal of individualism.

Neighbourhood Watch and Homewatch

The first of these schemes was established in 1982 in Mollington, Cheshire. According to the Home Office, there were by late 1989 well over 40,000 such schemes throughout England and Wales, covering an estimated 3.5 million households. Once again, we should emphasize that we are not concerned in this chapter with the effectiveness of these schemes in reducing crime or the fear of crime, but in the ways in which the rhetoric and power structures associated with crime prevention promote or sustain specific political interests and policies. While the principal objectives of these watch schemes is to encourage people to protect their homes and property and to provide information to the police about suspicious activity in the area, it is quite clear from the government's crime prevention literature and ministerial speeches that they have also been seen as a means of promoting neighbourliness and social cohesion. To this end *Practical Ways to Prevent Crime* reproduces at considerable length interviews with neighbourhood watch and homewatch co-ordinators which emphasize this aspect of the schemes.

> ... People have got to know each other much better – not as busybodies, but as *real neighbours* and there's a *real community atmosphere*. Each road has its own co-ordinator who is urged to organize a *community social life* with video parties, coffee evenings and other events.

> ... It's so fulfilling to get people to talk to each other and make them *aware of their neighbours*. (Coleen Atkins, a Neighbourhood Watch Co-ordinator in Bedford: 20)

> The watch has increased the *sense of neighbourhood*... There's a lot more social contact – a lot more interblock contact. (Leslie Pickles, Plymouth: 22)

> It's not run only for crime prevention purposes – it's also a *community exercise*. We do things like send flowers to people in hospital and the bereaved. (Arthur Jakins, Sheffield: 23) (emphasis added)

It is all rather reminiscent of the 'community spirit' which is supposed to have flourished during the war years and, as such, represents a nostalgic, idealized view of 'the community' and 'the neighbourhood', where, in the face of threats from an external, invisible enemy, everyone, regardless of class, colour, creed and political affiliations, gets together to repulse the enemy and to help and support one another through the difficult times.

In some ways this is similar to the idealized notion of *communauté* promoted by Bonnemaison and the French Socialist government, but whereas the Bonnemaison report recognized that French society marginalized certain social groups and acknowledged the failure of traditional social institutions to fulfil their socializing functions, the Home Office version portrays community and neighbourhood as a seamless web of like-minded people, all working together for the common good in co-operation with the traditional structures of criminal justice, education and family. To quote from the glossy brochure on the *Five Towns Initiative*, subtitled *A Community Response to Crime Reduction*, 'It is now widely recognized that preventing crime is not just a matter for police and central government: the co-operation and support of others in the community is essential to reduce opportunities for crime'.

However, both the rhetoric and the structural arrangements for neighbourhood watch go much further in promoting the government's political objectives than merely encouraging a nostalgia for an idealized past. As in the British government's 'opting out' policy in education and housing, crime prevention, as expressed in the watch schemes, effectively leap-frogs the local authority and goes straight to 'the people'. Here, the contrast with France could not be more complete, for the Mauroy government of 1982, it will be recalled, was firmly committed to a policy of devolving power to local government. The organization of crime prevention at a local level was, therefore, placed firmly in the hands of these elected representatives of the people under the leadership of the elected mayor. On the English side of the Channel, however, the British Conservative government has been engaged in a long and bitter political battle with local government, particularly with the Labour councils which control many of the country's large cities. It is perhaps not too surprising, therefore, to find local authorities largely ignored for the development and management of watch schemes and indeed in crime prevention generally, with the police being entrusted with these tasks.

Indeed, in its pictorial representation of 'Your Community' in *Practical Ways to Crack Crime* (p. 26) the police crime prevention officer is presented as the pivot of all crime prevention activity, while the Town Hall does not receive a mention and the local authority is only obliquely referred to as the 'planners' of building developments. All those social organizations involved in crime prevention whether planners, police, courts and probation service, crime prevention panels, the Manpower Services Commission Community Programme or the voluntary sector are shown as revolving around and depending upon the police crime prevention officer.

This view of the police's central role was endorsed by the Home Secretary: 'The police are the main inspirers and guides of crime prevention, but it is their strong view that they need energetic and well thought-out help from the community (Speech at launch of Crime Concern, 23 May 1988).

The use of the police as the main disseminators of target-hardening information to assist in the protection of people and property and as the collectors and collators of information about crimes committed in different areas is as common in the French system as it is in England and Wales. What has been totally absent in France is the use of the police as the local administrative body primarily responsible for crime prevention, including social crime prevention programmes involving young people. It is to these programmes that we shall now turn.

Helping the young
In keeping with the general principles which have guided Tory policies on crime and crime prevention, the Home Office have taken care to maintain a clear distinction between measures to control crime and social aid to young people. As if to guard against any suggestion that

the government might be admitting even the slightest causal relation between youth unemployment and crime, for example, the only mention of youth employment schemes in *Practical Ways to Crack Crime* is a reference to 'work for the community' and 'support for Neighbourhood Watch schemes' offered by the long-term unemployed on the Manpower Services Commission's Community Programme (p. 27).

When the official crime prevention discourse referred to children and young people it is in two specific contexts. The first, which we have already mentioned, sees children as potential victims, who must be taught to *say 'no' to strangers*, educated at school about crime prevention (p. 27) and encouraged to participate in 'junior' neighbourhood watch schemes. The second concerns helping young people 'to keep out of crime'. In a rare moment of 'softness', the Home Secretary at the launch of Crime Concern seemed close to admitting the possibility that not all 'criminals' or, at least, not all young 'criminals' are social pariahs: 'Most crime in this country is committed by young people and the peak age for offending is 15 years. These are *our young people and the whole community must have an interest in keeping them out of crime*' (23/5/88, emphasis added).

However, what should be done to keep them out of crime has never been spelt out with any precision in the government's crime prevention discourse. According to a full-time neighbourhood watch supervisor working for the Northumberland police, who is quoted in *Practical Ways to Crack Crime*, 'We could draw people closer by arranging things – to get the kids off the streets, for example. Maybe we could have a youth club' (p. 22), while the Home Office in its publicity statement on the introduction of the Safer Cities Programme gives as an example of ways of reducing crime, 'creating opportunities for personal and social development to tap the energies and enterprise, pariculary of young people, by providing youth sports and recreation initiatives...'

Steve Norris, then director of Crime Concern, saw parents and teachers as having 'a special responsibility for young people in their charge. But they need the help of every member of the community to help to deliver the good citizens of tomorrow' (Speech at the launch of Crime Concern, 23/5/88).

The fact that help for young people by the community has actually been happening outside the government's official crime prevention initiative, in programmes and projects organized by the voluntary sector, local authorities and the police is not simply a matter of convenient division of labour. Rather it represents, we suggest, part of a deliberate policy by the government to distance itself from any form of social intervention that could be construed by the public, and, more importantly, by the right wing of the Tory Party, as accepting social factors (as opposed to individual responsibility) explanations for the causes of crime and 'going soft on criminals'. Such distancing enabled government departments in 1986–7, for example, to give over £15 million to NACRO, the largest voluntary agency undertaking social crime prevention work, while maintaining the rhetoric of 'toughness' towards, and the 'social exclusion' of, 'criminals' in its official discourse on crime control and crime prevention.

The other politically 'acceptable' way which the government has found to support both morally and financially social crime prevention activities for young people has been through the criminal justice system. This has taken two main forms. The first is through the development of Intermediate Treatment (IT) in recent years, from a nebulous concept designed to provide largely unstructured activities run by local authority social workers charged by the courts with the supervision of young people found guilty of relatively minor offences to highly structured programmes offering an alternative to custody to youngsters who might otherwise have found themselves in detention or youth custody centres (Preston, 1982; Ely et al., 1987; Pointing, 1986). The use of IT to reduce dramatically the number of under-16-year-olds who receive custodial sentences has been a main plank of the government's policy towards young offenders. The DHSS made £15 million available for local authorities participating in the 'juvenile initiative' (White, 1988) and between 1978 and 1986 the Raynor Foundation has distributed to IT projects £2.5 million of government money (Raynor Project, 1986: 34).

It may seem strange that a government that began its first term of office by announcing tough measures against young criminals, should some six years later be applauding these programmes of treatment within the community. The answer to this enigma lies only partly in the economics that the price of a place on an IT scheme works out cheaper than board and keep at one of Her Majesty's youth custody or detention centres. The fact that the new version of Intensive IT has fitted in snugly with the New Right's recently developed approach to crime control, exemplifies the British government's tendency to use 'good housekeeping' arguments in tandem with explicitly ideological explanations (of criminals repaying their debt to the community) as justifications for what amount to major reversals of policy. In the case of IT, as in so many of the policy reversals effected by the Thatcher government, the change owes more to political pragmatism and expediency than to anything else.

For a start, it placed a large measure of control over the form and content of many Intensive IT schemes in the trusted hands of the magistrates. By applying the reduction in custodial sentences as one of the main measures of success, IT programmes came to depend increasingly on the approval of the juvenile court justices and, in general, this approval was likely to be forthcoming only if the magistrates were satisfied that the alternative offered by Intensive IT is 'not just a soft option'.

At the same time as the custody figures for young offenders have been falling, therefore, one saw a proliferation of these Intensive IT programmes offering structured behaviour modification and self-control where the efforts of the social work team concentrate on the offence – the criminal behaviour which gave rise to the court appearance. These range from strict control of young people's time (Ely et al., 1987), behaviour modification techniques (Preston, 1982: 187) to role-play methods where young offenders are asked to act out the sequence leading to the commission of the crime, to analyse the reasons for their behaviour and to rehearse ways of resisting temptation in the future.

What has been taking place, therefore, is the demands of the criminal justice system for self-control and individual responsibility imposing themselves upon social work policy and practice towards children and young people. Once again, the contrast with France is instructive. There, the crime prevention programmes aimed at young people operate quite independently of the courts and children's judges. Indeed, the movement has been in quite the opposite direction from that experienced in England and Wales with *éducation surveillée*, the court social workers, being increasingly involved in activities for young people which are part-financed, approved and co-ordinated, not by judges and the Ministry of Justice, but by the *conseils communaux* and *conseils départementaux de prévention de la délinquance* (Delatte and Dolé, 1987: ch. 1).

Crossing the Channel back again to the English side, one finds another example of this imposition of criminal justice upon social work practice in the development of cautioning panels and juvenile bureaux (Landau, 1981; Landau and Nathan, 1983; Thorpe and Finch, 1983). These consist of social workers and police, who decide together whether young offenders should be prosecuted and, if not, what sort of alternative intervention is necessary. Here the incentive for social workers' participation has been that of keeping young people out of the courts and away from what are perceived as the negative effects on their self-image and life chances of any involvement in the formal criminal justice system.

The proliferation of these filtering structures has been portrayed by many social workers and academic commentators as another victory against the repressive policies of the juvenile courts (Giller and Morris, 1987; Bowden and Stevens, 1986). An alternative interpretation, however, would be to see the involvement of police officers in decisions as to whether a particular child would benefit from social work help (with or without a formal caution) as an intrusion of what are essentially criminal justice principles of retribution and deterrence into areas of social intervention which were previously guided by the social worker's assessment of the needs of the child and family. Yet the debate as to who is invading whose territory is largely irrelevant to the argument of this chapter. What is important for our purposes is the fact that the line between social work and policing is becoming increasingly blurred and that the government has recently done much to blur it even further by encouraging the movement towards the reactive, policing aspects of social work practice in the area of both child abuse and juvenile justice. At the same time, through massive cuts in local authorities' social services, it has severely limited the scope of social workers for expensive preventive, welfare intervention. The growing influence of the courts and police over social work practice may be interpreted as an example of a more general policy of 'knocking social workers into shape' so that they can be seen as working towards the Thatcherite vision of a healthy British society rather than against it.

Whatever lingering doubts one may have about the view that social workers are becoming more like the police (Harris, 1982; Harris and Webb, 1987), the movement of the police into preventive social work has been clear and unambiguous. According to the publicity sheet issued by the Staffordshire Police Activity and Community Enterprise (SPACE), for example, the community programme which the police organize

> is an integral part of the crime prevention strategy operated within Staffordshire. Not only does it lead to a reduction in the number of criminal offences reported. The scheme also figures importantly in facilitating the establishment or reinforcement of good police and community relations.
>
> Over the summer holidays 25,000 children participated in 20,000 periods of sport and recreational activity at more than 30 centres staffed by police.

Moreover, both in multi-agency and community programmes the police through their increasing control of the purse-strings are able to have a significant influence over the nature and content of social activities for children and young people. The South Yorkshire Police Urban Action Scheme, for example, provided £50,000 for Urban Action Projects, where 'there is a significant amount of police involvement in the planning and execution.'

It could, of course, be argued that the participation of the police in organizing sporting and leisure activities for the young is nothing new. After all, the police have for many years been responsible for running attendance centres (Gelsthorpe and Tutt, 1986). Yet there is an important policy difference between deploying policemen to deal with young offenders who have been convicted by the courts and using police manpower and resources to engage in what is essentially preventive work, aimed not at known offenders but at disadvantaged youth. The South Yorkshire scheme's information sheet makes it clear that one of the agreed objectives of the scheme is 'to create opportunities for police officers and *young employed/disadvantaged people* to meet together and, hopefully, lead to a dialogue with the object of breaking down prejudices *to the benefit of society and the individual* (emphasis added).

The publicity blurb for the scheme goes even further in its attempt to promote the image of the police as a caring body which has the welfare of young people at heart, rather than solely as a force for repression and coercive control: 'These opportunities provided by a *concerned Police Authority* and pursued by trained and *caring police officers* throughout the County can create an environment in which disadvantage need not be an obstacle to one's contribution to a well-ordered society' (emphasis added).

The enthusiasm of the police in some parts of the country to undertake what can only be described as 'social welfare activities', while pre-dating the arrival of the New Right, may be seen now almost as official social policy, promoting as it does the government's desire to reduce the power of local government by giving authority and resources to those social structures 'which can be trusted'. Helping disadvantaged young people through childhood and adolescence through direct intervention to compensate for the inadequacies of their families and prevent the worst consequences of deprivation seems so obviously to fall within the remit of local authorities with their responsibilities for social services, education and sports and recreational facilities, that it is difficult to see how under any other government city and borough councils would not have been given this task and the resources to undertake it. Yet by defining such intervention as 'crime prevention' and at the same time massively reducing the power of local authorities, the Conservative government has in effect succeeded in legitimating a major expansion in the role of the police.

Crime Concern and Safer Cities

The exclusion of local authorities from any position of power has pervaded even those formal administrative structures of the Conservative crime prevention programme specifically designed to tackle crime through eliciting co-operation and partnership at a local level. While the rhetoric of both Crime Concern and Safer Cities speaks of partnership between local organizations, statutory and voluntary, public and private, and the encouragement of local initiatives, the reins of control for both these organizations are firmly in the hands of central government in the form of the Home Office and, more pre-cisely, Home Office ministers and those appointed directly by them. In neither of these organizations is there any accountability to the local electorate or any local control over which local projects should receive major funding. While Douglas Hurd in his written statement at the launch of Safer Cities emphasized the need for 'all sections of the community to work together in partnership' and 'drawing the max-imum effect from this local partnership', it was clear from the small print that the senior partner with the controlling interest would remain in his Whitehall office.

What has in fact been being offered to those local authorities that receive a Home Office invitation to participate in Safer Cities is responsibility with virtually no power. As 'a local lead agency', they may set up local steering committees which may include community and ethnic minority interests, but 'the membership of the steering committee will be a matter for discussion and agreement [with] the Home Office Safer Cities section'. The steering committee, once established, has to 'set priorities for the project, facilitate communica-tion and co-operation between the different agencies and oversee the implementation of measures against crime' (information received from Home Office Crime Prevention Division), but it depends for much of its information, policy advice, fund-raising activities and project evaluation on a professional team headed by a local co-ordinator who, according to the job description issued by the Home Office, is *'employed by the Home Office* and *under the direct line management of the Head of the Crime Prevention Unit'* (emphasis added). It would appear that the only clear power exercised by the local steering committee is, in consultation with the co-ordinator, to approve Safer Cities grants of up to £500. Grants above this amount may be awarded only by the Home Office. All that the committee may do in such cases is to make a recommendation on the grant proposal (information received from Home Office Crime Prevention Division).

Turning briefly to Crime Concern, the task of this organization, according to the information given to the press, is 'to undertake a series of practical initiatives which includes:

Identifying best practice in local crime prevention
Raising and distributing funds for local initiatives
Establishing a register of crime prevention initiatives
Monitoring research and
Establishing an information and advice service'.

Unlike Safer Cities, it can make no claim to be community based, since its operational headquarters are in Swindon and its chief executive and staff will operate from there rather than from local offices in different parts of the country. It does, however, claim to be independent of government. What this means in practice is that, although it receives initial Home Office funding, it will be self-financing 'as contributions are drawn from business'. Furthermore, it is not accountable to any minister and its policy and grant-funding decisions are made by a board which is outside the control of any government department. Yet it should perhaps be mentioned that its first director, Steve Norris, was a former Tory MP and has since re-entered parliament as the member for Epping Forest, and the original Advisory Board, appointed by the Home Secretary, contained in its ranks no representatives from Labour councils or ethnic minorities.

Conclusion

It should be clear from the evidence presented in this chapter that any similarities between the French crime prevention programme and the major crime prevention initiatives introduced by the British Conservative government are rhetorical rather than substantial. The political ideology which inspired the French Socialist government to launch the *conseils de prévention de la délinquance* could hardly be more different from the motives which inspired the policies towards crime and its prevention adopted by the British government. Moreover, the administrative structures which have been empowered in the United Kingdom to co-ordinate and finance crime prevention programmes, the Safer Cities local steering committees and the Crime Concern Board bear no resemblance to the locally autonomous and locally accountable structures responsible for organizing crime prevention programmes on the other side of Channel.

However, to suggest that all the British government has really been concerned with are the target-hardening and situational aspects of crime prevention is a gross over-simplification. It is certainly true that the government has been constrained by its own propaganda on crime and its causes from mounting, as part of its own official policy, the sorts of projects for young people that exist in France. However, it has nonetheless been able indirectly to promote and encourage intervention directed at improving community responsibility and the social behaviour of young people. Needless to say it has done this in ways which further enhance its own more general policies. These policies include harnessing the power of local authorities, restricting and controlling the role of social workers, and maintaining the autonomy of police chief officers free from the shackles of local authority-dominated police committees. At the level of political ideology the government has, not surprisingly, used the opportunity of crime prevention to promote those values of self-discipline, self-dependency and personal responsibility which it holds dear and to restrict the dissemination of values which it sees as leading to dependency on the state and an abnegation of personal responsibility. The police and courts are thus seen (perhaps not always correctly) as agencies likely to encourage these preferred values, while social workers pursuing their caring role and Labour-controlled local councils are not.

Now it could well be argued that, in pursuing these values and promoting these policies, the government has been doing no more than reflecting popular attitudes, as portrayed in the mass media and popular press, towards crime and its causes, just as the French Socialist government could be accused of ignoring these attitudes. However, this, once again, would be to oversimplify what is a complex web of power and influence, for as we have seen the British government through its spokespeople and publications has played no small part in promoting in the media a view of crime and its causality which enhances its interests. The attention drawn to 'lager louts' and 'shire town violence' is only one example of this process. Moreover, what is accepted as the public's view is very much a matter of taste. It is clear that local inner-city minority community groups on the Broadwater Farm (housing) Estate (Lea et al., 1987a) or in Hilldrop (Lea et al., 1987b) would take a very different view of the causality of crime and how to prevent crime than, say, the editor of a tabloid newspaper or members of suburban neighbourhood watch schemes, yet the attitudes of the former are nowhere echoed in ministerial speeches or Home Office crime prevention literature. Like all governments in modern societies, the British government, therefore, has constructed the crime problem and ways of controlling and preventing crime very much in its own image.

Note

I should like to thank Graham Howes of Cambridge University, Peter Ely of Kent University, Gerhard Baumann of the Human Science Department, Mohan Luthra of the Government Department and Christine Piper of the Law Department, Brunel University, for their helpful comments on earlier versions of this chapter.

References

Bonnemaison, G. (ed.) (1983) *Face à la délinquance: prévention, repression, solidarité.* Paris: La documentation française.

Bonnemaison, G. (1987) *La Sécurité en libertés.* Paris: Syros.

Bowden, J. and Stevens, M.J. (1986) 'Justice for juveniles – a corporate strategy in Northampton', *Justice of the Peace*, 2, 24 May.

Covington, C. (1979) *Evaluation of the Hammersmith Teenage Project: Summary of Research.* London: NACRO.

Delatte, J. and Dolé, P. (1987) *La recomposition du champ social et des pratiques de prévention.* Paris: Ministère de la Justice.

Dubet, F. (1987) *La galère*. Paris: Fayard.

Ely, P. et al. (1987) *The Medway Close Support Unit*. Edinburgh: Scottish Academic Press.

Gelsthorpe, L. and Tutt, N. (1986) 'The attendance centre order', *Criminal Law Review*, 146.

Giller, H. and Morris, A. (1987) *Understanding Juvenile Justice*. London: Croom Helm.

Haines, H. (1979) 'Cognitive enclosure and the depolitization of social problems', *Sociological Quarterly*, 20: 119–30.

Hall, S. (1988) *The Hard Road to Renewal: Thatcherism and the Crisis of the Left*. Verso: London.

Harris, R. (1982) 'Institutionalized ambivalence: social workers and the Children and Young Person's Act 1969', *British Journal of Social Work*, 12: 249–63.

Harris, R. and Webb, D. (1987) *Welfare Power and Juvenile Justice*. London: Tavistock.

Home Office (1988) *Practical Ways to Crack Crime*. London: HMSO.

King, M. (1987) 'Crime prevention in France', *Home Office Research Bulletin No. 24*.

King, M. (1988) *How to Make Social Crime Prevention Work*. London: NACRO.

Landau, S. (1981) 'Juveniles and the police: who is charged immediately and who is referred to the Juvenile Bureau?', *British Journal of Criminology*, 21: 27–46.

Landau, S. and Nathan, G. (1983) 'Selecting developments for cautioning in the London Met. Area', *British Journal of Criminology*, 23 (2): 128–49.

Lea, J., Jones, T., Woodhouse, T. and Young, J. (1987b) *Preventing Crime – The Hilldrop Project*, 1st Report. London: Centre for Criminology, Middlesex Polytechnic.

Lea, J., Jones, T. and Young, J. (1987a) *Saving the Inner City: Broadwater Farm – A Strategy for Survival*. London: Centre for Criminology, Middlesex Polytechnic.

Lotz, R. and Regoli, R.M. (1985) *Juvenile Delinquency and Juvenile Justice*. New York: Random House.

Marshall, T. (1985) *Alternative to Criminal Courts*. Gower: Aldershot.

Patten, J. (1988) 'Crime: a middle class disease', *New Society*, 13 May: 12–13.

Peyre, V. (1986) 'Une nouvelle politique de prévention en France, 1983–1985', *Annales de Vaucresson, No. 24: Politiques de prévention et action sociale*. Centre de Recherche Interdisciplinaire de Vaucresson.

Pointing, J. (ed.) (1986) *Alternatives to Custody*. Oxford: Blackwell.

Preston, M.A. (1982) 'Intermediate treatment: a new approach to community care', in P. Feldman *The Prevention and Control of Offending*. Chichester: Wiley.

Raynor Project Annual Report (1986). London: Raynor Project.

Ridell, P. (1984) *The Thatcher Government*. Oxford: Blackwell.

Schwartz, B. (ed.) (1981) *L'insertion professionelle et sociale des jeunes*. Paris: La documentation française.

Seeley, J.R. (1963) 'Social science? Some probative problems', in M. Stein and A. Vidaich (eds), *Sociology on Trial*. Englewood Cliffs: Prentice-Hall.

Skidelsky, R. (1985) *Thatcherism*. London: Chatto and Windus.

Thorpe, D. and Finch, F. (1983) *Does the Northamptonshire Model Work?* Lancaster: University of Lancaster.

White, T. (1988) 'In consideration of youth crime – an anti-custody strategy for young people', *Ajjust*, 17: 12–16.

5

The Politics of Prostitution and Drug Control

Neil Boyd and John Lowman

In contemporary Western societies, and many others, illegal drugs and prostitution reside in the darker recesses of human experience. As tainted hedonisms they are widely subject to criminal law sanctions, although the act of prostitution is quite legal in many countries, while such drugs as marijuana, cocaine and heroin are criminalized almost everywhere. It is the 'tainted' character of prostitution and certain drugs that brings them together as the subjects of this chapter, a discussion of the politics of censure (Sumner, 1983). In particular, we are interested in the way that various moral scripts and public health concerns interact to construct the rationales for censuring certain mind-altering substances and commercial sexual activities and how these rhetorics are, in turn, built into criminal law and help to shape law enforcement practices. For the most part, the chapter focuses on prostitution and drug control in Western societies, although it also considers some of the political–economic forces operating at a more global level.

The religious roots of moral opprobrium

Prostitution, in its broadest sense, finds a place in the literature of most civilizations and religions (Bullough and Bullough, 1978). Generally speaking, most references to prostitutes are to females, although male prostitution also has a long history (our discussion here will focus primarily on female prostitution). In some cultures the prostitute is revered, in some she is despised, and in others she is the subject of great ambivalence; attitudes may range from piety to pity, sympathy to revulsion, condemnation to resignation. Often, prostitution has been connected to religious ceremony and it is difficult to understand contemporary attitudes to the prostitute without understanding her religious role (Bullough and Bullough, 1978).

In Judaeo-Christian cultures prostitution has long been an object of censure, but even in the confines of these societies it would be a mistake to think of 'prostitution' as having a single trans-historical meaning (Shrage, 1989: 349–51). And although the practice has characteristically been an object of moral censure for most Christian sects, this sense of disapprobation has not been translated into the same types of criminal law control over prostitution. In most Western countries (with the notable exception of all but one state in the US) prostitution itself is quite legal, even if ancillary laws controlling various aspects of prostitution make it very difficult to practise the trade legally.

Most Christian sects consider prostitution to be a sin. And yet the prostitute finds a special place in Christian folklore. After the crucifixion it was Mary Magdalene, a reformed prostitute, who discovered that Christ's tomb was empty and it was she who first saw Christ after he had risen from the dead (Bullough and Bullough, 1978: 58). But as a temptress, the prostitute is only an exaggerated version of womanhood more generally, a sort of icon of male vulnerability to female deception. In the creation myth it was Eve, produced from Adam's spare rib and thus very much secondary to man, who tempted him with the apple and was responsible for their expulsion from the Garden of Eden; from the Book of Genesis forward, sex and sin are linked.

In contrast to the long history of the denunciation of prostitution, the emergence of various rationales for the censure of certain mind-altering substances has occurred mostly in the twentieth century and is largely a product of Western thinking. Although other cultures have certainly been aware of the damage that drugs could cause, it was, prior to the last century, the largely unrefined form of the drug that was consumed; possession and use were often tied to religious ceremony or restricted by custom. But in the mid-nineteenth century the technologies for extracting cocaine from coca leaves and morphine from opium were developed. These new and far more potent products were initially cast as medical panaceas (Weil and Rosen, 1983; Szasz, 1974). But in the early twentieth century, they came to be viewed as toxic demons. And from this point forward, a vast new array of mind-altering substances has been synthesized, many of which are now eagerly pursued on the black market, and in the doctor's office.

While there is considerable admonition of alcohol *over*-indulgence in the Bible, there is no censure of indulgence as such, and no obvious denunciation of other mind-altering substances. Nevertheless, religious scripts figure importantly in the distinction between licit and illicit drugs. Alcohol remains very much a Judaeo-Christian high, banned by other religions such as Islam. Alcohol was, after all, manufactured by Christ when he is said to have changed water into wine. And wine (metaphorically speaking, Christ's blood) is a consecrated component of the Eucharist. The naturally occurring drugs that we now find almost universally banned by criminal law – cannabis, cocaine and opium – originated in so-called pagan societies.

The origins of criminal censure

Substance criminalization is, in global terms, a relatively recent phenomenon, less than 90 years old. In North America, its beginnings were to be found in labour disputes, immigration issues and racial bigotry, as well as alarm about the addictive qualities of such substances as morphine and cocaine. Oddly, concern about the addictive nature of tobacco did not surface for another 50 years. The Chinese had been lured to North America to assist in the industrial development of British Columbia and California, and some brought with them the habit of smoking opium. The Chinese were a source of cheap labour, paid at only half the rate of the equivalent Caucasian. In British Columbia the Chinese set up municipally licensed smoking opium factories in various cities where they operated for over 40 years, seldom the focus of public concern. But once the labour shortage disappeared, the Chinese came to be viewed as a threat to white workers. In Canada, one of the first countries to outlaw opium, this legislation was, at least in part, a mechanism for controlling oriental immigration (Boyd, 1984).

There was also a more generalized concern at this time about alcohol, sexual morality and racial purity. This was a period when Christian moralism and new-found secular concepts of social engineering were merging in the 'Social Hygiene' movement. Social malaise was no longer conceived to be preordained; it could now be explained in the realm of such worldly 'causes' as genetic defect or racial inferiority. Certain forms of drug use were constructed as dangerous addictions and various sexualities were cast as pathological disorders. Alcohol was held responsible for every conceivable problem faced by the working classes and, for a short period, it was prohibited in the US and various parts of Canada.

In the case of other drugs, a number of international conventions, most notably the Shanghai Commission of 1909 and the Hague Convention of 1912, quickly led to a virtual global suppression of opium. The British, in two opium wars in the mid-nineteenth century, had first established their right to distribute the drug into China. But in the early twentieth century – at the behest of the Americans – the Chinese were told that they would now have to divest themselves of what had become one of their most valuable commodities (Szasz, 1974). It was also during this period that the cocaine in Coca-Cola was replaced by the more socially acceptable stimulant, caffeine (Szasz, 1974: 179). Over the next 15 years heroin, cannabis and cocaine were criminalized. Currently, over 150 synthetic and natural mind-active substances are banned in North America (de Brie, 1989b). With the end of alcohol prohibition in the US and Canada in the 1920s, the preeminence of alcohol and nicotine in Western nations was assured, if only by default.

From 1930 to 1970 imprisonment was the most common sentence for those convicted of possession or distribution offences. But in the 1960s, with the proliferation of illegal drug use and the development of a 'counter-culture' challenging stereotypes about 'dope fiends', courts were less willing to impose prison sentences. In most Western countries fines are now levied for possession offences, and distributors are not always imprisoned.

In the case of prostitution-related conduct, criminal censure has a longer history. In Britain, Canada and the US prostitutes and various activities associated with prostitution (particularly the running of 'disorderly houses') were controlled by provisions relating to vagrancy and lewdness, but prostitution as such was not criminalized. In the US the act of selling sexual services was criminalized at roughly the same time and in the same moral cauldron as mind-active substances.

Up to the early 1900s there had been various campaigns to suppress prostitution in North America and Britain, but a 'regulationist' strategy held sway. The prevailing feeling of police and medical authorities was that prostitution was not only inevitable, a natural reflection of male lust, but also an outlet for that lust, protecting respectable woman-hood (Rosen 1982). Prostitution was tolerated by policing authorities across North America as long as it was confined to certain 'restricted' or 'segregated' districts located in lower-class areas (and often as long as bribes were dutifully paid to the police by the operators of the brothels). Criminal law, in theory at least, was geared primarily towards the exploiters of prostitutes. In Britain, the regulationism took legal expression in the form of the Contagious Diseases Acts (1864, 1866, 1869), requiring that prostitutes, but not their clients, submit to venereal disease inspections. After concerted campaigning by feminists and others, the Acts were repealed in 1886, on the ground that they discriminated against women (Walkowitz, 1980).

In the early 1900s certain elements of feminist argument and moralist forces combined in Britain, Canada and the US to demand an end to regulationaism. As a sin, a source of disease, and a symbol of male domination of women, prostitution was referred to as the 'Social Evil'. It was argued that a 'white slave trade' existed, with sinister foreign men luring or enslaving white women into prostitution.

From 1900 onward, as part of the more general social purity movement that was washing across Britain and North America, the prohibitionists lobbied government to enact tougher laws against not only the exploiters of prostitutes, but also the prostitutes themselves. In the US and Canada this campaign led to the closure of the restricted districts, often with the result that prostitution would spring up elsewhere (Reckless, 1933). In most US states this campaign led to the criminalization of prostitution itself. In all but one state in the US prostitution remains a criminal offence, although only in some states does this law extend to the client. In Britain and Canada, forms of 'regulationist' strategy have prevailed.

In North America and Britain, pimping, procuring and offences related to the running of prostitution establishments are indictable or felonious offences, for which prison terms are common. Offences related to the public activities of prostitutes and (in some jurisdictions) their clients – crimes such as 'soliciting' – are usually dealt with less seriously in that they are either misdemeanours or summary offences. Nevertheless, many prostitutes are ultimately imprisoned either as repeat offenders or for failure to pay fines. In the US in 1978 more women were convicted of prostitution offences than of any other crime (Davis and Faith, 1987).

The politics of definition

While the selective criminalization of psychoactive substances has been successfully marketed as coherent social policy for almost 90 years, its premises and practices do not appear to be clearly founded in either pharmacology or any objective measure of harmfulness. Tobacco has been described as a more pharmacologically dangerous drug than heroin for most people and in most circumstances (Weil and Rosen, 1983; Brecher et al., 1972). The tripling of the incidence of lung cancer in Western countries between 1955 and 1980 has been directly tied to the tripling of tobacco consumption between 1930 and 1955 (Lee, 1975; World Health Organization, 1986).

Heroin also leaves a trail of death: overdose, and the violence of the illegal trade. But the violence of heroin is not primarily pharmacological; overdose is either an accident or a kind of suicide. The drug constipates the bowel, but it does not break down human tissue. In this important respect it differs from tobacco, alcohol, amphetamines, cocaine and many other drugs (Weil and Rosen, 1983). Health risks are associated with intravenous injection, the sedative effect of the drug and, quite separately, the often desperate lifestyle of the lucrative illegal trade.

Despite quite often vigorous public health and drug control measures in most Western countries the use of illicit drugs appears to be increasing. The criminalization of drugs such as heroin, cocaine and cannabis, when coupled with the legitimate promotion of alcohol and tobacco has, not surprisingly, led the public to believe that alcohol and tobacco are not as dangerous as illegal drugs. But even so, the dangers of tobacco have become painfully clear, and a concerted public health effort has been mobilized against the drug. Very rarely does anyone suggest that the criminal law be used to 'fight' tobacco use, much less distribution (some North American tobacco harvests are facilitated by government agricultural subsidies). But this has not always been the case – in the 1650s the use of tobacco was prohibited in Bavaria, Saxony and Zurich, and at about the same time in Russia tobacco users were tortured and executed (Szasz, 1974: 173).

Cannabis is smoked annually by an estimated 50 million North Americans and tobacco by almost 100 million (Health and Welfare Canada, 1989). There are no deaths that are directly attributable to marijuana consumption (although it, too, may cause lung disease); hundreds of thousands of deaths annually are directly attributed to tobacco (Lee, 1975). The point of these numbers is to suggest that the definition of certain mind-active substances as criminal is ultimately not only a claim about empirically demonstrable harm, but also a claim about the 'morality' of different types of consciousness alteration. A practice of social censure distances the legal smoker from the illegal drug (ab)user.

All forms of drug abuse, legal and illegal, remain as significant health and social problems, nonetheless. In terms of risk to health the most widely used dangerous drugs would seem to be alcohol, tobacco, and cocaine (Weil and Rosen, 1983). In most Western cultures the abuse of alcohol is associated with violence and violent death, automobile fatalities, deaths at work, and suicide (Statistics Canada, 1987). In Canada, recent data indicate that over 60 percent of all fatally injured drivers had blood alcohol levels of 0.15 and over – almost twice the legal limit (Donelson, 1985). These latter sorts of homicide are twice as common as all acts of murder and manslaughter.

While most users of alcohol are able to consume it without imposing a serious risk to health, there is a small minority who become 'problem drinkers', inflicting an empirically obvious social harm. With tobacco, most users quickly become dependent on the drug and escalate consumption to somewhere between 20 and 60 cigarettes per day. Controlled tobacco use – one or two cigarettes per day – may involve a relatively minimal risk to health, but only a small minority of users can exercise this sort of restraint.

Cocaine would appear to be much like alcohol, at least in the context of North American culture. It has been argued that most users are able to consume without imposing a serious risk to health (Erickson and Alexander, 1989) but there is a small minority who become highly dependent, and suffer the consequences typical of stimulant abuse: the risk of death from overdose, the risk of cardiac damage, agitation, unknowing paranoia, etc (Cox et al., 1983).

Marijuana is much like cocaine and alcohol in that most people who use it do not become drug dependent; for the small minority who do, the consequences appear to be less severe than in the instance of cocaine or alchol; the drug is much less toxic (Brecher et al., 1972; Weil and Rosen, 1983). In Canada, the 'average' marijuana smoker typically smokes less than five 'joints' per week (Erickson, 1980); consumption does not appear to be correlated with violence or other anti-social behaviours.

The moral images of illegal drugs are often quite different from their pharmacological representations. Marijuana was once thought to be every bit as addictive as heroin, and has been thought to be a stepping stone to other drugs. More recently it has been associated with political dissent. Timothy Leary's urging that Americans 'tune in, turn on, and drop out' inspired a certain amount of fear about this new (new in the Western world, that is) method for consciousness alteration. Marijuana was, in some senses, the drug of the liberal Left – it was a drug of protest in most Western societies, associated with the campaign against the Vietnam war, and other movements for progressive social change. Alcohol, in contrast, is tied to the more conservative and religious roots of our culture.

While drug legislation is about the 'appropriate' substances to be used in the pursuit of consciousness alteration, the decisive characteristic of almost any definition of prostitution is that it involves sex acts for payment; for the most part, where it is illegal, the actual sex acts involved in prostitution would be quite legal were it not for the element of payment. Where prostitution is criminalized it is because it is thought to be immoral and/or to constitute an unacceptable exploitation of (female) sexuality.

In abstract terms, what is noteworthy about the criminalization of prostitution on the ground that it is immoral is that other forms of sexual relationship which also are widely thought to be immoral are not criminally proscribed. For example, although infidelity is widely condemned, it is not criminally prohibited. Criminal laws against homosexuality and various types of sexual acts, be they homosexual/heterosexual (fellatio, cunnilingus, anal sex) or monosexual (masturbation), have largely disappeared from Western criminal codes.

What is noteworthy about the criminalization of prostitution on the ground that it is 'sexual slavery' (Barry, 1979) is that it selects out for criminal censure only one form of commodifying human activity from among the many commodifications that occur in market societies. More specifically, it selects one form of the commodification of women's sexuality for the application of criminal penalties. As Engels (1884) pointed out long ago, the traditional institution of marriage – whereby a man promised to support a wife financially while she promised to 'honour and obey' him – does not differ much from prostitution except in the sense that the wife might sell herself into sexual slavery once and for all, rather than only temporarily.

While we would not wish to speculate about the extent to which the lived experience of marriage takes this form, the point remains that gender relationships are often commercial in nature. Images of women ascending occupational hierarchies by 'sleeping with the boss' or marrying older men for their money are familiar fare on the daytime soaps and in popular pulp. But none of these sorts of sexual liaisons, even though they have a financial component to them, are the object of criminal prohibition, even if they are the object of opprobrium in some quarters. When criminal law prohibits prostitution, it is *promiscuous* multiple partner commercial sex that it targets. Since promiscuity itself is not subject to criminal sanction, and since no Western state seeks to limit the number of sexual partners an adult may have (although some do statutorily limit the number of sexual partners one may have in the same place at the same time), a government which criminalizes prostitution would thus seem to be saying that if men and women are going to have multiple sexual partners, the sex itself must be without compensation.

Competing law and policy models: drugs

There are three general, though not mutually exclusive, strategies for controlling mind-active drugs: *criminalization, therapeutic intervention*, and *education*. In legal terms, there are three primary models: *prohibition* of use and distribution; *decriminalization* (accommodating some measure of use but retaining some measure of control over distribution); and *legalization* (situating the drug as any other commodity in the marketplace).

Criminalization
Criminalization applies criminal sanctions to both the suppliers and possessors of certain drugs. Despite the pharmacologically capricious definition of these consciousness-altering substances as illegal, the United States has recently announced that it is embarking on an all-out effort against what public opinion and the government consider to be the single greatest threat to American society and security – 'drugs' (de Brie, 1989a). Ultimately, the main emphasis of this war, and the logic of criminalization from which it flows, is placed on the suppliers of illegal drugs; the basic premise is that *availability* is at the heart of the problem. By stopping the flow of illegal drugs into and within a given country the problem will disappear.

To this point, criminalization is the predominant strategy across the globe. With the growth of the industries of illegal drugs (principally in marijuana and cocaine) between 1967 and 1990, the cat and mouse manoeuvring between police and distributors has grown more sophisticated, telephone interceptions, room probes and satellite surveillance added to the more standard police arsenal of badge, gun and informant. The availability of cocaine, marijuana and heroin has increased over the past 23 years, the intentions of government compromised by the continuing economic value of the commodities. It has been estimated that even in the 1950s, however, there were 200 million marijuana users worldwide and in 1946, 40 million opium smokers in China (Szasz, 1974: 184–5).

Alternatives to criminalization

The dominance of demonic descriptions of the effects of certain drugs began to be challenged in the 1960s and thereafter. Lindesmith's *The Addict and the Law* (1965) was one of the first to question the notion that much of the behaviour of the users of drugs like heroin was a product of the drug itself. He suggested that prohibition has created a false scarcity for substances with a relatively inelastic demand. On the strength of this false scarcity, criminal networks have arisen to take advantage of lucrative markets, with some illicit drug users and abusers, in order to finance their consumption, turning to various other illicit activities. At about the same time, labelling theorists (such as Becker, 1963) were arguing that drug law itself amplified or even created some of the problems associated with illegal drug use. For those opposed to criminalization, more emphasis is likely to be placed on therapeutic intervention and education, though all three strategies typically coexist.

Therapeutic intervention conceives of drug use as primarily a medical problem. The user, suffering from drug dependence or addiction, is a person in need of assistance or treatment. In a correctional system which values social reintegration of offenders and offended, treatment is often more palatable than the rhetoric of punishment and retribution.

A strategy of education is one that suggests that the availability of a substance is not the only key to understanding and reducing drug abuse. In the case of alcohol and tobacco, the educational and medical models currently take precedence. Over the past decade, in particular, there has been an intensified effort in North America to educate the populace about the consequences of drug use and abuse generally, although the contemporary desire to reduce alcohol and tobacco abuse has occurred without any demand for the criminal prohibition of these two substances.

In the case of drugs not criminalized, two general types of legal regimes have been described (van Vliet, 1989); legalization, a relatively unregulated commercialization of a substance; and decriminalization, a system that typically regulates, in a non-criminal manner, both use and distribution, educating about problems of abuse and treating those who develop difficulties. Historically, alcohol and tobacco policies have fallen somewhere between these two types of regime.

Legalization   Legalization – the relatively unfettered commercialization of a mind-active substance – is problematic, given the individual and social costs of such substance abuse, and the significant increases in tobacco and alcohol consumption that accompanied such practices in most Western states between 1920 and 1980 (Health and Welfare Canada, 1989). Cigarette advertising in America in the 1950s actually extolled the health benefits of smoking, a doctor in a lab coat proclaiming in the pages of *Life* magazine that 'More doctors smoke Camels than any other cigarette'.

Decriminalization   Decriminalization involves a range of styles of state regulation, supplemented by educational and therapeutic programmes, both public and private. In the case of tobacco, North America and Britain have moved away from a model of legalization, towards a model of decriminalization. Tobacco advertising is restricted, places of consumption limited, and the product can only be sold with some form of health warning.

Criminalization and decriminalization in practice

With respect to drugs like marijuana, cocaine and heroin, the United States and the Netherlands represent two distinct styles and are thus worth comparing. While criminal law in the US differs from state to state, most jurisdictions impose lengthy jail terms, and in some instances life imprisonment, for the distribution of marijuana, cocaine, and heroin (some countries, such as Singapore and Malaysia, retain capital punishment for these offences). In the urban ghettos of the US those involved in the distribution of heroin, cocaine and crack are often armed. The distribution of these drugs is one of the few opportunities for wealth among North America's disadvantaged. As cocaine distribution and consumption expanded through the 1980s, so too did the unemployment rate among black men (Currie, 1990).

In the Netherlands the sale of marijuana and hashish is tolerated in about 300 coffee shops; customers may purchase small amounts (two to nine grams) to use on the premises, or to take away. The possession of cocaine and heroin is also tolerated, though police continue to take action against organized distribution of these drugs. One author has claimed that:

By setting up 'user-friendly'...services that were confidential, non-judgemental and not aimed at achieving immediate abstinence, yet providing treatment on demand, professionals began to see drug users who would otherwise stay beyond the reach of any drug assistance agency. They can now monitor and influence the health, social and legal status of the users and reduce some of the damage to society as well. (van Vliet, 1989)

There are approximately 300,000 marijuana and hashish users in the Netherlands, about 2 percent of the population (De Zwart, 1989); in North America the proportion of users is approximately five times as great (Health and Welfare Canada, 1989). Despite the high visibility of the marijuana and hashish trade in Amsterdam, less than 25 percent of the city's residents over the age of 16 have tried the drugs (Engelsman, 1989). Corresponding estimates in Canada and the United States vary between 35 and 50 percent (Health and Welfare Canada, 1989). It is difficult to know how much legal regimes influence these different drug use profiles, or how much they represent cultural differences.

Competing law and policy models: prostitution

Generally, there are three main types of prostitution control regime. In almost all Western European countries certain aspects of prostitution-related conduct – such as procuring, pimping and running prostitution establishments – are proscribed by criminal law but, in most of them, prostitution itself is legal. Where these countries differ is in the extent to which they allow the organization of prostitution as a business. In some of these countries, such as West Germany and the Netherlands, prostitution establishments and/or red light areas are legal; in others, such as the United Kingdom, a system of regulationism prevails in which much prostitution-related conduct is criminalized, but prostitution itself remains legal. Similar regimes exist in Canada and some Australian states. In most US states, in contrast, the sale of sexual services itself is illegal (the one exception is Nevada where, in some counties, brothel prostitution is legal). In some states it is also an offence to purchase such services.

Three genres of prostitution control policies can be identified in contemporary Western societies: *criminalization, regulationism* and *legalization*. A fourth model, *decriminalization*, which would take prostitution out of the criminal law altogether, has been advocated by prostitutes' rights organizations and some feminists.

Criminalization

Criminalization of prostitution itself represents a thoroughgoing denunciation of the act, primarily on the grounds that it is either 'immoral' or that it is an unacceptable form of exploitation. Opponents of criminalization suggest that it infringes the civil liberties of prostitutes, violates their right to privacy and, because the law until recently rarely applied to the customer, it also discriminates against prostitutes. Even in those legal regimes where clients are susceptible to prosecution, law enforcement efforts tend to concentrate on prostitutes (Barrows and Novak, 1986: 259; Barry, 1979: 125–6; Lowman, 1990). Critics of criminalization may also take the position that even if the goal of social policy is the eradication of prostitution, only fundamental changes to sexual institutions and economic structures will ultimately achieve this end. In the meantime criminal law only serves to further victimize prostitutes.

Alternatives to criminalization
Although they differ in certain key respects, alternatives to criminalization share at least one common premise: the state ought not to have the power to criminalize the sale or purchase of sexual services – a citizen should have the right to control the use of his or her own body. This position was articulated most clearly by the British Wolfenden Committee (1957) when it suggested that criminal law should not be concerned with sexual morality as such, but only with those aspects of sexual behaviour that are offensive or injurious to other citizens (and, in the case of prostitution, with the exploitation of prostitutes). If one accepts this premise, the question then becomes, how should prostitution be organized? It is in their answers to this question that the advocates of regulationism, legalization and decriminalization part company.

Regulationism   In contemporary writing (Matthews, 1986) the term 'regulationism' has been used to describe the type of criminal law regime that currently exists in England and Wales. Following the Wolfenden Committee's logic, this system of legislation allows the act of prostitution to take place, but prohibits prostitutes from meeting their customers in public places, criminalizes procuring and pimping, and outlaws 'bawdy houses'; a prostitute working alone out of a premise is, however, exempt from the last of these provisions.

A similar model of prostitution control operates in Canada, but here a single prostitute is not exempt from bawdy house laws, like her British counterpart. Canadian law would thus seem to enable legislators to say to the advocates of criminalization that prostitution is effectively criminalized, while saying to the advocates of legalization and decriminalization that prostitution is, nonetheless, legal.

Opponents of this system argue that it still caters to an old-style moralism by placing prostitutes in a legal no man's land where their status is unclear. In practice regulationism often turns out to be little different from criminalization (Matthews, 1986) with most law enforcement efforts directed at the visibility of the prostitute. If pushed out of sight, the prostitute may be more prone to exploitation by third parties. Under the regimes of both criminalization and regulation the prostitute is subject to a considerable amount of violence (in the US the 'Green River killer' alone has taken the lives of approximately 50 prostitutes).

Legalization In the literature on prostitution control models the term 'legalization' generally refers to regimes which permit the operation of state licensed 'brothels' (such as the Mustang Ranch in Nevada or the Eros Centers of West Germany), or permit licensed prostitutes to work in certain areas (as in the Netherlands). The advantages of legalized prostitution are variously touted as: (a) providing an important service for men who could not otherwise find sexual companions; (b) protecting non-prostitute women from potential rapists; (c) facilitating compulsory medical checks; (d) removing prostitution from city streets; (e) protecting prostitutes from pimps and violent clients; and (f) allowing the state to acquire revenue from prostitution in the form of taxes and licence fees.

Critics of legalization assert that there is no clear evidence that prostitution does protect non-prostitute women from male predation, that it does not necessarily remove prostitutes from city streets, since many of them view licensing as yet another form of stigmatization. Finally, many prostitutes would not want to work in brothels where they would have less autonomy and inferior working conditions (cf. Matthews, 1986; Shaver, 1985). Critics also suggest that prostitutes do not constitute a major source of venereal disease infection (many of them require their clients to use condoms), and that compulsory testing of prostitutes, but not clients, would be discriminatory. Perhaps most importantly of all, legalized prostitution would encourage the most crass commodification of women, a system in which the state becomes a 'pimp' (Barry, 1979: 124).

Decriminalization Decriminalization is the position advocated by most prostitutes' rights organizations and many women's groups. They propose a system in which prostitutes could either work in small collectives or independently, on a self-employed basis. In this system all references to prostitution would be removed from the criminal law since many prostitution-related offences are defined according to the status of the offender rather than a specific type of behaviour. In Canada, for example, the law which makes it an offence to communicate in a public place for the purpose of buying or selling sexual services allows a person to stand on a street corner, proposition any number of passers-by and have sexual intercourse with them –

provided, of course, that the act takes place in private and that they do not get paid for the sex. To avoid creating a status offence the problem of prostitute and client nuisance would be covered by generic public nuisance laws (Shaver, 1985). Similarly, laws which criminalize people for living wholly or in part on the proceeds of prostitution have been criticized by the advocates of decriminalization for being overly paternalistic, applying to any person (including husbands and off-spring) cohabiting with a prostitute (McLeod, 1982). Under a system of decriminalization coercive pimping would be controlled by generic laws prohibiting threats, assault and extortion.

Critics of decriminalization have sometimes assumed that it amounts to no control whatsoever, perhaps a reflection of the failure of some of its advocates to specify just what sort of regulations should apply to prostitution. Thus Wilson (1983) concluded that decriminalization would create a sexual 'free-for-all' for men. But according to certain advocates (Shaver, 1985, 1988), a system of decriminalization would allow control of prostitution in the same way that other businesses are regulated, and with these regulations, prevent the establishment of exploitative prostitution businesses.

Prostitution is a contradictory issue for feminists and anyone else concerned with gender equality. On the one hand supporters of civil libertarian arguments in favour of decriminalization suggest that it is possible to develop non-exploitive and non-degrading forms of prosti-tution (Ericsson, 1980; Shaver, 1988). In its most romanticized form this argument provides the image of the positively 'happy hooker' (Hollander, 1972). Against this is the view that prostitution is 'morally undesirable, no matter what reforms are made, because it is one of the most graphic examples of men's domination of women' (Pateman, 1983: 561; see also Shrage, 1989). Because of these contradictions, feminists and sex trade workers are not always in accord (cf. Delacoste and Alexander, 1987; Bell, 1987).

The political economy of drugs and prostitution

It is impossible to understand the politics of drugs and prostitution outside the context of international market mechanisms, gender struc-tures and a global class system.

Illegal drugs are produced primarily in the largely unindustrialized South, legal drugs (including pharmaceuticals) in the industrialized North. In the case of illegal drugs, the geography of profit is similar. Some of the profits go to drug barons and corrupt politicians in the producing countries; the bulk goes to drug distributors in Europe and the US. The peasant farmers actually producing the raw material get comparatively little for it. For example, of the $30 billion estimated to be generated by coca leaf farming, only about $60 million (or one-fifth of 1 percent) goes to the farmers (de Brie, 1989b). Over the past decade there appears to have been a considerable increase in the amount of land devoted to drug production resulting, in part, from the destruction of traditional economic structures and from the consequences of the vast debt that many of the drug-producing countries have incurred by borrowing from the International Monetary Fund – debt that there is no foreseeable means of repaying. The turning over of lands to coca production in South America is itself a reflection of the effect of the failure of countries like the US to renew an international agreement supporting the price of coffee. The decline in coffee prices has been dramatic (it was estimated that if the trend in prices persisted it could cost Colombia $4 billion in 1990) thereby diminishing the ability of many South American peasants to eke out a living (de Brie, 1989b). As de Brie puts it, 'The coffee crisis was passed over in silence by the leading industrialized countries. By way of contrast, plenty of brash publicity surrounded Bush's promise to give the Colombian government $65 million... so that it could equip itself with American made equipment for its fight against the drug barons.'

Drug production is further implicated in the financing of local political conflicts, a problem often exacerbated by US foreign policy. On the one hand, the US government wages a war on drugs urging other regimes to do the same, while on the other it has supported certain political factions who depend on drug money to finance their political struggles. So it was that much of the Afghan hashish smuggled into North America through the 1980s bore the stamp 'Freedom Fighters'. In some small measure each hashish consumer thus helped to support the Afghan resistance to Russian occupation and, in the process, to line the coffers of international arms dealers.

Although official discourse about drug problems rarely includes any discussion of what to do about the economic plight of Third World countries it would seem that until there are viable economic alternatives to coca, marijuana or poppy production, the war on drugs will not have much of an impact on production patterns. Similarly, when it comes to drug distribution and consumption patterns within countries like the US, the black market in illicit drugs is intimately tied to the economic and social circumstances of the inner city. While solutions to the problems confronting the urban poor might not, in and of themselves, result in immediate changes in drug use and abuse patterns in the inner city, it may be that not much can be changed in these areas without such initiatives. But given the occurrence of drug use at all levels of society, it will take much more than poverty to explain the phenomenon of drug use and shape policies designed to deal with abuse.

In the case of prostitution we again find that patterns of supply and demand reflect economic disparities at an international level. Throughout South East Asia, prostitution has become a particularly big business, fuelled mostly by foreign demand. One study estimated that 700,000 women are involved in prostitution in Thailand, and 200,000 in the Philippines and South Korea (Gay, 1985, cited in Messerschmidt, 1986). At least part of the supply of women into the ranks of prostitution in these countries is a reflection of the disruption of traditional economies caused by the growth of foreign-sponsored industries taking advantage of cheap labour, the demand created by the existence of large American military installations, and the development of a large sex industry catering to West European, North American, Australian and Japanese businessmen and tourists. In the context of this demand, women and girls turn to prostitution because of unemployment or because they do not want to take the low-paying and menial jobs generally available to them (Messerschmidt, 1986: 95).

In an important sense in Western societies it is these same sorts of conditions – the marginal position of females in the labour force combined with a substantial male demand – that provide the context in which the decision to become a prostitute is made. If the goal of social policy is to reduce prostitution, it is these factors that will have to be dealt with. If one takes the position that our goal should not be to censure prostitution as such (on the ground that it is no more exploitive than many other forms of labour), the primary goal of social policy would seem to be to ensure that women are not forced into the trade because of a lack of economic or social alternatives.

Note

Our thanks to Mimi Ajzenstadt for comments on this paper.

References

Barrows, S. and Novak, W. (1986) *Mayflower Madam: The Secret Life of Sydney Biddle Barrows*. New York: Arbor House.

Barry, K. (1979) *Female Sexual Slavery*. New York: New York University Press.

Becker, H. (1963) *Outsiders: Studies in the Sociology of Deviance*. Glencoe: Free Press.

Bell, L. (ed.) (1987) *Good Girls/Bad Girls: Sex Trade Workers and Feminists Face to Face*. Toronto: The Women's Press.

Boyd, N. (1984) 'The origins of Canadian narcotics control: the process of criminalization in historical context', *Dalhousie Law Journal*, 8: 102–36.

Brecher, E. and the Editors of Consumer Reports (1972) *Licit and Illicit Drugs*. Boston: Little Brown.

Bullough, V. and Bullough, B. (1978) *Prostitution: An Illustrated Social History*. New York: Crown Publishers.

Cox, T.C., Jacobs, M.R., Le Blanc, A.E. and Marshman, J.A. (1983) *Drugs and Drug Abuse*. Toronto: Addiction Research Foundation.

Currie, E. (1990) 'Retreatism, minimalism and realism: three styles of reasoning on crime and drugs in the United States'. Paper presented at the conference on 'Realist Criminology: Crime Control and Policing in the 1990s', Vancouver, Simon Fraser University, 24/25 May 1990.

Davis, N.J. and Faith, K. (1987) 'Women and the state: changing models of social control', in J. Lowman, R.J. Menzies and T.S. Palys (eds), *Transcarceration: Essays in the Sociology of Social Control*. Aldershot: Gower.

de Brie, C. (1989a) 'Shadow boxing in the drug ring', *Manchester Guardian Weekly*, 19 November, p. 14.

de Brie, C. (1989b) 'World evil with its roots in the north-south divide', *Manchester Guardian Weekly*, 19 November, p. 14.

Delacoste, F. and Alexander, P. (eds) (1987) *Sex Work: Writings by Women in the Sex Industry*. Pittsburgh: Cleis Press.

De Zwart, W.M. (1989) *Alcohol, Tobacco, and Drugs in Figures*. Amsterdam: Netherlands Institute of Alcohol and Drugs.

Donelson, A. (1985) *Alcohol and Road Accidents in Canada: Issues Related to Future Strategies and Priorities*. Ottawa: Policy, Programs and Research Branch, Department of Justice.

Engels, F. (1884) *The Origin of the Family, Private Property and the State*. Moscow: Progress Publishers.

Engelsman, E.L. (1989) 'Dutch drug policy in Western European perspective', in M.S. Groenhuijsen and A.M. van Kalmthout (eds), *Nederlandse Drugbeleid in West-europees Perspectief*. Amsterdam: Arnhem.

Erickson, P. (1980) *Cannabis Criminals*. Toronto: Addiction Research Foundation.

Erickson, P. and Alexander, B.K. (1989) 'Cocaine: an addictive liability', *Social Pharmacology*, 3: 249–70.

Ericsson, L.O. (1980) 'Charges against prostitution: an attempt at a philosophical assessment', *Ethics*, 90: 335–66.

Gay, J. (1985) 'The "patriotic" prostitute', *The Progressive*, February: 34–6.

Health and Welfare Canada (1989) *Licit and Illicit Drugs in Canada*. Ottawa: Ministry of Supply and Services.

Hollander, X. (1972) *The Happy Hooker*. New York: Dell Publishing.

Lee, P.N. (ed.) (1975) *Tobacco Consumption in Various Countries*. London: Tobacco Research Council.

Lindesmith, A. (1965) *The Addict and the Law*. Bloomington: Indiana University Press.

Lowman, J. (1990) 'Notions of formal equality before the law: the experience of street prostitutes and their customers', *The Journal of Human Justice*, 1 (2): 55–73.

Matthews, R. (1986) 'Beyond Wolfenden? Prostitution, politics and the law', in R. Matthews and J. Young (eds.), *Confronting Crime*. London: Sage. pp. 188–210.

McLeod, E. (1982) *Women Working: Prostitution Now*. London: Croom Helm.

Messerschmidt, J.W. (1986) *Capitalism, Patriarchy and Crime: Toward a Socialist Feminist Criminology*. Totawa, New Jersey: Rowman and Littlefield.

Pateman, C. (1983) 'Defending prostitution: charges against Ericsson', *Ethics*, 93: 561–5.

Reckless, W. (1933) *Vice in Chicago*. Chicago: University of Chicago Press.

Rosen, R. (1982) *The Lost Sisterhood: Prostitution in America, 1900–1920*. Baltimore: Johns Hopkins Press.

Shaver, F. (1985) 'Prostitution: a critical analysis of three policy approaches', *Canadian Journal of Public Policy*, 11 (3): 493–503.

Shaver, F. (1988) 'A critique of feminist arguments against prostitution', *Atlantis*, 14 (1): 82–9.

Shrage, L. (1989) 'Should feminists oppose prostitution?', *Ethics*, 99: 347–61.

Statistics Canada (1987) *Historical Homicide Data Relevant to the Capital Punishment Issue*. Ottawa: Canadian Centre for Justice Statistics.

Sumner, C. (1983) 'Rethinking deviance: towards a sociology of censure', *Research in Law, Deviance and Social Control*, 5: 187–204.

Szasz, T. (1974) *Ceremonial Chemistry*. New York: Anchor Press.

van Vliet, H. (1989) 'The uneasy decriminalization: a perspective on Dutch drug policy'. Paper presented to the 41st Annual Meeting of the American Society for Criminology, November, Reno, Nevada.

Walkowitz, J.R. (1980) *Prostitution in Victorian Society: Women, Class and the State*. Cambridge: Cambridge University Press.

Weil, A. and Rosen, W. (1983) *Chocolate to Morphine: Understanding Mind Active Drugs*. Boston: Houghton Mifflin.

Wilson, E. (1983) *What Is To Be Done about Violence against Women?* Harmondsworth: Penguin.

Wolfenden Committee (1957) *Report of the Committee on Homosexual Offences and Prostitution*. London; Her Majesty's Stationery Office.

World Health Organization, *Annual Reports, 1950–1986*. New York: World Health Organization.

PART TWO

ALTERNATIVE APPROACHES TO PREVENTION AND CONTROL

6

Freedom, Responsibility and Justice: The Criminology of the 'New Right'

Chris R. Tame

The term 'New Right' is label that has, in the last few decades, been applied to intellectual and political movements ranging from racism, fascism, socio-biology, the 'moral majority' and Christian fundamentalists and the like to any expression of anti-socialism, and to the revivals of both classical liberalism and traditionalist conservatism.

Indeed, it is hard to see the logic behind the customary categorization of 'left' and 'right'. Why, for example, are collectivist, anti-individualist and anti-capitalist exponents of racism, anti-semitism, national socialism/fascism lumped together with anti-collectivist, pro-individualist exponents of free markets and individual liberty as being on something called 'the right'? The moral, political and economic premises, and indeed the practices, of fascists and national socialists are virtually identical to those of Marxist and Socialist collectivists (Weber, 1969; Piekoff, 1982). This use of the left–right spectrum appears to be a result of, at best, ignorance or confusion, or, at worst, partisan and propagandistic obfuscation.

Unfortunately, the term 'New Right' has of late been once more applied to a very real phenomenon, the rise of schools of thought and writers whose common characteristic is a rejection of, or critical stance towards, the dominant worldview of socialism/Marxism in myriad forms, of doctrines of social determinism and social engineering, and of state interventionism in personal, political and economic life. Since it is hard to alter established usage, no matter how misleading, what is understood by the term 'New Right' in this chapter is essentially the broad phenomenon of a school, or rather schools, of thought whose primary analytical, and normative, orientation, is to the concepts of freedom, justice and responsibility.

Within criminology the established paradigm, with some variations, is arguably one characterized by an anti-punitive ethics and juris-prudence and a determinist model of the causes of crime and of criminal responsibility. The New Right as it is understood herein represents a rejection, albeit not a totally unified one, of this paradigm. It can largely be seen as consisting of four major streams of thought, namely:

1   A radical restatement of natural rights classical liberalism, or libertarianism
2   A vigorous application of the conceptual tools of liberal, free market economics
3   An restatement of 'traditionalist' conservatism
4   An empiricist, primarily *wertfrei* (value-free) critique of the failure of the established policies.

I shall examine each of these four streams of thought in turn.

The natural rights libertarians

Although frequently called the New Right (Green, 1987; King, 1987), a more appropriate description of this school of thought would be the New Liberalism or, as I have argued elsewhere, the New Enlighten-ment (Tame, 1985). It is a revival of nineteenth-century 'classical' liberalism, the revolutionary rationalist radicalism of the major En-lightenment figures (Tame, 1977; Barry, 1987; Gray, 1990; Sampson, 1984). Because of a strange linguistic evolution in America, whereby the term 'liberal' is applied to doctrines of state interventionism, in contradiction to its historical (and elsewhere, contemporary) usage, most adherents of this approach now favour the term 'libertarian'.

The major school of libertarian thought is a reassertion of Aristotelian, natural rights/natural law philosophy. On the basis of an analysis of the nature of humans as rational entities with free will it develops a moral philosophy of rational egoism (selfishness) and self-actualization and a political philosophy of 'life, liberty and property'. Individual freedom should be limited only by the duty not to initiate force against others (what Herbert Spencer in the nineteenth century termed the 'law of equal freedom'). The primary source of this radical Aristotelianism has been the work of the Russian-born philosopher and novelist Ayn Rand (1964, 1967), which has been applied and extended by writers like Tibor Machan (1975), Eric Mack (1976), John Hospers (1971), Murray Rothbard (1973, 1978, 1982), Leonard Peikoff (1982), and David Kelley, among others.

The relevance of this approach to both criminology and legal philosophy is obvious. In the words of Rothbard:

> The key to the theory of liberty is the establishment of the rights of private

property, for each individual's justified sphere of free action can only be set forth if his rights of property are analysed and established. 'Crime' can be defined and properly analysed as a violent invasion or aggression against the property of another individual (including his property in his own person). The positive theory of liberty then becomes an analysis of *what* can be called property rights and therefore *what* can be considered crimes ... Since questions of property and crime are essentially *legal* questions, our theory of liberty necessarily sets forth an ethical theory of what law concretely *should* be. (Rothbard, 1982: vi)

Thus libertarians reject the whole panoply of 'victimless crimes' as not really crimes, and the subsequent criminalization and stigmatization of individuals engaged in acts which in reality range from foolish or self-destructive, perhaps personally immoral, to the completely legitimate and productive.

In 1977 well over five million Americans were arrested not for attacks upon the other people or property, but for victimless crimes, acts which the government violently (although very selectively) disapproves of, but which do not violate anyone's rights; drunkenness, possession of drugs, prostitution, homosexuality, vagrancy, loitering, pornography, and the like ... In order to police the morals of America and 'protect' these men, women and children from themselves, many will be forcibly separated from their homes, families and jobs and thrust into a brutal sub-human prison environment, from which they will emerge as real threats to others, rather than simply the imagined threats that they were to themselves before incarceration. (Wollstein, 1967: 4)

Indeed, it is the state itself which is seen as the major perpetrator of criminal acts, by its criminalizing of non-criminal behaviour, and by such coercive acts as conscription, taxation, regulation of the economy, censorship and the like. 'The disgraceful reality', writes Wollstein, 'is that justice in America today is more often than not injustice; that the aggressions committed by police, judges, juries and jailers are vastly greater than all private American violence; and that the American "justice" system produces more wholesale destruction and carnage than it even remotely begins to prevent' (Wollstein, 1967: 2).

Some English and US libertarians have attempted to trace in detail the historical genesis of 'victimless crimes'; for example, the criminalization of sexual 'immorality' as a result of medical paternalism, coercive preventive medicine and various forms of 'right-wing' and 'left-wing' Social Darwinism, bureaucratic statism, moral purity movements (in conservative and feminist guises), and paternalist health crusades (Hamowy, 1977; Szasz, 1975; Gabb, 1990; Davies, 1991).

Libertarians also vehemently reject the assertions of both authoritarian conservatives and socialist feminists that pornography 'causes' rape or violent behaviour. Such claims are not only refuted by the existence of free will, but the alleged scientific studies sometimes cited have been shown to be unfounded or misleading (Thomson et al., 1990).

The most prolific writer in regard to the stigmatization of the innocent has been the psychologist Thomas Szasz. The core of his critique has been the concept of free will and its negation by concepts of mental illness. In his view, with very few exceptions of physically caused pathologies, 'mental illness' (although he rejects even the term itself) is a largely volitional process over time. Individuals are responsible for their actions, and these are not determined by inner or outer forces. The consequence of doctrines of mental illness has been 'to conceal conflict as illness and to justify coercion as treatment' (Szasz, 1974: xi). In both the East and the West unpopular minorities of every sort, whether sexual or political, have been labelled as mentally ill. The language of orthodox psychiatric diagnosis is rejected as either meaningless, fallacious and always 'used to stigmatize, dehumanize, imprison, and torture those to whom they are applied' (Szasz, 1974: xiii).

Moreover, the harmful consequences of psychiatric degradation of individualism are twofold. On the one hand it destroys the civil liberties of 'offenders', real ones as well as the perpetrators of 'victimless crimes': 'The thesis that the criminal is a sick individual in need of treatment . . . is false. Indeed, it is hardly more than a refurbishing, with new terms, of the main ideas and techniques of the inquisitorial process' (Szasz, 1974: 108). But the discrediting of the individual as a 'self-responsible human being' also exposes society to the depredations of the truly wicked and coercive:

> The American government is now a threat to the freedom of its own people not because it punishes the innocent, nor because its punishments are too harsh, but rather because it does not punish the guilty. One result is an ever-increasing army of thieves and thugs, muggers and murderers, abroad in the land, preying on a people unprotected by their own police and judiciary. Another result is an ever-increasing tendency not to punish those who are evil and who commit evil acts but instead to treat them for nonexistent illnesses. (Szasz, 1977: 119)

The rejection of the idea of individual responsibility and free will has led to an unwillingness 'to shoulder the responsibilities for punishing men, women and children who deprive other individuals of their life, liberty and property' (Szasz, 1977: 120). Of course, in reality no real 'rehabilitation' or 'treatment' goes on in prisons, which, in the USA especially, have become nightmare realms of violence and instruction in crime, governed by their inmates. Nevertheless, in plea bargaining, absurd rules of evidence and procedure, lax sentencing and parole, punishment is minimized.

In Szasz's view, then, the remedy for crime is to 're-embrace the ethics of a truly dignified system of criminal sanctions consisting of minimal but fitting punishments meted out as inexorably and as fairly as possible. In proportion as a decent punitive penology would be realized, people would be safe from crime' (Szasz, 1977: 120).

The attack on orthodox criminology becomes even more vigorous in the work of Robert James Bidinotto. Demonstrating that a real 'crime explosion' has occurred, he argues that this is primarily a result of the 'excuse-making industry', the social-science establishment as a whole, philosophers, psychologists, political scientists, legal scholars, sociologists, and criminologists alike. The legal system has increasingly embodied a view that criminals are not to blame for their own actions, that they are determined by environment, poverty, injustice, or by psychological forces beyond personal control, or by alleged sociobiological drives. Punishment, in the orthodox view, is seen as unjust and immoral, deterrence doesn't work, and 'rehabilitation', 'treatment' or large-scale social reform (of a collectivist nature) are the only rational answers to crime. It is this ideology, in Bidinotto's view, that has undermined the legal system:

> The issue of free will versus determinism is *the* key to resolving any argument about the causes and cures of crime.... By not taking into account the free will of the criminal, it's ignoring the very factor which is *decisive* to his criminality: his responsibility for his actions. Instead, it has shaped the institutions of law to excuse him from justice. (Bidinotto, 1989: 10–11)

While not denying that individuals are influenced by social 'forces' and the social environment, nothing can remove freedom of will. 'To excuse criminals because of poor social environments leaves unexplained the crimes of those from good social environments. And the sociological excuse is an insult to millions of others from the poor backgrounds, who have not turned to crime' (Bidinotto, 1989: 6). Ironically, the culture of excuses, constitutes exactly the sort of environment which encourages crime. Against those who assert 'the crime of punishment', Bidinotto sees the victims of crime as the 'forgotten people', whose 'cries for justice must be heard' (Bidinotto, 1989: 1).

What sort of solutions do the libertarians offer to the problem of crime?

On the one hand, the traditional concept and practice of incarceration is defended. It serves the 'goals of retribution, deterrence, incapacitation, and punishment' (Bidinotto, 1989: 28). The removal of the criminal 'from free association with a large segment of society', whether in prisons or some sort of geographical 'exile', is not seen as either 'old-fashioned' or irrelevant. And even if it served no deterrent function, punishment is seen as a good in itself, an inherent part of justice as retribution (Lee, 1974). Capital punishment is also generally defended on primarily moral grounds, although its clash with the possibility of extracting material restitution to heirs and dependants tends to downgrade it as a mandatory punishment (Rothbard, 1978).

A more radical aspect of the libertarian approach, however, is its emphasis on the importance of enforcing restitution upon the criminal. With the rise of the nation state and doctrines of statism, (both in the 'King's peace' or 'debt to society' form) the older, allegedly more 'primitive' common law view of crime as an act whereby the criminal incurred a debt to the victim (or his/her heirs and dependants) was superseded. Libertarians favour the reversal of this development. A central concern of law should, then, be the attempt to ensure the proper restitution by the aggressor to the victim.

It is worth noting that a minor dispute does occur here between pure restitutionists, like Barnet and Hagel (Barnet and Hagel, 1977; Barnet, 1977), and those like Rothbard, Lee and others (Rothbard, 1982; Lee, 1982; O'Keeffe, 1989) representing the mainstream of libertarian thought, who see restitution as an essential, but not exhaustive, function of law. Although less concerned with abstract philosophical issues, the influential British free market think-tank, the Adam Smith Institute, has also campaigned for emphasizing restitution within a privatized prison service (Elliott, 1990).

Insofar as the state can have any rightful powers (a premise attacked by the anarcho-capitalist wing of libertarianism) they can only be derived from the rights of individuals, and certainly do not deprive them of right to exercise them individually. Libertarians have defended not only the morality but the effectiveness and value of private law enforcement, detection agencies and 'vigilance societies' (Anderson and Hill, 1979). The radical anarchist wing of Libertarianism argues that ultimately only a fully privatized system of market anarchism can fully preserve freedom and prosperity. The feasibility of such a system is defended and outlined in a growing body of literature (Rothbard, 1973; Tannahill and Wollstein, 1972).

Similarly, the private ownership of firearms is vigorously defended. Contrary to popular belief the evidence demonstrates that ownership of firearms exercises an effective deterrence against aggression and that 'gun control' (in practice, the disarming of the victims but not the aggressors) is both undesirable and ineffective. Women, minorities and 'lower-class' individuals are especially harmed by gun control measures, it is argued (Kates, 1979, 1984; Kope, 1988). The broader issue of a disarmed citizenry facing ever more mighty state power also lies behind the libertarian defence of the desirability of an 'armed citizenry' (Gabb, 1988; Botsford, 1990).

Even libertarian exponents of a 'limited state', rather than anarchist, position have a sceptical attitude towards the efficacy and honesty of state police forces. Private sector responses to rising crime, in the form of private security, private patrols, voluntary neighbourhood watches and initiatives like the Guardian Angels have been widely welcomed (Tame, 1989). Groups like Adam Smith Institute have thus called for the encouragement, rather than discouragement or persecution, of such private initiatives. Similarly, the privatization of 'public' space, housing estates, and streets is favoured in itself and as it lends itself to the extension of effective private security (Elliott, 1989).

The more militant forms of socialist criminology, which sees 'capitalism as the cause of crime', and no fundamental solution outside a broader radical social transformation, also find their polar opposite in the libertarian position. For the libertarians it is not only the determinist premises that underlie most variants of collectivism and statism that cause crime, but all the ramifications of collectivist economic, social and political policies.

In a historic and comparative account the sociologist Christie Davies (drawing upon Clinard, 1978) has described the remarkable achievement of what he calls 'Respectable Britain' in the nineteenth century, a close approximation of a crime-free society, insofar as that is humanly possible. That condition was attained, in his view, by a 'moralizing of society' along very specific lines, the rise to predominance of a morality rooted in individualism and free market values, and in an ethos of personal responsibility and self-control:

> The decline of Respectable Britain, the eclipse of the era of the law-abiding British, can ultimately be traced to the ever-increasing bureaucratic centralization of British society in the twentieth century and the linked, but independent, rise of a corrosive ethic of socialist egalitarianism. Both these changes undermined the moral fabric of Respectable Britain and eroded its central belief in individual personal responsibility. (Davies, 1983: 68).

The rise of crime is seen as essentially the result of what libertarians generally see as the victory of the state in the never-ending conflict between state power and 'social power', between imposed 'order' and control and spontaneous order and natural social control (Mack, 1976). In Davies' words: 'The state has been pitted against society and the liberty of the ordinary citizen constrained by the "liberation" of violent and anti-social elements ... disciplined freedom has been replaced by anomie liberated delinquency' (Davies, 1989: 15, 8).

The return to a market-based order, and the promulgation of a similar morality of autonomy and individualism is the ultimate social route to the minimization, if not total eradication, of crime. Historian Stephen Davies came to the same conclusion. The nineteenth century, in his view, faced exactly the same sort of crisis of civil disorder and crime that we face today. The rise to dominance, intellectually, morally and politically, of a capitalist ethos of individualism, self-responsibility and self-help was what created – for a time – an amazingly crime-free society. The remoralization of society is the only cure for crime, and means the complete overthrow in every sphere of policy and life, of socialist values and policies (Davies, 1987).

This analysis in fact links up with the broader libertarian analysis of the problem of what has become called the 'underclass'. This is a restatement of the problem of the phenomenon the nineteenth-century liberals termed 'pauperization' (Mackay, 1896; Loch, 1890; Strachey, 1906; Fawcett, 1871; Mason, 1974). The effect of indiscriminate welfare provision on a small but significant group in the 'working class', is to elicit a quite rational response from individuals who already share a 'high time preference' (or unwillingness to defer gratification) and value system best characterized as a 'culture of poverty'. A moral ethos of irresponsibility, passivity, family break-down, and crime is nurtured and subsidized. When combined with a reduced risk of arrest and punishment the effects are exactly what we observe in Britain and America, and anywhere else such policies are adopted.

Ironically, it is the 'honest poor' and the working classes who are the first and worst victims of pauperization, which, in the words of Charles Murray, represents 'an extraordinary range of transfers from the most capable poor to the least capable, from the most law-abiding to the least law abiding, and from the most respectable to the least respectable' (Murray, 1984, 1990).

It should be noted that there are a minority of libertarians who take a different view from that outlined above. A notable example is the Australian social psychologist John Ray. Accepting a utilitarian ethic he argues that 'the protection of the community be the sole criterion of what is done with any convicted criminal' and that 'whenever a criminal is caught, he never be released unless there is good reason to believe that he will in future abstain from crime' (Ray, 1989: 3, 2).

The economic liberals

Simultaneously with the revival of classical liberal political and moral philosophy, an even more widespread revival of classical, free market economics has taken place. The work of the countless adherents of the Chicago School of Milton Friedman and his colleagues has established itself as a cutting edge within the discipline of economics. The Austrian School of free market economics of von Mises and Hayek has had a lesser, but no means insignificant impact (Butler, 1985; Dolan, 1976).

One of the demonstrations of the vigour of this revival has been the phenomenon of 'economic imperialism', as it has been labelled

(Radnitzky and Bernholz, 1987). The Chicago School has attempted to apply economic analysis to problems and issues customarily conceived as being outside its traditional subject matter and scope. Social and political institutions, politics as a whole, how we treat our bodies, sexual behaviour, love and marriage, crime and honesty have become part of the 'new world of economics'.

Not surprisingly, since the characteristics of economic reasoning are its analysis of purposeful individual and institutional behaviour, of rational action related to objectives to be achieved, and the concepts of choice, price, alternatives, and trade-offs, criminality is seen in a very different light from the orthodox criminological view (Veljanovski, 1990). The criminal is seen as no less a rational utility maximizer, responsive to incentives and disincentives, than any other human being: 'Crime, far from being the result of a sickness or mental disorder, in most cases is simply a business oriented economic activity which is undertaken for much the same reasons as other types of economic activity' (Meiselman and Tullock, 1973).

By applying economic analysis, it is argued, 'the amount of crime actually committed can be determined in the same manner as is the amount of any other activity'. Moreover, it appears 'that professional criminals seem to have made sensible career choices. In other words, crime pays' (McKenzie and Tullock, 1975: 131, 155).

The economists have devoted considerable efforts to analysing the issue of deterrence. They have examined the existing 'anti-deterrent' sociological research and judged it 'very inferior work' (McKenzie and Tullock, 1975: 152). More recent research, especially when inspired by economic perspectives, Gordon Tullock argues, arrives at a more favourable view, although its writers have difficulty in getting it 'accepted in the more conventional sociological journals' (Tullock, 1974: 107). Such findings are, for the economists, hardly surprising (the reverse would be) since 'the deterrence theory of punishment is, after all, simply a special version of the general economic principle that raising the price of something will reduce the amount purchased' (McKenzie and Tullock, 1975: 152).

Although many of the economists also favour libertarian policies on moral grounds, their economic analysis alone leads to the advocacy of the decriminalization of 'victimless crime' laws. The 'considerations of expediency', as Friedman has put it, attest to the counter-productive effect of any act of prohibition, its worsening of the situation for addict and non-addict alike, and its corrupting effect on all institutions of law enforcement (Friedman and Friedman, 1984: 136–41: Horton, 1973: 16). Along with the libertarians the free market economists now constitute the strongest lobby for drug legalization and have produced a large body of literature on the issue (Boaz, 1990; Ostrowski, 1989; Hamowy, 1987).

Economic analysis has also produced some unusual perspectives on the nature of crime. On the one hand, Godfather-fed visions of the prevalence of 'organized crime' seem to be unfounded. 'Organized crime' does not appear to be extensive, and the market structure of criminal enterprise tends to small and relatively ephemeral enterprises (Reuter, 1968, 1983). Ironically, this may not be a good thing. From society's point of view 'organized', and consequently monopolized crime, would be better than disorganized crime. Monopoly results in the restriction of output. While we do not favour restriction in the supply of goods, we certainly do favour restriction in the supply of 'bads' (Buchanan, 1973).

It should also be noted that application of economics to law has a much wider scope than that of criminology. In such works as the seminal *Economic Analysis of Law* (Posner, 1986) and a growing body of literature, legal doctrines and procedural rules can be given explanations, rationalizations and improvement in the light of economic analysis (Posner, 1987). There are also interesting disputes between what we might term 'economic efficiency' theorists (adhering to a utilitarian or pragmatic ethic) and natural rights-based analysts (Epstein, 1980).

The economists' arguments have not been without effect upon sociologists. In their work *The Honest Politician's Guide to Crime Control* (1970) Norval Morris and Gordon Hawkins accept a large part of the economic critique, albeit in somewhat less rigorous form. The limitations of mental illness as a legitimate plea, the general efficacy of deterrence, and the disastrous nature of victimless crime laws are all highlighted. It is the latter area, however, in which their advocacy is most spirited and clear:

> The prime function of the criminal law is to protect our persons and property; these purposes are now engulfed in a mass of other distracting, inefficiently performed, legislative duties. When the criminal law invades the spheres of private morality and social welfare, it exceeds its proper limits at the cost of neglecting its primary tasks. This unwarranted extension is expensive, ineffective, and crimogenic. (Morris and Hawkins, 1970: 2)

Traditionalist conservatives

In Europe conservatism was ideologically a collectivist movement, sharing with socialism an opposition to the individualistic, allegedly 'atomized' society of capitalism. The radical rationalism and individualism of capitalism was rejected in favour of the 'organic society' and the alleged wisdom of tradition (Nisbet, 1944, 1952). Anglo-American conservatism has been rather a different creature, symbolized by the ambiguities in its founder, Edmund Burke, between his acceptance of Adam Smith's liberal economics and his own endorsement of certain illiberal social values. Anglo-American conservatism has largely eschewed extreme and mystical forms of anti-rationalism and traditionalism, favouring instead a more defensible view of spontaneous order akin to that held by liberals. While rejecting a consistent libertarianism or individualism, it has, in the face of such enemies as fascism and Marxism, been increasingly driven to an orientation towards liberty, albeit not without ambiguities.

Not surprisingly there are many similarities between post-war conservative thought on crime and that of the libertarians. Much of the work of the leading conservative writer on these issues, Ernest van den Haag, has been characterized by a defence of the efficacy of deterrence and a reaffirmation of the existence of individual free will and responsibility (van den Haag, 1975, 1985).

In line with the greater emphasis on 'social order' generally found in conservative rhetoric, there tends to be a greater emphasis in conservative writing on the role of punishment as a broader sanction of social mores, its symbolic effect in establishing 'moral solidarity' and stimatizing criminal behaviour (although this aspect is not ignored by libertarians, as evidenced by Lee, 1982): 'Because most offenders are not significantly different from the rest of the population, society must reinforce resistance to temptation by punishment and by stigmatizing crime as odious, so that most people will not yield to the temptation no society can eliminate' (van den Haag, 1975: 62, 88).

Capital punishment is vigorously defended. Its abolition, van den Haag argues, is 'perceived symbolically as a loss of nerve: social authority no longer willing to pass an irrevocable judgement on anyone. Murder is no longer thought grave enough to take the murderer's life. Respect for life itself is diminished, as the price for taking it is. Life becomes cheaper as we become kinder to those who wantonly take it' (van den Haag, 1975: 213).

The conservatives also tend to emphasize the moral crisis involved in the widespread (especially among intellectuals generally, and criminologists specifically) manifestation of sympathy for criminals beyond that shown (if at all) for victims. In the words of Walter Berns, 'compassion is felt for the criminal and . . . anger is directed at society' (Berns, 1979: 81). (Although libertarians have also noted and criticized what it sees as an anti-life transvaluation of values at work in sympathy with criminality.) 'A just society', the conservatives very vigorously proclaim, 'is one where everyone gets what he deserves, and the wicked deserve to be punished – they deserve "many sorrows"', as the Psalmist says – and the righteous deserve to be joyous' (Berns, 1979: 147).

However, it should not be assumed that the conservatives are merely embodiments of an excessively punitive tough-mindedness, as some opponents would like to portray them. The determinist and rehabilitationist approach is also seen by the conservatives, as by the libertarians, as a real threat to justice and liberty. For example, writing about the Children and Young Persons Act of 1969 in Britain, which lays out the 'treatment' of juvenile delinquency, Colin Brewer makes two points. 'Treatment' programmes have been demonstrated to be ineffective: 'The old fashioned approach was much more effective than giving the child to the care of social workers, in terms of reducing both truancy and associated crime' (Brewer, 1981: 16).

Moreover, the system is horrendously *unjust*. The allegedly humanitarian decriminalization of juvenile offences, the granting of impunity to crime, has actually provided a total mandate for potentially unlimited intervention into the lives of children and parents. Children can be imprisoned (although it is not called that) as the result of non-judicial kangaroo courts, on an evidential basis that would not convict an adult. 'Compulsory measures of care', as the Act's terminology would have it, appear as euphemistic as the 'treatment' for political dissidents in the Soviet Union. Indeed, the two juvenile Acts in Britain are, as Patricia Morgan puts it, 'examples of the tendencies of rehabilitative systems to destroy legal rights and spawn injustices, while essentially segregating a large measure of society's crime into realms of impunity' (Morgan, 1981: 65).

In reality, the extravagant claims regarding rehabilitation and therapy are fanciful. Social work practice is generally characterized by 'tolerance of unhelpful behaviour as part of the diagnostic and healing process'. The evidence regarding rehabilitative endeavours, it is argued, demonstrates that 'none are more effective than traditional penalties in reducing recidivism' (Morgan, 1981). Similarly, with respect to adults, the parole system rests upon positivist assumptions, sanctioning an indeterminacy of sentencing which is 'predicated upon an acceptance of executive justice that is inconsistent with a concept of open justice' and more consistent with totalitarian states (Morris, 1981: 37).

The key to understanding both the cause and cure of crime lies for the conservatives in the undermining of moral values by the myriad forms of socialism and interventionist statism. In Patricia Morgan's words, the 'quasi-moral distaste for the imposition of norms' (Morgan, 1978: 136) characterizes theory and practice in much sociology, criminology and jurisprudence, as well as in the welfare and administrative practice of the contemporary state. The result has been a massive failure of socialization into civilized and moral behaviour, the toleration of a 'new barbarism', the endorsement of moral relativism and the unwillingness to publicly affirm real moral values in the face of aggression and insulting behaviour.

In Morgan's view it is especially ironic that many sociologists and criminologists seem to view crime and violence as revolutionary expressions of the 'working class'. In reality, it is the 'working class' which suffers first and worst. The elements romanticized by some writers are not the real working class, characterized by an ethos of productiveness, but the underclass of petty criminals, thugs and parasites on the labour of others.

The answer to this moral crisis can only be, in the words of David Marsland, 'at least a degree of re-moralisation of social life' (Marsland, 1988: 70). 'We have to challenge immoralist permissivism with beliefs and values to which young people can commit themselves positively and actively' (Marsland, 1988: 71; see also Marsland, 1991).

Although there is clearly much common ground between the libertarians and the conservatives, there are equally clearly differences. In van den Haag's work there is a willingness to accept the use of law to attain ends other than justice. 'Thus', he declares, 'justice may be impaired to preserve or enhance another value, or the social order as a whole' (van den Haag, 1975: 36). Elsewhere he has explicitly rejected the concept of natural rights, has endorsed censorship of pornography, and called for the death penalty for drug pushers. However, in this latter area it is interesting that he has more recently, in company with a growing number of prominent conservatives, recognized that the 'war on drugs' has been lost, that prohibitionist policies have proved both futile and disastrous, and that the pragmatic case for drug decriminalization made by the libertarians and the economists was correct (Buckley, 1986).

Although libertarians would accept much of the argument made by the conservatives for a 'remoralization' of society, one suspects that there would be some disputes as to what constitutes morality in certain areas (especially relating to sexual behaviour). Moreover, the libertarians adhere to a stronger belief in the beneficence of spontaneous order. In the absence of the perverse incentives and disincentives established by state interventionism, libertarians would have confidence in the evolution of socially beneficial and harmonious practices. Among conservatives, however, there is a tendency towards a more activist support for particular practices. This is manifest in Patricia Morgan's endorsement, for example, of stricter laws concerning divorce (1988).

The new realists

While both the libertarians and the conservatives started out from a clear commitment to particular rival values, and the economists did so with a conceptual apparatus already methodologically at variance with determinism, another group of writers arrived at a similar critique of the reigning paradigm from a very different starting point.

In his model of 'paradigm' change Thomas Kuhn argues that at a certain time any established scientific worldview or 'paradigm' will begin to confront 'anomalies' that cannot be explained in its own terms. What happened in the 1960s in America was precisely the emergence of such anomalies in the Great Society, state interventionist model. Interventionist policies were widely followed in welfare policy, housing, race relations, economic regulation, etc, but the expected beneficial results did not occur. Quite simply it became obvious that interventionist policies were not working as they were supposed to and that there was something wrong with the fundamental philosophy that underlay them.

Faced with these policy failures a small but growing number of scholars and writers who had previously accepted the ruling assumptions became increasingly critical of them. These were individuals whose criticisms of the established paradigm came not from the premises of a rival system but largely or entirely from an empirical and pragmatic observation of the failures of orthodoxy. Subsequently, some of these writers have been termed 'neo-conservatives' (some of them accepting the label, some of them not). A better term, in my view, would be 'New Realists'. Although some have come to endorse a rival ideology many still share the basic assumptions of interventionist statism. What they reject are the *specific* policies favoured by orthodox interventionists.

Who are these writers? They include individuals like Martin Anderson, Norman Podhoretz, Irving Kristol, Daniel P. Moynihan, Edward Banfield, Jay Forrester, Theodore Lowi, James Q. Wilson and Jane Jacobs, among others. In relation to criminology the most relevant are Jacobs, Banfield and Wilson.

Thus, Jacobs demonstrated the counter-productive role of planning and regulation (Jacobs, 1964). As well as being economically detrimental such planning had a directly crime-creating result by its destruction of natural social controls exercised in natural neighbourhoods. Similar observations on the crimogenic consequences of 'modern movement' municipal housing were made in Britain by Alice Coleman (Coleman, 1985, 1988). Furthermore, Banfield outlined an analysis of the problems created by the 'lower-class' value system (that is a culture of poverty), of the pauperizing effects of welfare, and the rational effects of incentives and disincentives to crime (or the reality of deterrence).

However, by far the most significant writer in relation to criminology is James Q. Wilson. Certainly no libertarian, he explicitly accepts paternalist and welfarist duties by the state, opposes individual ownership of firearms, and still supports the criminalization of drugs to this day. Neither were conservative values obviously prominent in his work.

Nevertheless, his empirical observations fully support the criticisms offered by libertarians, economists and conservatives. Poverty does not cause crime, he declared (Wilson, 1975): indeed, crime has risen with increasing affluence. Instead, crime is seen as resulting from the breakdown of civic socialization of young people, a 'failure of community' and by family disorganization. The 'subjective forces – ideas, attitudes, values' must also be taken into account. The orthodox view of the inefficacy of deterrence is rejected, and is not borne out, in his view, even by the scholarly work of the orthodox themselves (Wilson, 1975: 47–70). Wilson thus concludes his work:

> Wicked people exist. Nothing avails except to set them apart from innocent people. And many people, neither wicked nor innocent, but watchful, dissembling, and calculating of their opportunities, ponder our reaction to wickedness as a cue to what they might profitably do. We have trifled with the wicked, made sport of the innocent, and encouraged the calculators. Justice suffers, and so do we all. (Wilson, 1975: 235–6)

Although from within psychology and psychotherapy a whole new wave of anti-determinist thinkers has also arisen since the war (like Abraham Maslow and Carl Rogers, and diverse forms of 'humanistic', 'third force', existentialist, self-actualization and 'human potential' schools) surprisingly very few have devoted any attention to criminological issues.

The one major exception to this consists of the work of Samuel Yochelson and Stanton Samenow in their two-volume study *The Criminal Personality* (Yochelson and Samenow, 1976/77), and the one-volume popularization, *Inside the Criminal Mind* (Samenow, 1984). Both started as orthodox Freudians, committed to the mental illness theory of criminality and to their work in the 'rehabilitation' of prisoners. As a result, however, of their decades of work inside prisons, both became what they termed 'reluctant converts' to a philosophy of autonomy and non-determinism. According to Samenow:

> ... criminals choose to commit crimes. Crime resides within the person and is 'caused' by the way he thinks, not by his environment. Criminals think differently from responsible people. From regarding criminals as victims we saw that instead they were victimizers who had freely chosen their way of life ... Criminals cause crime – not bad neighbourhoods, inadequate parents, television, schools, drugs, or unemployment. Crime resides within the minds of human beings and is not caused by social conditions. (Samenow, 1984)

Habits are not compulsions, there are no overpowering forces, within or without, that cause criminals to act. What causes criminal activity is simply the freely chosen actions of individuals, and the ideas they develop about themselves, others and the world at large. The criminal mind is characterized by ideas which are coercive, self-delusory, irrational and irresponsible.

Conclusion

Although there are differences in analytical emphasis and moral orientation among libertarians, economists, conservatives and New Realists, there is also sufficient common ground among them all to justify gathering them under one label. Whether their shared critique of the existing paradigm in criminology is found convincing, and whether it will be more fully developed and refined, is yet to be seen.

References

Anderson, T. and Hill, P.J. (1979) 'An American experiment in anarcho-capitalism: the not so wild wild west', *Journal of Libertarian Studies*, 3 (1).

Banfield, Edward (1968/2nd edn. 1974) *The Unheavenly City*. Boston: Little, Brown.

Barnet, R.E. and Hagel, J. (eds) (1977) *Assessing the Criminal: Restitution, Retribution, and the Legal Process*. Cambridge, MA: Ballinger.

Barnet, R.E. and Hagel, J. (1977) 'Assessing the criminal: restitution, retribution and the legal system', in R.E. Barnet and J. Hagel (eds), *Assessing the Criminal: Restitution, Retribution, and the Legal Process*. Cambridge, MA: Ballinger.

Barnet, R.E. (1977) 'Restitution: A New Paradigm of Criminal Justice', in R.E. Barnet and J. Hagel (eds), *Assessing the Criminal: Restitution, Retribution, and the Legal Process*. Cambridge, MA: Ballinger.

Barry, Norman (1987) *On Classical Liberalism and Libertarianism*. London: Macmillan.

Berns, Walter (1979) *For Capital Punishment: Crime and the Morality of the Death Penalty*. New York: Basic Books.

Bidinotto, James (1989) *Crime and Consequences*. Irvington-on-Hudson, New York: Foundation for Economic Education.

Boaz, David (ed.) (1990) *The Crisis in Drug Prohibition*. Washington DC: Cato Institute.

Botsford, David (1990) *The Case against Gun Control*. London: Political Notes No. 47, Libertarian Alliance.

Brewer, Colin (1981) 'Compulsory Therapy for Crime: Bad Habits Are Not Diseases', in Colin Brewer, T. Morris, P. Morgan, M. North (eds), *Criminal Welfare on Trial*. London: Social Affairs Unit.

Buchanan, James (1973) 'A defense of organized crime?', in Simon Rottenberg (ed.), *The Economics of Crime and Punishment*. Washington, DC: American Enterprise Institute.

Buckley, William F. (1986) 'Legalize drugs and reduce crime', syndicated widely and reprinted in *Southern Libertarian Messenger*, October.

Butler, Eamon (1985) *Milton Friedman*. London: Maurice Temple Smith.

Clinard, Marshall B. (1978) *Cities with Little Crime: The Case of Switzerland*. Cambridge: Cambridge University Press.

Coleman, Alice (1985) *Utopia on Trial: Vision and Reality in Planned Housing*. London: Hilary Shipman.

Coleman, Alice (1988) *Altered Estates*. London: Adam Smith Institute.

Davies, Christie (1983) 'Crime, bureaucracy, and equality', *Police Review*, No. 23.

Davies, Christie (1989) 'Society versus the state: freedom versus liberation'. Paper delivered to Liberal Democratic Societies: Their Present State and Their Future Prospects, 4th International Congress of Professors World Peace Academy, London, August.

Davies, Stephen (1987) 'Towards the remoralization of society', in Martin Loney (ed.), *The State or the Market: Politics and Welfare in Contemporary Britain*. London: Sage.

Davies, Stephen (1991) *The Historical Origins of Health Fascism*. London: FOREST.

Dolan, E.G. (ed.) (1976) *The Foundation of Modern Austrian Economics*. Kansas City: Sheed and Ward.

Elliott, Nick (1989) *Streets Ahead*. London: Adam Smith Institute.

Elliott, Nick (1990) *Making Prison Work*. London: Adam Smith Institute.

Epstein, Richard A. (1980) *A Theory of Strict Liability: Toward A Reformulation of Tort Law*. Washington, DC: Cato Institute.

Fawcett, Henry (1871) *Pauperism: Its Causes and Remedies*. London: Macmillan.

Friedman, Milton and Friedman, Rose (1984) *The Tyranny of the Status Quo*. London: Secker and Warburg.

Gabb, Sean (1988) *Gun Control in Britain*. London: Political Notes No. 33, Libertarian Alliance.

Gabb, Sean (1990) *Smoking and Its Enemies*. London, FOREST.

Gray, John (1990) *Liberalisms: Essays in Political Philosophy*. London: Routledge & Kegan Paul.

Green, David (1987) *The New Right*. Hassocks, Sussex: Wheatsheaf.

Hamowy, Ronald (ed.) (1987) *Dealing With Drugs: Consequences of Government Control*. Lexington, MA: Pacific Research Institute for Public Policy/Lexington Books, D.C. Heath.

Horton, Paul B. (1973) 'Problems in understanding criminal motives', in Simon Rottenberg (ed.), *The Economics of Crime and Punishment*. Washington, DC: American Enterprise Institute.

Hospers, John (1971) *Libertarianism*. Los Angeles: Nash Publishing.

Jacobs, Jane (1964) *The Life and Death of Great American Cities*. Harmondsworth, Middlesex: Penguin Books.

Kates, Don B. (ed.) (1979) *Restricting Handguns: The Liberal Skeptics Speak Out*. n.p: North River Press.

Kates, Don B. Jr. (ed.) (1984) *Firearms and Violence: Issues of Public Policy*. San Fransisco: Pacific Institute for Public Policy Research.

King, D.S. (1987) *The New Right*. London: Macmillan.

Kope, David B. (1988) *Trust the People: The Case against Gun Control*. Washington, DC: Cato Institute.

Lee, J. Roger (1974) 'Reflections on punishment', in Tibor Machan (ed.), *The Libertarian Alternative: Essays in Social and Political Philosophy*. Chicago: Nelson Hall.

Lee, J. Roger (1982) 'The arrest and punishment of criminals: justifications and limitations', in Tibor Machan (ed.), *The Libertarian Reader*. Totowa, NJ: Rowman and Littlefield.

Loch, C.S. (1890) *Charity Organization*. London: Swan Sonnenschein.

McKenzie, Richard B. and Tullock, Gordon (1975) *The New World of Economics: Explorations into the Human Experience*. Homewood, Illinois: Richard D. Irwin.

Machan, Tibor (1975) *Human Rights and Human Liberties*. Chicago: Nelson Hall.

Mack, Eric (1976) 'Society's foe', *Reason*, 8 (5).

Mackay, Thomas (1896) *Methods of Social Reform*. London: John Murray.

Marsland, David (1988) 'Young people betrayed', in Digby Anderson (ed.), *Full Circle: Bringing up Children in the Post-permissive Society*. London: Social Affairs Unit.

Marsland, David (1991 forthcoming) *Understanding Youth*, London: Institute of Economic Affairs.

Mason, J.W. (1974) 'Thomas Mackay: the anti-socialist philosophy of the charity organization society', in K.D. Brown (ed.), *Essays in Anti-Labour History*. London: Macmillan.

Meiselman, David and Tullock, Gordon (1973) 'Preface', in Simon Rottenberg (ed.), *The Economics of Crime and Punishment*. Washington, DC: American Enterprise Institute.

Morgan, Patricia (1978) *Delinquent Fantasies*. London: Maurice Temple Smith.

Morgan Patricia (1981) 'The Children's Act: sacrificing justice to social workers' needs?', in Colin Brewer, T. Morris, P. Morgan and M. North (eds), *Criminal Welfare on Trial*. London: Social Affairs Unit.

Morgan Patricia (1988) 'For the Sake of the Children', in Digby Anderson (ed.), *Full Circle: Bringing up Children in the Post-permissive Society*. London: Social Affairs Unit.

Morris, Terence (1981) 'The parole system: executive "justice"', in Colin Brewer et al., *Criminal Welfare on Trial*. London: Social Affairs Unit.

Morris, N. and Hawkins, G. (1970) *The Honest Politician's Guide to Crime Control*. Chicago: Chicago University Press.

Murray, Charles (1984) *Losing Ground: American Social Policy 1950–1980*. New York: Basic Books.

Murray, Charles (1990) *The Emerging British Underclass*. London: IEA Health and Welfare Unit.

Nisbet, Robert A. (1944) 'De Bonald and the concept of the social group', *The Journal of the History of Ideas*, V (3).

Nisbet, Robert A. (1952) 'Conservatism and sociology', *American Journal of Sociology*, LVIII (2).

O'Keeffe, Matthew (1989) *Retribution versus Restitution*. London: Legal Notes No. 5, Libertarian Alliance.

Ostrowski, James (1989) *Thinking about Drug Legalization*. Washington, DC: Policy Analysis No. 121, Cato Institute.

Peikoff, Leonard (1982) *The Ominous Parallels*. New York, Stein and Day.

Posner, Richard A. (1986) *Economic Analysis of Law*. Boston: Little, Brown.

Posner, Richard A. (1987) *The Economics of Justice*, Harvard MA: Harvard University Press.

Radnitzky, G. and Bernholz, P. (eds) (1987) *Economic Imperialism*. New York: Paragon House.

Rand, Ayn (1964) *The Virtue of Selfishness: A New Concept of Egoism*. New York: New American Library.

Rand, Ayn (1967) *Capitalism: The Unknown Ideal*. New York: New American Library.

Ray, John (1989) *Towards a More Pragmatic Penal System*. London: Legal Notes No. 7, Libertarian Alliance.

Reuter, Peter (1968) *The Organization of Illegal Markets: An Economic Analysis*. US Dept of Justice/National Institute of Justice, reprinted by Loompanics Unlimited, Port Townsend, Washington, nd.

Reuter, Peter (1983) *Disorganized Crime: The Economics of the Visible Hand*. Cambridge, MA: MIT Press.

Rothbard, Murray (1973) *For a New Liberty*. New York: Macmillan.

Rothbard, Murray (1978) 'The Capital Punishment Question', *Libertarian Review*, 7 (5).

Rothbard, Murray (1982) *The Ethics of Liberty*. Atlantic Highlands, NJ: Humanities Press.

Samenow, Stanton (1984) *Inside the Criminal Mind*. New York: Times Books.

Sampson, Geoffrey (1984) *An End to Allegiance: Individual Freedom and the New Politics*. London: Maurice Temple Smith.

Strachey, J. St Loe (ed.) (1906) *The Manufacture of Paupers*. London: John Murray.

Szasz, Thomas (1974) *Law, Liberty and Psychiatry*. London: Routledge & Kegal Paul.

Szasz, Thomas (1975) *Ceremonial Chemistry: The Ritual Persecution of Drugs, Addicts and Pushers*. London: Routledge & Kegan Paul.

Szasz, Thomas (1977) 'Psychiatric diversion in the criminal justice system: a critique', in R.E. Barnet and J. Hagel (eds), *Assessing the Criminal: Restitution, Retribution, and the Legal Process*. Cambridge, MA: Ballinger.

Tame, Chris R. (1977) 'The revolution of reason', *The Journal of Libertarian Studies*, 1 (3).

Tame, Chris R. (1985) 'The new enlightenment', in Arthur Seldon (ed.), *The 'New Right' Enlightenment*. Sevenoaks, Kent: Economic and Literary Books.

Tame, Chris R. (1989) *On the Side of the Angels: A View of Private Policing*. London: Political Notes No. 40, Libertarian Alliance.

Tannahill, M.L. and Wollstein, J. (1972) *Society without Government*. New York: Arno Press/New York Times.

Thompson, Bill, Annetts, Jason, Egan, S., Shilton, C., Sappiah, S., King, A., Lee, N. (1990) *Soft-Core*. London: GJW Government Relations.

Tullock, Gordon (1974) 'Does punishment deter crime?', *The Public Interest*, No. 36.

van den Haag, Ernest (1975) *Punishing Criminals: Concerning a Very Old and Painful Question*. New York: Basic Books.

van den Haag, Ernest (1985) *Deterring Potential Criminals*. London: Social Affairs Unit.

Veljanovski, Cento (1990) *The Economics of Law: An Introductory Text*. London: Institute of Economic Affairs.

Weber, Eugene (1969) *Varieties of Fascism: Doctrines of Revolution in the Twentieth Century*. New York: Van Nostrand.

Wilson, James Q. (1977; orig. 1975) *Thinking about Crime*. New York: Vintage Books.

Wollstein, Jarrett (1967) *The Case against Victimless Crimes*. Silver Springs, Maryland: Society for Individual Liberty.

Yochelson, Samuel and Samenow, Stanton (1976/77) *The Criminal Personality*. Northvale, NJ: J. Aronson.

7

Left Realism and the Priorities of Crime Control

Jock Young

Left Realism in criminology is a social democratic approach to the analysis of crime and the development of effective policies of crime control. At the heart of this approach is the recognition that crime is now a very real source of suffering for the poor and the vulnerable, particularly in the inner cities. Ironically, for too long it has been the parties of the Right that have gained most benefit from this at the ballot box. They have claimed, with some justification, that the liberals and the Left have cared more for the offender than for the victim. This has provided a rationale for right-wing administrations expanding the budgets of the crime control industry, without adequately ensuring that citizens get value for the public money so spent, while simultaneously reducing spending on other public services. At the same time they have shown scant interest in investigating the deeper causes of crime and tackling those socioeconomic conditions which help to provide fertile soil for the growth of crime; in fact their policies seem almost designed to promote it. Furthermore, when their policies clearly fail to halt the rising tide of crime, as in Britain, they are not above making tactical shifts in claiming that the problems have been exaggerated and that since there is little the police and justice systems can do in any case, it is better for citizens to do more to protect themselves!

Yet, for too long, many voices on the Left have found the kinds of crime which cause greatest public alarm to be an embarrassment, since most of these crimes occur within poor neighbourhoods and involve both poor victims and assailants. It is difficult to romanticize this type of crime as some kind of disguised attack on the privileged. The response by the Left has often been to shift attention away to the anti-social behaviour of the powerful and to the discriminatory and stigmatizing behaviour of the agencies of control. This position, in effect, denies the external reality of crime and tends to reduce it to a set of labels imposed on the behaviour of the allegedly powerless (Young, 1986).

A social democratic approach to crime must avoid the mistakes of those on the Right and the Left and, using empirical research, take care to discover the experiences and concerns of ordinary citizens. Through this, it should encourage the move towards more accountable strategies of crime prevention and control, in which fairness and non-discrimination should be founding principles. This may help to build up confidence among the poor in reformed official agencies. Only by developing a genuine partnership between official agencies and the public can real progress be made towards a more civilized way of life. Left Realism offers the hope that something *can* be done about crime.

In this chapter I will first outline the structure of realist theory, in particular, the role of surveys and the linkages between four key factors: the police and other agencies of control; the public; the offender and the victim. Then I will examine the role of the agencies involved in crime control.

Britain, like most advanced industrial countries, has faced a seemingly inexorable rise in crime since the Second World War, and this is in spite of better living standards and a vast increase in expenditure on police, judiciary and prisons.

Some crime control measures work, some do not, and some are simply counter-productive, but precious little research is available to sort out the wheat from the chaff. This is extraordinary, given the vast amount spent on crime control in Britain. In 1988, for example, £3500 million went to the police force, £698 million to the prisons and £1000 million to the criminal justice system. In the private sector, £1000 million was spent on security equipment alone, while local authorities spent as much again on crime-related areas.

Yet this expenditure seems to have little effect on the rise in crime, and more research is urgently needed. At present, policy decisions can only be based on the last 15 years of substantiated findings. We need, for example, to know the success rate of relatively new crime control measures, such as the neighbourhood watch schemes, and how this differs between, say, inner-city areas and the suburbs.

A consensus exists as to the need for a multi-agency approach to crime control. Partly, this comes from the obvious fact that crime has always been controlled through the family, through schools, and by the police. But it also, more importantly, stems from how all of society can co-operate in preventing crime; every crime control agency or social institution needs support from the others.

A further reason why research needs to be updated is that the public's attitude must be gauged. Many crimes, such as attacks against members of ethnic minorities or cases of domestic violence, are under-reported, because the victims feel that the police will not treat them sympathetically. Only some very probing social surveys can reveal what the public expect from crime control agencies and, until this is done, effective policies cannot be made.

Obviously the task of any crime control policy is to reduce crime in general. In this, it is like a community health project: success cannot be measured by how much a well-off person can jump the queue for care, but how such indicators as reduction of infant mortality and increased life expectancy for adults reflect the effectiveness of the service.

Both crime and ill-health, while being universal problems, affect some sectors of society more than others. Therefore we must target our resources in order to reduce the general rate of crime. Unfortunately – and this has always been a problem with welfare provision in Britain – resources have been distributed more to those people with political muscle and social power, rather than to those in most need. The history of the National Health Service and state educational provisions are adequate evidence. Crime control has parallel problems.

The survey and the citizen

For Left Realism, the social survey is a democratic instrument (Painter et al., 1989; Jones et al., 1986, 1987; Crawford et al., 1990): it gives a detailed picture of consumer demand and satisfaction. Without such research, policy makers have little to go on. Many crimes are un-reported and the aggregate statistics for the whole country do not give enough information. Rates of crime and types of crime will obviously vary between inner-city, suburban and rural areas, so without local surveys there is no basis for appropriate crime control measures.

Unless the views of the public are made clear in this way, experts and politicians will advise and act on their own. For example, crimes against women – from harassment to rape or murder – are often ignored because of under-reporting by victims. This is ascribed to 'irrationality' on the part of women, yet it seems rational, if a woman is attacked by her partner, that she will not report it for fear of further violence.

Generalized national research produces figures of little worth. More invidiously, it allows politicians to talk of irrational fears of crime when compared to the average risk rate of the 'average' citizen. The 1982 British Crime Survey showed that the risk of experiencing robbery in England and Wales was once every five centuries; an assault resulting in injury once every century; a burglary once every 50 years. But 'irrational' fears are not so, for people who live in circumstances where there is a high risk of being a victim of crime.

The left realist approach to crime control sees social surveys as crucial. Without them, we cannot know the 'lived reality' of people at risk, which in turn affects key policy decisions such as the role and effectiveness of beat policing or neighbourhood watch schemes. However while research can help in the direction and prioritization of crime control, its results cannot provide us with a blueprint. The process of moving from input to policing involves four stages: identification of problems, assessment of priorities, application of principles, and ascertaining possibilities.

The victimization survey accurately provides a map of the problems of an area. Although based on public input, it delivers what any individual member of the public is ignorant of: that is how private problems are publicly distributed. In this task, it shows which social groups within the population face the greatest risk rates and geographically pinpoints where these occurrences are most frequent. In this it directs crime intervention initiatives towards those people and places which are most at risk. It therefore reveals the concealed crime rate and it ascertains its social and spatial focus. But it goes beyond this, for risk rates alone, however delineated, do not measure the true impact of crime and hence the actual patterning of crime as a social problem. To do this we must advance beyond the one-dimensional approach of aggregate risk rates and place crime in its social context. The myth of the equal victim underscores much of conventional victimology with its notion that victims are, as it were, equal billiard balls, and the risk rate merely involves the calculation of the chances of an offending billiard ball impacting upon them. People are, of course, not equal; they are more, or less, vulnerable, depending on their place in society.

First of all, at certain parts of the social structure, we have a compounding of social problems. If we were to draw a map of the city outlining areas of high infant mortality, bad housing, unemployment, poor nutrition, etc, we would find that all these maps would coincide and that further, the outline traced would correspond to those areas of high criminal victimization (Clarke, 1980). And those suffering from street crime would also suffer most from white-collar and corporate crime (Lea and Young, 1984).

Further, this compounding of social problems occurs against those who are more or less vulnerable because of their position in the social structure. That is, people who have least power socially suffer most from crime. Most relevant here are the social relationships of age, class, gender and race. Realist analysis, by focusing on the combination of these fundamental social relationships, allows us to note the extraordinary differences between social groups as to both the impact of crime and the focus of policing.

There are two tendencies within contemporary victimology. The 'objectivists' conduct surveys which calculate the risk of crime and contrast this with public fear of crime. They are thus in a position to assign to various groups degrees of rationality. In particular, women and the elderly have been conventionally designated as irrational in that their levels of fear are higher than their supposed risk rates. More generally, the fear of crime in the population as a whole is seen to be greater than the average risk rates. As a corollary, fear of crime is seen as a separate problem from crime itself or, indeed, taken to extremes, that fear of crime is more of a problem than crime itself. Such a position has ready resonances among more radical writers, who will readily talk of moral panics regarding crime, for example, with regard to mugging and juvenile delinquency. The causes of fear of crime are thus, to a degree, separated from experience of crime.

The 'subjectivists', in contrast, believe that public perceptions of crime are ipso facto the problem of crime. There is no distinction between fear of crime and actual criminal victimization, and if one requires a rational input into the crime control policing machine, then public opinion itself is the prime yardstick. The task of researchers is to show that public opinion is rational. And there is no doubt by employing more sympathetic interviewers and exploring the 'dark' figure of crime, they have shown that much of what is seemingly 'irrational' has a rational basis. Both feminist research and the earlier work in the past decade of radical victimologists have exhibited this tendency.

Thus, the realist position differs from both objectivism and subjectivism. Objectivism, with its use of aggregate crime rates and its unwillingness to focus on the way in which crime affects particular subgroups of the population, is too prone to making accusations of irrationality. It belongs to the old social tradition of Fabianism, where experts readily bestow problems on a population supposedly ignorant of the true nature of their own suffering (see Corrigan et al., 1988). Subjectivism, on the other hand, is only too ready to believe that what people subjectively experience as their problem is the problem. It grants too much rationality to the citizens surveyed.

In contrast to both these perspectives, realism:

1 Notes that rationality and irrationality relate to the experience of crime and crime control. In the majority of serious crimes, inner city dwellers, their neighbours and their friends have a surfeit of experience: irrationality is unlikely here. As far as a minority of crimes is concerned, the lack of direct experience may well generate irrational responses. In terms of crime control, lack of knowledge of what goes on either in police or local authority intervention, can generate incorrect evaluations.

2 Points out that individual respondents are aware of the crime experienced by themselves or their acquaintances. They have only a rudimentary knowledge of the overall picture.

3 Emphasizes that the nature of crime involves behaviour and evaluation: an objective action and a subjective assessment of this action as criminal. Over time, between different groups of people

and in different countries, evaluation varies. All societies stigmatize violence, but intolerance of violence may differ. What was
considered the normal chastisement of children in Victorian Britain
would be considered child abuse today. Realists recognize that
differences in evaluation have to be taken into account. Women
and old people, for example, may have higher fears of crime than
young men, while young men are actually more at risk. But to call
women's and old people's fears 'irrational', taking the fear rate of
men as being the standard for rationality, denies people's right to
choose how far they are willing to tolerate the threat of violence.
4   Indicates that the individual may be unaware of the real impact of
crime on his or her life. A middle-class woman, for example, might
feel safe from risk because she moves from her car, to her friends'
houses, or to a 'protected' place such as a restaurant. A working-
class youth may well be part of a street subculture which never
admits to worrying about crime. A working-class woman, trapped
in a situation of domestic violence, might see her predicament as
individual. All these people will reply to a questionnaire on the
level of their everyday perceptions, without an understanding of
how or why they see things in the way they do. All of them will be
either unconscious or falsely conscious of the reality of their
predicament (see Walklate, 1989).

Therefore the expert, the social analyst, has a vital role in putting crime
into context. The social analyst must uncover problems and then give
weight to their severity. This is the basis for a rational input into the
system of crime control.

Focusing on lived realities

People's understanding of crime and policing cannot be reduced to
global figures of the average risk rates of particular crimes or the
'normal' citizen's experience of policing. All evidence indicates that the
impact of crime and policing is geographically and socially focused: it
varies enormously by area and by the social group concerned. The
reason for selecting an inner-city area is to enable us to detail such
experiences at the sharp end of policing, while comparing this to data
derived from wider-based surveys of total cities and the country as a
whole. The reason for the use of extremely high sampling is to be able
to break down the impact of crime and policing in terms of its social
focus. That is, on social groups, based on the combination of age, class,
gender and race. Such a high social focus corresponds more closely to
the lived realities of different groups and subcultures of the population.
Thus, just as it is inaccurate to generalize about crime and policing
from gross figures based on large geographical areas, it is incorrect,

even within particular areas, to talk in terms of, for example, 'all' young people, 'all' women, 'all' blacks, 'all' working-class people, etc. Generalizations which remain on such global levels frequently obfuscate quite contradictory experiences, generating statistics which often conceal vital differences of impact.

The introduction of age into the analysis of fear of crime by gender changes the usual generality of men's fear of crime being low and women's high. In fact, older women have a fear of crime rather like men in the middle age group, and younger women have a fear rather like old men. And, in the case of foot-stops by the police, it becomes evident that differentials based on race are much more complicated than the abstraction that blacks are more likely to be stopped than whites. No older black women in our crime survey samples were stopped. Young, white, women were over three times more likely to be stopped than older black men. And even the differential between young black men and young white men becomes remarkably narrowed when class is introduced into the equation. The realist method stresses the need to base analysis on specific areas and social groups. It is in marked contrast to the approaches which try to explain differences in experience in terms of only one of the major social ones: age, class, gender, or race. Such reductionism simply does not fit the reality of social experience. This approach enables us to be more discriminate about changes in modes of policing and methods of crime control.

Explaining crime – the realist square

The simplest equation in crime control is that which envisages the police directly controlling crime rates. This equation, enshrined in conventional wisdom, is, in the face of the last 20 years of research, palpably untrue, because it is too abstract, because it only embraces part of the process omitting essential variables, because it is phrased in terms of quantities and not relationships, and because it puts too much onus on the police.

At heart, realism points to the fact that crime rates are a product of four interacting factors: the police and other agencies of social control, the public, the offender and the victim. Any changes in one of these factors will affect the crime rate: the police are only one factor in the equation. The point here is that crime rates cannot be explained simply in terms of crime control agencies, and that the agencies involved in crime control are much wider than the criminal justice system.

The degree of impact of an intervention about crime by one agency is dependent on the other agencies. To take a simple example: no amount of propagation by the police of crime prevention advice in terms of better locks and bolts will be effective on estates if the local authority does not simultaneously strengthen the doorframes of its tenants' houses.

Realism, then, points to a square of crime involving the internal understanding between police and the other agencies of social control, the public, the offender and the victim. It is the relationship between points of this square which determines the crime rates (see Figure 7.1) (Young, 1987).

Police multi-agencies ————————————————	*Offender*
Social control	The criminal act
The public ————————————————	*Victim*

Figure 7.1

The police–public relationship is central. But the interaction between all the parts is also important. For example, the police and agency response to victims greatly affects the actual impact of victimization and in certain instances, such as rape and sexual assault, can even involve what has been termed 'secondary victimization'. That is where the victim herself becomes further stigmatized by police and courts. All of this, particularly in terms of willingness (and wariness) to report to the police, affects the official crime rate and the possibilities of clear-up. Similar relationships occur between the offender and the public. In the case of burglary, for example, the close relationships of certain sections of the public to the purchase of stolen good creates an illegal hidden economy which supports and encourages the crime.

Reversing the retreat from causality and the realist agenda

It is of vital importance that we face up to the problem of crime in our inner cities. To do this will involve social crime prevention, better design, public involvement and more effective policing. Two tasks face us: our first is to re-open the question of the causes of crime. Common sense tells us that the reality of crime involves offenders and victims. Intervention can, therefore, occur at two points: that of protecting the victim and that of thwarting offenders. Present government policy has over-focused on the victim: it seeks, through target-hardening and the increasing privatization of security, to make the public responsible for their own safety, while dealing with offenders only after the offence has been committed through the courts and a strong police force.

But to prevent offending before it occurs by removing the causes of crime itself has become anathema. What is needed are resources directed at the likely offenders, frequently adolescent boys, in terms of anti-crime education in schools, massively greater youth employment possibilities, and better leisure facilities. The French government has given a lead in its energetic social crime prevention policies. (see Chapter 4; King, 1988). The failure of the social democratic consensus of the 1950s that better conditions would reduce crime was based on notions of the reduction of absolute deprivation. But it is not absolute but relative deprivation which causes crime (Lea and Young, 1984). It is not the absolute level of wealth, but resources perceived as unfairly distributed which affects the crime rate. The structural unemployment of youth, cheek by jowl with a wealthy middle class that occurs within our gentrified inner cities, is a recipe for a high crime rate (see Lea et al., 1987). To reduce crime we must reduce relative deprivation by ensuring that meaningful work is provided at fair wages, by providing decent housing which people are proud to live in, by ensuring that leisure facilities are available on a universal basis, and by insisting that policing is equally within the rule of law, both for working class and middle class, for blacks and for whites.

Our second task must be to stress that the prime role of the police is to fight crime. Not to act as traffic cops – a separate force as in most of Europe should do that – not to act as lost property agents nor to act as the secret social services. And, in order to fight crime, they must gain public support, for this is the lifeline of effective policing. In over 90 percent of cases, the police depend on the public for identifying the culprit, providing evidence and witnessing in court. Without public support policing fails or lapses into a desultory authoritarianism. The goal must be to bring policing priorities into line with the public that pays for policing (see Kinsey et al., 1986). In 1989, Britain spent £3½ billion on the police force. It is important to consider whether we are getting value for money. Of the 3.7 million crimes reported to the police, one-third were cleared up: some two million crimes every year, representing public demands upon the police, are not solved. As the clear-up rate has fallen by about one percentile point per year during the lifetime of the present UK government, this figure of unresolved crime has risen faster than the crime rate itself.

The main problem is the extremely low rate of productivity per police officer. In all, 1.25 million crimes were cleared up: about ten crimes per police officer per year. Of course, the police do other things besides attempt to control crime – this, indeed, is perhaps the crux of the matter – but even so, such a performance is scarcely reassuring. And in the metropolitan areas, where crime hits hardest, performance is lowest. Just 4.5 crimes cleared up per police officer in London in a year; indeed, if the sizeable civilian back-up were to be taken into consideration, the true figure would be less than 3 (see Lea et al., 1987).

A realist policy acknowledges that there are various methods which, if properly tested, monitored and costed, can reduce crime. But any one method, however effective, will have declining marginal returns if taken too far and too exclusively. Furthermore, any one method, be it public surveillance through neighbourhood watch, extra police on the streets, or target-hardening, will have costs which impact on the quality of life and the freedom of citizens. Britain's present government policy, by putting too great an emphasis on target-hardening and ignoring the conditions which give rise to crime, has created an imbalance.

I have considered the possibilities of intervention in the control of crime. In the final section, I wish to look at the institutions involved.

The institutions – multi-agency control

The existing system of crime control

Multi-agency intervention is the planned, co-ordinated response of the major social agencies to problems of crime and incivilities. The central reason for multi-agency social intervention is that of realism: it corresponds both to the realities of crime and to the realities of social control. Social control in industrial societies is, by its very nature, multi-agency. The problem is that it is not co-ordinated and represents a series of other disparate policy initiatives, with little overall rationale for the allocation of resources, and institutions which are often at loggerheads with each other.

The agencies and crime

If we compare burglary to child abuse we see immediately the differences between the involvement of the various agencies. Burglary will, in general, have a high police involvement in terms of catching the criminal. The local council, on the other hand, will have the greatest role in the 'target-hardening' of the local housing project. If the culprit is an adult, social services will be unlikely to be involved, but they will, of course, do so if the offender is a juvenile. For child abuse, by contrast, schools will be major institutions of detention; social services and the medical profession will play an important role.

One glance at Table 7.1 demonstrates the multiplicity of agencies involved and underlines the contrasts with the traditional approach which highlights the police and the courts and focuses on only one part of the process.

A realist approach to offenders sees the development of criminal behaviour over time. It breaks down this trajectory of offending into its component parts and notes how different agencies can and should be operative at different stages. Thus we can talk of (1) the *background causes* of crime; (2) the *moral context* of opting for criminal behaviour;

Table 7.1   *The multi-agencies involved in crime control*

Stages in the Development of Crime	Factors	Agencies
Causes of crime	Unemployment Housing Leisure	Local authority Central government Business
The moral context	Peer group values Community cohesion	Schools Family Public Mass media
The situation of commission	Physical environment Lighting Home security	Local authority Public Police
The detection of crime	Public reporting Detective work	Public Police
The response to the offenders	Punishment Rehabilitation	Courts Police Social services Probation
The response to the victim	Insurance Public support	Local authority Victim support The public groups Social services

(3) the *situation of committing* crime; (4) the *detection of crime*; (5) the *response to the offender*; (6) the *response to the victim*. Let us examine these one by one, noting the factors involved and the agencies with the power to intervene.

Background causes   These lie in relative deprivation as witnessed in poverty and unemployment, in overcrowded housing conditions, in poor leisure facilities and in inadequately funded families (particularly single parent). Here central government, the local authorities, and local business have responsibility.

The moral context   Here we have particularly the family, the education system, the mass media, youth organizations and religious organizations. The public themselves, the councils, in their provision of education and youth facilities, the media professionals in terms of their negative judgements of adolescents; and local religious and youth leaders, have their roles.

The situation of commission   Target-hardening, lighting, public willingness to intervene and police patrols are all important. Thus the important agencies are the council, the police and the public themselves.

The detection of crime Here, as discussed above, the co-operation of police and public is paramount, both in terms of informing the police and witnessing in court.

The response to the offender The role of the police and the court is paramount in their dual aim of punishment and rehabilitation. A rehabilitated offender, of course, should not be a recidivist. Here the social services are prominent in their role of caring for young people, but also in terms of possibilities of employment, and the shoring-up of unstable family situations.

The response to the victim Up until now we have discussed the whole process of multi-agency social intervention as if it was just concerned with dealing with offenders and preventing offences. We must never forget, however, the victim. Here again, it is obvious that various agencies must be involved in tackling the problem of criminal victimization. Social services, for example, may have to deal with the after-effects of a mugging of an elderly person, the council has to repair doors after burglary, staff in battered women's refuges have to deal with domestic violence, the police have to deal with the victims' fears on the spot. Victim support has a vital role to play throughout. Thus our measurement of success – or failure for that matter – is not solely in terms of the levels of offending (or crime), but in the levels of victim support provided.

Our approach views crime as a developing system, from its initial causes to the impact on the victim. In doing this it places the responsibility for crime control on a wide range of agencies and the public themselves.

Multi-agencies and the public

The literature on multi-agency intervention is dominated by a discussion of the relationship between the institutions involved. This analysis quite correctly focuses on the possibilities of co-operation and likely conflicts between the agencies. It omits, however, a crucial link in the scheme, namely the relationship between the agencies and the public. We have noted the vital role that the public plays in policing. The recognition of this is, if anything, a major part of modern criminological thinking. And we must not restrict our attention to police–public relations, but must include the relationships between the public and the various agencies concerned with crime control. For the social services, education, probation and the local council, no less than the police, are dependent on public co-operation.

What emerges clearly from our crime survey data is the role of the police as the leading agency of first referral. This is not, of course, identical with a view that the police should be the dominant agency in the multi-agency set-up, merely that they are seen as an essential element in intervention. Indeed, in areas such as crime prevention, the local authority in particular is seen as having a more important role than the police, perhaps, and in tackling juvenile offences social services are given a prominent role.

A crucial element in the relationship between agencies and the public is accountability. Discussion in this area has been overwhelmingly dominated by the topic of police accountability. This must, of course, be extended to all agencies, with performance indicators based on public demand being devised for the array of crime control institutions.

The relationship between agencies
We have delineated three dimensions of multi-agency intervention:

1   The relationship between the agencies and particular crimes.
2   The relationship between the agencies and the public.
3   The relationship between the agencies.

Most of the discussion has been in terms of the last area: the need for multi-agency social intervention, where all agencies are involved in their clearly defined roles, relating to each other in a democratic fashion. This is in contradiction to the notion of multi-agency policing, where the agencies meet together on a platform dominated by the police, in which the latter have the central co-ordinating role. Elsewhere we have argued for a conception of minimal policing which incorporates the following features:

1   A restriction of police intervention solely to crime control activities.
2   A restriction to only certain parts of the criminal justice process, (for example in the case of child abuse only to those limited times and occasions where coercive force is necessary: all else is social work).
3   A clear delimitation of spheres between the various parts of the control apparatus. Social work is social work and policing is policing, etc.
4   That, because of the different foci of points of the control apparatus, the absolute democratic necessity of conflict and debate between different sectors should take priority over any overreaching corporate agreement (Kinsey et al., 1986; Young, 1987).

Conclusion

The democratic relationship between agencies must be based on their specialist knowledge and purchase on particular crimes. A juvenile delinquent, for example, may be regarded from the point of view of whether guilty or not by the police, the context of a family with problems by the social services, and as part of a family which causes problems for others in the estate by the housing officers. There has to be pre-agreed consensus as to specialism, although in some cases more than one agency will be involved at the same point. Lighting, for example, will be under the auspices of both the local authority's architect's department and their housing officers.

Having brought together these agencies there will, despite an agreement on acknowledged specialisms, be a necessary conflict of interests. In child abuse, for example, social work will, by necessity of its brief, focus on the general welfare of the child within the family; the police more on the actual issues of culpability; the paediatrician on the extent of physical contact and harm. What is necessary, in the co-ordination of such expertise, is that in the final analysis a corporate decision must be made, after listening to the contributions of each agency, and backed with sufficient executive power in order to come to an agreed decision. As it is, the agencies discuss together, yet then too often merely proceed upon their own paths. Local authorities should provide this co-ordinating role. It is the ultimate task of national government to ascertain how the funding of resources to each agency is based on the actual cost-effective contribution of each part, rather than, as present, allow resources to be decided by the separate agencies themselves.

Such a conception of minimal policing has clear implications for the legitimation of crime control. We have seen that there is widespread community support for such a proposal. It does not involve a domination by the police of the multiple agencies, and room has to be made for a healthy debate and conflict of perspectives within a consensus delineated by public demands. Finally, in terms of the concern hitherto largely omitted in discussion of multi-agency intervention – the priority is to ensure efficiency and the need for public bodies to fall in line with the demands of the public whose support is necessary for their effectiveness and who, out of their rates and taxes, pay these bodies for the task of achieving a reasonable level of community safety.

All of this, with due regard to the three dimensions of multi-agency intervention, suggests the basis for a restructuring of these institutions to ensure a maximum level of service delivery, while protecting the rights and dignity of the offender.

References

Clarke, R. (1980) 'Situational crime prevention', *British Journal of Criminology*, 20 (2): 136–47.

Corrigan, P., Jones, T., Lloyd, J. and Young, J. (1988) *Socialism, Merit and Efficiency*. London: Fabian Society.

Crawford, A., Jones, T., Woodhouse, T. and Young, J. (1990) *Second Islington Crime Survey, 1990*. Centre for Criminology, Middlesex Polytechnic.

Jones, T., Lea, J. and Young, J. (1987) *Saving the Inner City: The First Report of the Broadwater Farm Survey*. London: Centre for Criminology, Middlesex Polytechnic.

Jones, T., Maclean, B. and Young, J. (1986) *The Islington Crime Survey*. Aldershot: Gower.

King, M. (1988) *How to Make Social Crime Prevention Work: The French Experience*. London: NACRO.

Kinsey, R., Lea, J. and Young, J. (1986) *Losing the Fight against Crime*. Oxford: Blackwell.

Lea, J. and Young, J. (1984) *What is to be Done about Law and Order?* London: Penguin.

Lea, J., Matthews, R. and Young, J. (1987) *Law and Order: Five Years On*. London: Middlesex Polytechnic, Centre for Criminology.

Painter, K., Lea, J., Woodhouse, T. and Young, J. (1989) *The Hammersmith and Fulham Crime and Policing Survey*. London: Middlesex Polytechnic, Centre for Criminology.

Walklate, S. (1989) *Victimology*. London: Unwin Hyman.

Young, J. (1986) 'The failure of criminology: the need for a radical realism', in R. Matthews and J. Young (eds), *Confronting Crime*. London: Sage.

Young, J. (1987) 'The tasks facing a realist criminology', *Contemporary Crises*, II: 337–56.

8

The Theoretical and Political Priorities of Critical Criminology

Phil Scraton and *Kathryn Chadwick*

Since 1979 British society has been dominated by the political and economic doctrines of Thatcherism. The New Right's rise to power during the 1970s was built on a broad appeal to the 'logic' of social authoritarianism. Its four cornerstones were: the collapse of 'community' structures through creeping criminality within the inner cities and towns; the increased militancy and inordinate power of the unions; the dependency on welfare and the encouragement of fecklessness by the 'nanny' state; the decline of moral values, Christian ethics and the sanctity of the family. Just as the 'enemies within' were easy to name and identify – terrorists, criminals, scroungers, militants, feminists, homosexuals, atheists, etc. – so equally were the explanations for their ascendancy. The New Right did not differentiate in naming its 'enemies': trade unionists, political terrorists, militant caucuses, sexual 'deviants' or divergent cultures, each had achieved the capacity to 'hold the state to ransom' (Moss, 1976).

In the USA and in Britain the New Right reaffirmed its commitment to individualism, to ambition and to the 'free' market. Its rhetoric hijacked the principle of freedom: to choose, to own, to spend, to save, to opt out, etc – targeting public housing, schooling, health care, public sector industries and local government. Alongside Reaganism, Thatcherism declared war on state interventionism, pursuing an agenda of legal reform, unprecedented in its severity and punitive intent. The issues were shifted from the political–economic realities of the free market with its relative surplus populations locked into structured, long-term unemployment, to create the illusion that the marginalization of particular groups was self-inflicted, brought on by individual pathologies, moral degeneration and social contagion.

On both sides of the Atlantic the rhetoric of the radical right presented classical assumptions giving 'the law and order crusade much of its grasp on popular morality and common-sense conscience' (Hall, 1979: 19). Essential to the Right's programme is the assumption of *voluntarism* – that individuals choose to commit crime, take part in disorder or industrial conflict. Classically, crime is then portrayed as pathological and contagious with a potential of *universal* contamination and moral degeneracy. Thus it is left to the radical right to confront crime, preserve order, reaffirm traditional values and safeguard the nation's moral identity. A 'crime is a crime is a crime', resonated Thatcher, regardless of the perpetrator, the content or the intent. The assumption is that a spectrum of violence and lawlessness exists ranging from 'intimidatory' behaviour to severe acts of interpersonal violence and political terrorism.

Within this context police powers have been extended, police accountability diminished (Scraton, 1985; Reiner, 1985; Spencer, 1985), civil liberties eroded and the use of imprisonment expanded to inconceivable levels with spectacular consequences (Sim, 1990; Scraton et al., 1991). What has been most dramatic is that so many fundamental changes have been achieved with minimal public debate or public opposition. By capitalizing on the 'fear' of crime the terrain shifted and the ideology of endemic criminality has become internalized within communities (Hough and Mayhew, 1983). While not underestimating the impact of certain crimes on individuals and the complexity of victim/survivor support (Walklate, 1988), the public/political debate has remained trapped within the construct of ever-increasing spiral violent crime, the inevitable road of lawlessness and the popular rejection of authority.

The Radical Right's programme has had a dynamic impact on the politics of reform and the struggle for rights. Those campaigning for progressive reforms have undergone public castigation and condemnation as being politically subversive, sympathetic to terrorism and, at best, naive idealists. Against this the self-styled Left Realists (Lea and Young, 1982, 1984), disassociating themselves from those they name 'left idealists' (Young, 1979), have courted favour with centrist Labour politics searching for a new realism for new times (Sivanandan, 1990). As Sim et al. (1987: 57) state: 'in its acceptance of the rhetoric of law and order and in its uncritical response to the official statistics the new realist approach reinforced the very fears it was seeking to alleviate'.

This chapter, by returning to the initial critique of the criminological traditions, sets out to reaffirm the principles and direction of critical analysis. It concentrates on the complex relations of power, legitimacy and knowledge in terms of the primary determining contexts of production, reproduction and neocolonialism and maintains that 'crime', 'disorder' and 'conflict' at the level of interpersonal relations and specificity require structural location and analysis within these determining contexts.

Criminology and its discontents

> Here, then, the proper study of criminology is made thoroughly clear: it is
> the *critical understanding* of both the larger society and of the broadest
> social theory; it is not simply the study of some exotic or esoteric group, be
> they criminals or criminologists... Clearly what this work is saying and
> exhibiting is that what matters is not crime and deviance studies but the
> larger critical theory on which they must rest. (Gouldner, 1973: x)

In 1973 the *New Criminology*, a benchmark work in critical theory,
delivered a fierce attack on traditional, correctionalist criminology as
the 'empirical emasculation of theories' which had supervised the
'depoliticisation of criminological issues' (Taylor et al., 1973: 278–80).
Their objective was to emphasize the significance of the everyday
world of 'criminals' or 'deviants' and their relationship with state
institutions geared to their regulation or control, but in the context of a
broader, historical and structural framework.

The emergence of a 'new' criminology owed much to social movements and politics of the 1960s. The first radical break came with the
challenge to mainstream criminology in the USA and in Western
Europe. Its architects were the 'new deviancy theorists' whose foci were
the diverse worlds of the ascribed 'deviant', the relativity of social
rules and the meaning implicit in acts labelled as criminal or deviant. In
challenging explanations which emphasized individual or social pathology the new deviancy theorists were concerned to demonstrate that
crime and deviance had to be considered in terms of the processes
through which specific acts were defined, labelled and punished, that
'social reaction' was located in state institutions and their professional
practices as essential to the maintenance of social and political order.

Becker (1963: 8) proposed that deviance was created 'by making
rules whose infraction constitutes deviance, and by applying those
rules to particular people and labelling them as outsiders'. Thus
deviance was not to be found in the 'quality of the act' committed but
as a 'consequence of rules and sanctions'. His concern was to question
who has the power to label and thereby define and whose definitions
stand highest in the 'hierarchy of credibility' (Becker, 1967). Lemert
(1967: 49) affirmed this position in concluding that, 'social control
becomes a "cause" rather than an effect of the magnitude and variable
forms of deviation'. Within this context he introduced the construct of
secondary deviation as a means of understanding social reaction as
part of the transactions or negotiations between the labelled and the
labellers. The problem with this essentially social interactionist perspective, however, was that it appeared to deny the structural relations
of power and the political processes of legitimacy. To argue, as did
Lemert, that social control created deviance provided no more insight
into the dynamics and relations of control than had structural func-

tionalist theory. The 'power of the definers', however, was placed firmly on the map and it was as much the critique within academic social sciences as it was the social and political movements outside which came to inform the radical debate.

Students had grown frustrated by the anti-communist propaganda generated by the 1950s Cold War, especially the political hysteria generated by McCarthyism in the United States, and its impact on intellectual critique and academic freedom. The move to re-establish what C. Wright Mills (1959) argued was the reforming and liberative potential of sociological analysis was sharpened by social and political movements around poverty, institutionalized racism, women's exploitation, misogyny and homophobia. International conflicts over Korea, Vietnam, South Africa and South America generated strong opposition to the 'imperialism' of powerful Western nation-states and their multinational economies. Gouldner (1969) laid bare the vested interests of structural–functionalism and its inherent conservatism, revealing the underlying 'domain assumptions' of academic social research and enquiry. It was a critique extended to the new deviancy theorists: 'His critique bore down especially sharply on criminologists. Helping to operate programmes of social control without questioning their wider objectives, they had made themselves into "technicians of the welfare state"... the "zoo-keepers of deviance"' (Hall and Scraton, 1981: 464–5).

Others (Chambliss, 1969; Quinney, 1970) revitalized a conflict analysis directly challenging the pluralist assumptions central to 'consensus theory' and clearly responding to Becker's (1967) invitation to social researchers to indicate 'whose side' they were on. The shift to a conflict analysis suggested that if the established order imposed regulation and control as *the* key functions in its maintenance and reproduction then law-breaking or deviant behaviour were acts of resistance or rebellion. What the academic traditions had contributed was the 'consecration' of the social order (Blackburn, 1969: 163), via the 'indissoluble practical [and theoretical] bonds between social sciences and the very material structure of modern society' (Shaw, 1972: 33). As the academic professional bodies came under attack, Nicolaus (1972: 45) called the American Sociological Association the 'house-servants of civil, military and economic sovereignty'. Sim et al. (1987: 3) conclude:

> The significance of these critiques of academic social sciences was that they turned attention to the work and utility of applied social research. Much of this work was based on the structural–functionalist assumption that 'crime', 'deviance' and 'conflict' were aberrations in an otherwise efficient, fair and just social system. In that scenario the 'corrective' or rehabilitative function of applied social sciences, particularly criminological or deviancy analyses, was a perfectly legitimate academic, interventionist function.

Within criminology alternative and radical initiatives, such as the Union of Radical Criminologists in the United States and the National Deviancy Conference in Britain, developed (Cohen, 1981). The 'new criminology' was rooted in the 'diverse and unique' world of everyday life, the claimed location of the interactionists, yet it adapted and contextualized new deviancy theory within the structural dynamics of power and social control. The capacity and ability to criminalize – to define and confer criminality – was to be found in the social relations, state institutions and political economy of advanced capitalism.

While these propositions were central to achieving the 'radical break' within criminology there was immediate criticism of the over-emphasis on the established theoretical premises of Marxist analysis. In prioritizing the mode of production, the primacy of the economic, the politics of distribution and the dynamics of class conflict, radical criminology was severely criticized for drifting back or regressing into the crude formulae of economic determinism. In calling for, 'a state of freedom from material necessity – a release from the constraints of forced production, an abolition of the forced division of labour, and a set of social arrangements, therefore, in which there would be no politically, economically, and socially induced *need* to criminalize deviance' (Taylor et al., 1973: 270), the new criminologists were portrayed as reducing *all* 'crime' to the materialism inherent within advanced capitalist economies. While criticism rained down from a wide range of perspectives, Hirst (1975: 204) brought radical deviancy theory to task for failing to question 'its own position, assumptions and interests'. The point was, he argued, that 'crime and deviance are no more a scientific field for Marxism than education, the family or sport'.

Yet the 'radical break' returned to prominence the significance of structural relations, the question of power and the processes which underpinned its legitimacy. Immediately, and related to other work developing in political economy, new explorations emerged: the role of law in advanced capitalist societies and the relationships between class, crime and the law. With these developments critical criminology entered a 'second phase'. The emphasis of the critical approach was to analyse the *contexts* of social action and reaction rather than to persist with the crude reductionist obsessions with causation. Balancing the lived experiences of people and the immediacy of daily interaction with the often less-visible structural arrangements – the political, economic and ideological management of social worlds – set the radical agenda for the consolidation of critical analysis within criminological theory.

It was, however, an agenda which was already under fire from other radical or progressive positions. Advanced industrial societies, East as well as West, were riven by their imperialist legacies manifested in the racism implicit, and often fiercely explicit, in the relations of neo-colonialism. While racism remained complex and distinctive in form between and within societies its presence as part of the structural relations of advanced industrial societies indicated a universality in which institutionalized racism differed only by degree. Similarly, the global domination of women provided clear evidence of the universality of patriarchy and the prevalence of misogyny. The feminist critiques argued that patriarchies were all-encompassing and durable, defining and delimiting male–female roles and potential in terms of the structural relations of reproduction as well as production. Not only were patriarchies universal, however, but they gained their legitimacy within societies at all levels – economic, state, religious, cultural institutions (Millet, 1970; Rich, 1977). This led directly to the proposition that 'sex-class' was as, if not more, significant than 'economic class' (Firestone, 1977). The work of women such as Simone de Beauvoir (1972) and Dorothy Smith (1973, 1975) demonstrated sharply that the social relations of reproduction and the political-economy of patriarchy had produced not only the material dependency of women on men but also had legitimated and enshrined 'male knowledge' as '*the* knowledge'. If the new, critical version of criminology was to read any differently from its predecessors then it had to consider *all* structural forms of oppression: their interrelationships and their mutual dependency. For questions of power, legitimacy, marginalization and criminalization could only be addressed with reference to the structural relations of production, reproduction and neocolonialism as *the* primary determining contexts.

Establishing a framework for critical analysis

> We should admit that power produces knowledge (and not *simply* by encouraging it because it serves power or applying it because it is useful); that power and knowledge *directly* imply one another; that there is no power relation without the correlative constitution of a field of knowledge, or any knowledge that does not presuppose and constitute at the same time power relations (Foucault, 1977: 27–8, emphases added)

Gouldner's (1969, 1973) devastating indictment of Western sociology established that the 'domain assumptions' of academic disciplines and their pre-eminent theoretical perspectives had been influenced massively by those powerful vested interests who commissioned research. Academic research was identified as essential to the management of advanced capitalism's inherent contradictions and conflicts. For Foucault, however, power is not uni-dimensional nor is it restricted to those formal relations of dominance in the economic or political spheres. As Sim (1990: 9) remarks, power is 'dispersed through the body of society' and exercised through the processes of 'discipline, surveillance, individualization and normalization'. Crucially the power–knowledge axis permeates all formal or official discourses, their language, logic, forms of definition and classification, measurement techniques and empiricism as essential elements in the technology of discipline and the process of normalization. 'Professionals', as key interventionists in societal relations and in the political management of social arrangements, pursue a 'logic and language of control' revealing a daunting 'power to classify' with clear consequences for the reproduction of 'bodies' of knowledge and for the maintenance of dominant power relations (Cohen, 1985: 196).

Foucault's work demonstrates that the challenges to mainstream theoretical traditions have adopted the agendas of those traditions, taking their premises as legitimate points of departure. While starting with 'knowledge-as-it-stands', that which is 'known', a radical alternative must also contextualize knowledge – its derivation, consolidation and recognition – within dominant structural relations. Undoubtedly professionals, be they employed in the caring agencies, the military, the criminal justice system or private industry, operate on the basis of professional training and work experience enjoying discretionary powers in accord with their rank and status. Yet whatever the quality and implications of decisions formulated and administered at the interpersonal level of 'agency', their recognition and legitimacy are rooted in the determining contexts of 'structure' and their manifestation in the professional ideologies of control and political management (Giddens, 1979, 1984).

The dynamics and visibility of power, however, are not always so obvious. For, 'power may be at its most alarming, and quite often at its most horrifying, when applied as a sanction of force' but it is 'typically at its most intense and durable when running through the repetition of institutionalized practices' (Giddens, 1987: 9). As power is mediated through the operational practices of institutions their daily routines become regularized, even predictable. It is important to establish that the routine world of 'agency', of interpersonal relations, is neither spontaneous nor random. Personal reputations and collective identities are ascribed and become managed via official discourses, themselves derived within the dominant social relations of production, reproduction and neocolonialism. For these represent the primary determining contexts which require and reproduce appropriate relations of power and knowledge.

The structural contradictions of advanced capitalist patriarchies require political management. While grassroots resistance has remained a persistent feature in Western social democracies their great achievement has been to contain opposition through relying on 'consensus' rather than 'coercion'. Relations of domination and exploitation, both material and physical, have become redefined and broadly accepted as the justifiable pursuit of competing interests. The smooth and successful operation of power in this context is dependent on social arrangements, forms of political management and cultural traditions which together contribute towards hegemony (Gramsci, 1971). Dissent and disorder are regulated by social forces and cultural transmission rather than by physical coercion. To challenge orthodoxy, to question the established order or to raise doubts concerning formal authority are not perceived as acts of progression towards worthwhile change but are presented in official discourses as acts of subversion which undermine shared identities and common interests.

While 'power', 'regulation' or 'control' can be identified in personal action and social reaction as part and parcel of the daily routine of *agency*, critical analysis seeks to bring to the fore *structural* relations, involving the economy, the state and ideology, in explaining the significance of the power–knowledge axis and relating it to the processes by which dominant ideas gain political legitimacy. Discrimination on the basis of class, gender, sexuality and perceived ethnicity clearly operates at the level of attitude, on the street, in the home, at the workplace or at social venues. Once institutionalized, however, classism, sexism, heterosexism and racism become systematic and structured. They become the taken-for-granted social histories and contemporary priorities which constitute state institutions, informing policies and underwriting practices, and which provide legitimacy to interpersonal discrimination. Through the process of institutionalization, relations of dominance and subjugation achieve structural significance. Critical analysis of crime and the criminal justice process must be grounded in these theoretical imperatives.

Class analysis and the determining context of production

Much of the post-war optimism over capital reconstruction and economic growth was derived in the 'Butskellite' compromises which married Keynesian principles concerning state management of the economy to a protected programme of capital investment and development in the private sector (Taylor-Gooby, 1982; Gamble, 1981). This programme was made possible through the initiation of effective, albeit often illusory, programmes of state welfare and social justice. Through initiatives in public housing, access to health care and medicine, new educational priorities and state benefits the popular assumption, also embodied in academic accounts of welfarism, was that benevolent reformism and its commitment to social justice had broken the hold of the free enterprise economy and its market forces over the social well-being of the nation. The era of 'welfare capitalism' had arrived, led by entrepreneurs of conscience who claimed 'people before profit'.

A cursory glance, however, at the relationship between the public and private sectors which emerged during this period reveals the grand illusion through a series of ambiguities and contradictions. In all sections of public service and ownership – schooling, housing, health and medicine – a strong and privileged private sector, bolstered by the inheritance of wealth, was maintained. Property ownership continued to become more centralized and concentrated within fewer hands. The expansion of state interventionism, local and central, ensured that the state became the largest employer and also the primary customer of private capital. Those industries which came under 'state ownership' were those essential to the reconstruction and consolidation of private manufacturing capital yet those deemed to be the least profitable or in need of the most reinvestment: coal, roads, railways, steel, communications, etc. The optimistic portrayal of this new pluralist society – based on equality of opportunity and access, on cradle-to-grave welfarism – disguised the structural contradictions inherent within the social arrangements and relations of the new dawn of economic expansionism.

Friend and Metcalfe (1981) graphically illustrate the divisions, well-established and noted during the depression of the 1920s and 1930s, of regional decline. Although unemployment in the 1950s remained relatively low so too did wages, job security, working conditions and living standards (Nightingale, 1980). The growth in immigration during the 1950s provided further evidence of this apparent expansionism. What was never made clear, however, was that throughout this period emigration exceeded immigration and that many immigrants, particularly from black Commonwealth countries and from Ireland were fed directly into the worst jobs with the lowest pay and the fewest prospects (Hall et al., 1978; Miles, 1982; Sivanandan, 1983; Cashmore, 1989).

The 'attack on poverty' meant the virtual end of widespread destitution and starvation and there were major advances in housing, health care, schooling and the general 'quality of life' – but the divisions remained. Capital reconstruction, despite the veneer of state interventionism in the management of the economy, meant capital accumulation and this, in turn, delivered the further centralization and concentration of capital. National monopolies became multinational conglomerates and, despite the institution of tiers of executive management as the 'controllers' of industry, ownership – and *effective* control – of industry became even more focused.

Parsons (1951) proclaimed the success of 'integration' of diverse elements within the social system, and Lipset (1960) announced that the fundamental conflicts of early capitalism had been resolved. The argument was that through the decomposition of capital and labour and the 'end of ideology' (Bell, 1960) more affluent and secure workers had taken on the characteristics, lifestyle and ambitions of the middle-class white-collar workers – the consolidation of contemporary industrial societies as essentially classless (Dahrendorf, 1959). This gave academic legitimacy to the dubious claim that the period of economic reconstruction was also one of significant political reconstruction. Class conflict represented a politics of the past matched by class analysis as a theoretical endeavour of the past. In its rush to bury Marxism and to proclaim the arrival of a new, meritocratic form of industrialism, structural functionalism replaced class analysis with stratification theory. Effectively this work failed to recognize that the post-war reconstruction of capital brought with it the reconstruction of class relations including the consolidation of the new professional and managerial class forms, in both the private and public domain, and their internal hierarchies. It also produced new hierarchies of labour within the transitional working class. These were complex developments, particularly as the dynamics of intra-class location encompassed divisions around gender, ethnicity and region as new contexts of class fragmentation.

The broadsides fired by stratification theorists and 'grand theorists' such as Parsons led to the reappraisal of Marxist analysis. Ten years after Dahrendorf's requiem for Marxism, Miliband (1969) and Quinney (1970) published their influential analyses of the advanced capitalist state. There followed a decade of important commentary on the state which picked up and developed the complexities of Miliband's central thesis that those who have occupied the key positions of state power for generations have been drawn from a different class position than those to whom the state administers, and that the legitimacy for that power is found within the dominant political–economic relations and not in the body politic. It proposed that in its mediation of existing class relations and conflict the state, through the rule of law, intervenes to protect, maintain and reproduce the very contradictions which it sets out to mediate (Thompson, 1975). Class rule, claimed Therborn (1978: 132), 'is exercised through state power ... through the interventions or policies of the state'.

Braverman (1974: 110) noted that the complexity of the class structure of advanced capitalism lay in the fact that 'almost all of the population has been transformed into employees of capital' through 'the purchase and sale of labour power'. For Braverman, as with Thompson, the historical relations of production have given rise to class formations within modes of production, each set of relations bearing the birthmarks of the previous mode. Given that productive relations create shared positions within the process of production it is logical to conclude that the social relations of production are structurally determined. Thus, while class represents a social process reflected in the concrete world of 'human relationships', it represents also a *structural location* within capitalist modes of production. It is precisely because class relations are in process, historically determined yet *responsive* to human relationships, that specific class locations shift as capitalism develops, refines and reconstructs through its stages of accumulation. Any interpretation of the political economy demands the theorization of class relations, for these relations are part of the essential foundations of contemporary social policy, of welfare programmes, of family relations, of culture and subculture of 'community' and of government.

The reaffirmation of class analysis produced important work on class location (Poulantzas, 1973, 1975; Wright, 1976, 1978; Carchedi, 1977; Miliband, 1977; Hunt, 1977) in which the process by which classes were conceptualized and class location established was explored. Braverman and Wright each indicated that class boundaries are located in terms of the economic demands of capital while emphasizing the structural significance of ideological and political criteria. As Poulantzas argued, the divisions which arise out of supervisory or managerial functions occur at the political level. Functionaries of capital, be they in the factory, the state or the police, occupy ambiguous and contradictory class locations. Classes, however, remain 'in motion', they organize and disorganize, they extend and retract their capacities and they are fixed permanently in struggle. The fundamental criteria for the location of classes are economic, however, and this has been clearly evident in the 1980s as the free market economy has expanded but not required a comparable expansion of labour, and substantial numbers of workers have been forced into the relative surplus population.

Marginality, and the process of marginalization, is an important concept in the structural analysis of contemporary class location, class fragmentation and Wright's discussion of contradictory class locations. Implicit in this analysis is the premise that during periods of economic recession part of the total workforce is used as the disposable surplus of wage-labour essential to the reconstruction of capital. During the 1980s while international companies enjoyed unprecedented profits and those with secure incomes took part in a decade of unchecked consumerism, approximately one-third of the population sat, marginalized, on or below the poverty line (Walker and Walker, 1987). While the private sector in housing, education, health care and transport flourished, the National Health Service, state schools, council housing and public transport offered a reduced service staffed by disillusioned workers.

Set within the context of the structural location of class the concept of marginality is both rigorous and significant. Marginality is manifested not only in terms of economic relations but also in terms of the subsequent political and ideological responses to those relations. Just as certain groups occupy 'contradictory class locations' so groups are pushed beyond the marginal locations of the relative surplus population. A range of identifiable groups and individuals, while relying on the capitalist mode of production and social democracy to provide them with an economic opportunity structure, live outside the 'legitimate' social relations of production. Marx (1961: 644) identified those condemned to 'pauperism', 'the hospital of the active labour army . . .' as the 'demoralized and ragged'. They constituted the 'dangerous classes' because their conditions were seen as the breeding ground of dissension and a real threat to civil order and social stability.

The link – unemployment, destitution, crime – has provided an important starting point for research which has developed the 'surplus population' thesis and its relevance in explaining not only certain categories of crime but also the process of criminalization of certain groups of people. While the 'immiseration thesis' cannot explain fully 'all' crimes it has demonstrated that the broader structural contexts of production and distribution, of poverty and unemployment, are significant in the involvement of people in 'crime' but also in the processes which define, adjust, enforce and administer the criminal law. The policy of targeting identifiable and vulnerable groups through heavy or saturation policing, for example, often precipitates a quasi-political resistance from marginal groups. While street crime might arise out of social, political and economic conditions it is not a progressive 'political' expression. Not only is it unlikely to stimulate long-term solutions to structural problems but inevitably it carries negative consequences. It divides the working class, nourishes racism, popularizes 'law-and-order' campaigns, victimizes the poor, consolidates the threat of violence towards women and increases the vulnerability of poor neighbourhoods. Consequently street crime, burglary and assault are often intra-class, and exacerbate problems and sharpen contradictions. Clearly poverty and long-term unemployment increase the propensity of the poor to commit 'survival' crime (Franey, 1983; Box, 1987) but this process of immiseration has divisive and threatening consequences as well as the potential for sharpening political consciousness and action.

Criminalization, the application of the criminal label to an identifiable social category, is dependent on *how* certain acts are labelled and on *who* has the power to label, and is directly limited to the political economy of marginalization. The power to criminalize is not derived necessarily in consensus politics but it carries with it the ideologies associated with marginalization and it is within these portrayals that certain actions are named, contained and regulated. This is a powerful process because it mobilizes popular approval and legitimacy in support of powerful interests within the state. As Hillyard's (1987) discussion of Northern Ireland illustrates clearly, public support is more likely to be achieved for state intervention against 'criminal' acts than for the repression or suppression of a 'political' cause. Further, even where no purposeful political intention is involved, the process of criminalization can divert attention from the social or political dynamics of a movement and specify its 'criminal' potential. If black youth is portrayed exclusively as 'muggers' (Hall et al., 1978) there will be less tolerance of organized campaigns which emphasize that they have legitimate political and economic grievances (Gilroy, 1987a). The marginalization of women who campaign for rights or for peace and the questioning of their sexuality is a further example of the process by which meaningful and informed political action can be undermined, de-legitimized and criminalized (Chadwick and Little, 1987; Young, 1990). Fundamental to the criminalization thesis is the proposition that while political motives are downplayed, the degree of *violence* involved is emphasized. In industrial relations, for example, it is the violence of the pickets which is pinpointed (Scraton and Thomas, 1985; Fine and Millar, 1985; Beynon, 1985), rather than the importance, for the success of a strike, of preventing supplies getting through to a factory. The preoccupation with the 'violence' of political opposition makes it easier to mobilize popular support for measures of containment.

In many of these examples, 'criminalization' is a process which has been employed to underpin the repressive or control functions of the state. This compounds further the difficult distinction between 'normal' and 'social' crime, since criminalization fuses the categories. The problem remains that even when violence is only used tactically it is double-edged. It breaks the assumed agreement to pursue conflicts by 'democratic', 'parliamentary' means which is the basis of the social contract and the legitimacy of the liberal–democratic state. The state is then certain to react, by fair means or foul (Poulantzas, 1975). Consequently it becomes difficult to disentangle those instances in which criminalization is part of the maintenance of social order, and where it is not. Theoretically, however, it highlights a significant function of the law in the ideological containment of class conflict. Married to the process of marginalization, through which identifiable groups systematically and structurally become peripheral to the core relations of the political economy, criminalization offers a strong analytical construct. Taken together these theses provide the foundations to critical analyses of the state, the rule of law and social conflict in advanced capitalist society.

Racism, crime and the politics of neocolonialism

> ... if you were to ask a taxi driver, hotel clerk or news vendor in London
> they would explain the increase in violent crime, especially robbery, by the
> presence of West Indians. (Wilson, 1977: 69)

This statement, made by one of the leading New Right criminologists
in the USA, directly attributes the escalation of street crime – and other
'predatory' crime – to the behaviour of a clearly identifiable group. It
consolidated the media-hyped imagery of the 1970s which first named
'mugging' and then located it within the actions of black Afro-
Caribbean youth. What this confirmed, according to Gilroy (1987b:
108), was a generally held assumption that 'undesired immigrants' are
infected by a 'culture of criminality and inbred inability to cope with
that highest achievement of civilization – the rule of law'. That these
views are prevalent in popular culture, the media coverage of 'hard
news' and political commentaries is sufficient evidence of the breadth
and depth of racism in Britain, but it is their institutionalization as all-
pervasive (Gordon, 1983) which transforms imagery into ideology.
The ideological construction of the race–crime–black criminality debate has been an essential condition upon which the differential
policing and discriminatory punishment afforded to specific neighbourhoods has been based.

Following the serious disturbances in Toxteth, Liverpool, during
the summer of 1981 the then Chief Constable of Merseyside Kenneth
Oxford justified the well-established principle of heavy policing of
Liverpool's black population by direct references to immigration.
Immigrants, from as early as 1335, had contributed to the 'turbulent
character of the Liverpool populace': 'Each of these new communities
brought with them associated problems, disputes and tensions, which
on occasion spilled over into outbreaks of violence' (Oxford, 1981: 4).
On this basis Oxford defended differential policing and discriminatory
practices and discounted allegations of racial harassment or violence.
These views, combining traditional criminological theories of individual pathology with those of social pathology, create a 'neat dovetail
of genetic characteristics and environmentalism' (Scraton, 1982: 35).
They are commonly held throughout the criminal justice process
(Gordon, 1983), and inform the decisions and actions of powerful
definers throughout all institutions of the British state. While evidence
of this was overwhelming in the police-commissioned Policy Studies
Institute study of police–community relations in London (PSI, 1983),
Scarman (1981) denied the existence of 'institutionalized racism' either
in the police or in other state agencies.

Essential to understanding the process of institutionalized racism,
however, is the proposition that:

...marginalisation is not a 'condition' suddenly inflicted on the Afro-Caribbean or Asian community simply by a downturn in the economy. It is written into the statutory definitions of immigration law and reflected in the political management of identities throughout state practices. (Sim et al, 1987: 44)

In constructing an analysis of the social relations of neocolonialism as a determining context, clearly the connection has to be made with class and the relations of production. Advanced capitalism persistently has required relations based on national domination as well as the provision of a ready supply of cheap materials, fuel and labour power. Central to this is the historical development of class fragmentation, particularly the use and abuse of immigrant or migrant labour as 'reserve armies'. Ironically named 'guest workers', the exploitation of cheap labour from the colonies has been a key feature in the construction of European and US labour forces throughout the twentieth century. Sivanandan's (1982) work, as with the excellent Institute of Race Relations' journal *Race and Class*, has done much to remind critical theorists that the connection between 'race' and labour power has formed an essential basis for the consolidation of multinational capitalism. Certainly the relationship between immigrant/migrant labour and the 'core' working class has created a complex dynamic in the interpretation of class locations. With the political and ideological criteria referred to earlier clearly evident in the politics of racism, black workers, like their late nineteenth-century Irish equivalents, have been allocated the least desirable, most insecure and poorest paid work. Their marginalization (some authors argue that they constitute an underclass) is primarily economic and the political and ideological struggles around this process have certainly contributed to the fractionalizing of the working class (Miles, 1982). As Sivanandan suggests, the process of economic marginalization, manifest at all material levels, has brought with it organized resistance and spontaneous rebellion. In his 'reversal' of the orthodoxy Gilroy (1987a) is not as far away from this position as it first seems when he emphasizes the reciprocity of race and class as determining contexts. His concern is to free racism of its subservience to classism, that racism is simply reduced to its function for capital. Racism *can be* and often is implicated in intra-class struggle but it has become central in establishing rational explanations, in the minds as well as the hearts of working class white communities, for diminishing circumstances. Racism, in that sense, is part of British hegemonic consciousness – it carries convincing explanations, it offers plausible accounts and its *logic* must not be underestimated (Cashmore, 1987).

What has become clear during the 1980s, however, is the simple proposition that the differential policing and targeting of particular communities has not only led to rebellion (Scraton, 1987) but has also completed the process of marginalization. While it is incorrect to homogenize groups under the ascribed labels of 'black', 'brown' 'people of colour', this is precisely what racism does and organized resistance has emerged. Yet these are the very groups that remain targeted and, as with the earlier discussion on class, the process of criminalization has been hand-in-glove with that of marginalization. Even if identifiable groups have a greater propensity to commit crimes than other comparable groups, and there is no evidence to suggest that 'black crime' is any more prevalent than 'crime' in other communities, that does not explain the ferocity with which the criminal justice process has reacted to the black people with which it deals.

A House of Lords debate in March 1989 on violent crime brought claims by Conservative peers that 61 percent of all street robbery was committed by black people. It was alleged that in London boroughs where only 14 percent of the population were black 72 percent of rapes were committed by black men. This brought renewed calls to identify the racial background of offenders. Given that further crime surveys in Britain have found that 49 percent of people 'feared' personal attack on the streets it is clear that the renewed campaign directed towards connecting race and crime has encouraged people to fear young blacks on the streets.

Black defendants are more likely to go to prison earlier, for longer periods and their social workers' reports are more likely to be ignored by the courts, than in the case of comparable offences committed by whites. Afro-Caribbean youths are given custodial sentences more readily and are remanded in custody, despite fewer convictions, than whites. In 1987 83.8 percent of the male and 72.7 percent of the women's prison population was classified as 'white'. The increase in black and 'ethnic' imprisonment has been rising by 1 percent per year since the mid-1980s. In all offence categories black people are sentenced for longer periods, have fewer previous convictions and less serious charges. While the number of young people in black/ethnic groups is approximately 4.3 percent of the population in most detention or remand centres they number 20 to 30 percent of those incarcerated.

The main conclusion to be drawn from the above material is that the reassurances given by the Home Office, by government inquiries and by the liberal commentaries of academics – that racism in the criminal justice process is an issue of the attitudinal approach of individuals and not an institutional problem – are false. It is clear that in terms of access, recruitment, training and development the criminal justice institutions and their professions have failed to deal with their well-established traditions of discrimination. Further, it is clear that racism is endemic in the policies, priorities and practices of the criminal justice institutions.

The shift from labour-intensive production and the uneven distribution of the effects of economic crisis in Britain have contributed significantly to the imposition of long-term, structural unemployment. The inevitable consequences of the economic, political and ideological location of black communities is that they are overrepresented in this surplus population.

> As with the late nineteenth century constructions of moral degeneracy and social contagion, black people have found themselves on the wrong end of the rough–respectable and nondeserving–deserving continua. This series of factors have created the preconditions in which black communities can be identified as the new 'dangerous classes'. (Sim et al., 1987)

The feminist critiques and the determining context of patriarchy

> Women appear in a sociology predicated on the universe occupied by men ... its methods, conceptual schemes and theories has been based on and built up within the male social universe. (Smith, 1973: 7)

Patriarchy, as the systematic domination of women by men both in the public and private spheres, embodies more than material and physical processes of power. It legitimates its rule, its politics, its universalism through knowledge forms based on 'themes, assumptions, metaphors and images' (Smith, 1975: 354) which underpins academic discourse, as self-evident truths. One such truth is fundamental, that is the defining and differentiating of women with reference to men: 'He is the Subject, He is the Absolute ... She is the Other' (de Beauvoir, 1972: 16). What academic discourse has assumed is the 'fixed and inevitable destiny' of women as daughters, wives, mothers, mistresses and servicers to their menfolk whose consolidation of power rests on the cultural–legal regulation of paternity (O'Brien, 1981).

Undoubtedly patriarchies develop distinctive and unique characteristics which produce complex institutional forms and social arrangements (Segal, 1987) but the subordination of women is both universal and structural (Morgan, 1986; Connell, 1987). The marginalization of women within patriarchies takes a variety of political and economic forms: the unwaged and unrecognized domestic mode of production (Delphy, 1984); the 'control of women's labour power' (Hartmann, 1979: 14) and the all-pervasiveness of masculine values and processes in paid work (Cockburn, 1986; Walby, 1986); the threat and reality of physical violence (Stanko, 1985; Kelly, 1988). While the caveat of 'false universalism' (Eisenstein, 1984: 141) has recognized the diversity of women's experiences, needs and desires the project of the feminist critiques of patriarchy has been the deconstruction of the power–knowledge axis within advanced capitalist societies.

While the standpoints and priorities of feminist analyses remain distinctive, particularly in the debates around the relationship between advanced capitalist relations and patriarchal relations, the critiques have been successful and progressive in challenging 'the assumptions which historically have normalised and subordinated political relations based on perceived natural constructs of gender and sexuality ... assumptions etched deep in the institutional fabric of the political economy which form part of the national consciousness and which become central to the professionalisation of knowledge' (Scraton, 1990: 15). In terms of the earlier discussion of power these assumptions not only underwrite, even encourage, the institutionalized sexism and heterosexism of state institutions but also form part of the daily, hourly round of interpersonal relations which deny women access to social space, silence their voices, violate their bodies and denigrate their resistance.

While state institutions 'coercively and authoritatively constitute the social order in the interest of men as a gender' (Mackinnon, 1983: 44) and advanced capitalism has been eminently successful in its assimilation of quite diverse forms of patriarchies, academic knowledge has provided both the legitimacy and justification for the determining contexts of gender and sexuality (Harding, 1986; Sydie, 1987; Smith, 1988). Within criminology, as Carol Smart first noted in 1976, the 'wider moral, political economic and sexual spheres which influence women's status and position in society' has been neglected or seen as irrelevant to the priority of studying men and crime (Smart, 1976: 185). More recent feminist research and publication has posed 'fundamental questions about the adequacy' of criminological analyses which has taken for granted the 'exclusion of women' (Gelsthorpe and Morris, 1990: 7). The substantive debates have prioritized: the relationship between patriarchy, the rule of law and the underpinnings of theoretical criminology (Smart, 1989); the universality of violence against women and the persistent reluctance of the state to intervene (Kelly and Radford, 1987); women's incarceration in prisons (Carlen, 1983) and in mental institutions (Showalter, 1987); family law and its 'role in enforcing women's position in society' (Bottomley, 1985: 184).

In addition to this work there has been further critical research into women and crime (Carlen, 1988; Carlen and Worrall, 1987; Heidensohn, 1985). Hilary Allen's (1987: 1) work, for example, confirmed previous research in showing that women are 'twice as likely as a man to be dealt with by psychiatric rather than penal means'. Further, the trend – first reported in 1988 – of a sharp increase in the imprisonment of women, more readily and for longer sentences, has consolidated as courts have become more severe on women offenders. This trend applies also to women with dependent children. In June 1988, 58 percent of women taken into custody had committed offences involving theft, handling stolen property or fraud. Twenty-five percent of women prisoners admitted were black. The average sentence increased by 36 percent on 1987. Of the 1765 women in prison over half had dependent children and most were convicted of non-violent crimes.

What this range of work has achieved has been to locate these issues within the material base of patriarchy demonstrating the diversity of women's oppression and the dynamics of male dominance. This includes 'women's access to production' and 'control over biological reproduction' but also through 'control of women's sexuality through a particular form of heterosexuality' (Mahony, 1985: 70). For 'male identity' and 'male sexuality' are 'crucial to the maintenance of male power' (Mahony, 1985). The determining context of patriarchal relations is based on the material and physical power appropriated by – but also ascribed to – men, and this is supported by a 'hegemonic form of masculinity in the society as a whole' with women 'oriented to accommodating the interests and desires of men' (Connell, 1987: 183). While women fight back individually and collectively, 'emphasized feminity' internalizes the ideology of servicing and use-value, and feeds the politics of dependency. It is within this process that gender divisions and ascribed sexualities become legitimated as 'natural' and, therefore, inevitable.

As with Connell's work, Brittan (1989) and Segal (1990) have explored the importance of hegemonic masculinity or masculinism in its subordination not only of women's sexuality, but also other male sexualities. As Mort (1987) observes, it is the historical processing of medico-legal discourses concerning 'dangerous sexualities' which has rendered alternative expressions of sexuality unacceptable, abnormal and unnatural. The broad consensus around what Rich (1977) labelled 'compulsory heterosexuality' has had a major impact on legislation but also has lessened significantly official responses to crimes against lesbians and gay men. Once again, the duality of marginalization is clear: the criminalization of the 'outcrop' (prostitutes not clients, homosexuals nor harassers, etc), and the reluctance to regulate or act against the oppressors.

Clearly all women are controlled by the public and private realities and fears inherent within male power relations but when they assert their rights, contest their oppression or organize against the discriminatory practices of the law, they become the threat. These are the women, already economically marginalized by the dependency relations of advanced capitalist patriarchy, who are further marginalized by their politics of opposition. Ultimately, as Chadwick and Little (1987) show, they are criminalized. The feminist critiques of criminology, both old and new, have demonstrated that critical criminology must have at its core the marginalization and criminalization of women, women's experiences of the criminal justice process and relationship of women to crime. They provide not only an essential contribution to critical analysis but also to the realization of a critical methodology which interprets the interpersonal experiences of women within the broader structural relations of advanced capitalist patriarchy.

Conclusion

What this discussion has pursued is the central argument that critical criminology recognizes the reciprocity inherent in the relationship between *structure* and *agency* but also that structural relations embody the primary determining contexts of production, reproduction and neocolonialism. In order to understand the dynamics of life in advanced capitalist societies and the institutionalization of ideological relations within the state and other key agencies it is important to take account of the historical, political and economic contexts of classism, sexism, heterosexism and racism. These categories do not form hierarchies of oppression, they are neither absolute nor are they totally determining, but they do carry with them the weight and legitimacy of official discourse. They reflect and succour the power–knowledge axis both in popular culture and in academic endeavour.

While the state, as a series of often contradictory relations, negotiates with oppositional forces and develops administrative and professional strategies/alliances to deal with political struggle, its essential objective is the maintenance of the established order. The politics of liberal democracy demands room for manoeuvre, some discretionary possibilities and occasional progressive reform but the state's legacy is essentially conservative. It is that of containment, caution and political management. As Sim et al. (1987: 62) state:

> Advanced capitalism, with the added complexity of managerial relations and class fractions, is served and serviced but rarely confronted by the state's institutions whose members share its ends, if not always its means, in a common ideology. It is at this level that the function of institutions, exemplified by the rule of law, tutors and guides the broad membership of society.

The above discussion demonstrates the basis upon which class fragmentation occurs and how those economically marginalized are exposed to the processes of criminalization. Additionally the post-colonial exploitation of migrant and immigrant labour has served capitalism and has led to a form of immiseration connected directly to racism. Finally, patriarchy has been functional for capital both in the public and private spheres. The interpretation and analysis of these primary determining contexts, however, cannot be limited to economic imperatives. Patriarchy and neocolonialism are also political forms which give rise to opposition and challenge. Yet, at the ideological level, their construction as oppressive social and political orders is justified and reinforced. The criminal justice process and the rule of law assist in the management of structural contradictions and the process of criminalization is central to such management. While maintaining the face of consent, via negotiation, the tacit understanding is that coercion remains the legitimate and sole prerogative of the liberal democratic state. Liberalism and authoritarianism do not form distinctive regimes or administrations within the context of democracy, they constitute a well-established spectrum of legitimate state rule and its use of legal censures.

Note

With many thanks to our undergraduate and postgraduate students who have helped us to develop critical criminology at Edge Hill College and to Deena Haydon, Barbara Houghton and Sheila Scraton for their critical contributions and technical support in producing the chapter.

References

Allen, H. (1987) *Justice Unbalanced: Gender, Psychiatry and Judicial Decisions*. Milton Keynes: Open University Press.

Becker, H.S. (1963) *Outsiders: Studies in the Sociology of Deviance*. New York: Free Press.

Becker, H. (1967) 'Whose side are we on?', *Social Problems*, 14 (3).

Bell, D. (1960) *The End of Ideology*. New York: Free Press.

Beynon, H. (1985) *Digging Deeper: Issues in the Miners' Strike*. London: Verso.

Blackburn, R. (1969) 'A brief guide to bourgeois ideology', in A. Cockburn and R. Blackburn (eds), *Student Power: Problems, Diagnoses, Action*. Harmondsworth: Penguin.

Bottomley, A. (1985) 'What is happening to family law? A feminist critique of conciliation', in J. Brophy and C. Smart (eds), *Women in Law*. London: Routledge & Kegan Paul.

Box, S. (1987) *Recession, Crime and Punishment*. London: Macmillan.

Braverman, H. (1974) *Labour and Monopoly Capital*. New York: Monthly Review Press.

Brittan, A. (1989) *Masculinity and Power*. Cambridge: Polity.

Carchedi, G. (1977) *On the Economic Identification of Social Classes*. London: Routledge & Kegan Paul.

Carlen, P. (1983) *Women's Imprisonment*. London: Routledge & Kegan Paul.

Carlen, P. (1988) *Women, Crime and Poverty*. Milton Keynes: Open University Press.

Carlen, P. and Worrall, A. (1987) *Gender, Crime and Justice*. Milton Keynes: Open University Press.

Cashmore, E.E. (1987) *The Logic of Racism*. London: Allen and Unwin.

Cashmore, E.E. (1989) *United Kingdom? Class, Race and Gender since the War*. London: Unwin Hyman.

Chadwick, K. and Little, C. (1987) 'The criminalisation of women', in P. Scraton (ed.), *Law, Order and the Authoritarian State*. Milton Keynes: Open University Press.

Chambliss, W.J. (1969) *Crime and the Legal Process*. New York: McGraw-Hill.

Cockburn, C. (1986) *Machineries of Dominance*. London: Pluto.

Cohen, S. (1981) 'Footprints in the sand: a further report on criminology and the sociology of deviance in Britain', in M. Fitzgerald, G. McLennan and J. Pawson *Crime and Society*. London: Routledge & Kegan Paul.

Cohen, S. (1985) *Visions of Social Control*. Cambridge: Polity.

Connell, R.W. (1987) *Gender and Power*. Cambridge: Polity.

Dahrendorf, R. (1959) *Class and Class Conflict in Industrial Society*. Stanford: Stanford University Press.

de Beauvoir, S. (1972) *The Second Sex*. Harmondsworth: Penguin.

Delphy, C. (1984) *Close to Home: A Materialist Analysis of Women's Oppression*. London: Hutchinson.

Eisenstein, H. (1984) *Contemorary Feminist Thought*. London: Counterpoint.

Fine, B. and Millar, R. (eds) (1985) *Policing the Miners' Strike*. London: Lawrence & Wishart.

Firestone, S. (1977) *The Dialectic of Sex*. London: Paladin.

Foucault, M. (1977) *Discipline and Punish: The Birth of the Prison*. London: Allen Lane.

Franey, R. (1983) *Poor Law*. London: CHAR/NCCL.

Friend, A. and Metcalfe, A. (1981) *Slump City: The Politics of Mass Unemployment*. London: Pluto Press.

Gamble, A. (1981) *Britain in Decline*. London: Papermac.

Gelsthorpe, L. and Morris, A. (1990) *Feminist Perspectives in Criminology*. Milton Keynes: Open University Press.

Giddens, A. (1979) *Central Problems in Social Theory*. London: Macmillan.

Giddens, A. (1984) *The Constitution of Society*. Cambridge: Polity.

Giddens, A. (1987) *The Nation-State and Violence*. Cambridge: Polity.

Gilroy, P. (1987a) *There Ain't No Black in the Union Jack*. London: Hutchinson.

Gilroy, P. (1987b) 'The myth of black criminality', in P. Scraton (ed.), *Law, Order and the Authoritarian State*. Milton Keynes: Open University Press.

Gordon, P. (1983) *White Law*. London: Pluto Press.

Gouldner, A.W. (1969) *The Coming Crisis in Western Sociology*. London: Heinemann.

Gouldner, A.W. (1973) 'Foreword' in I. Taylor, P. Walton and J. Young, *The New Criminology*. London: Routledge & Kegan Paul.

Gramsci, A. (1971) *Selections from the Prison Notebooks*. London: Lawrence & Wishart.

Hall, S. (1979) 'The great moving right show', *Marxism Today*, January.

Hall, S. et al. (1978) *Policing the Crisis*. London: Macmillan.

Hall, S. and Scraton, P. (1981) 'Law, class and control', in M. Fitzgerald, G. McLennan and J. Pawson (eds), *Crime and Society*. London: RKP.

Harding, S. (1986) *The Science Question in Feminism*. Milton Keynes: Open University Press.

Hartmann, H. (1979) 'The unhappy marriage of Marxism and feminism: towards a progressive union', *Capital and Class*, 8.

Heidensohn, F. (1985) *Women and Crime*. London: Macmillan.

Hillyard, P. (1987) 'The normalization of special powers: from Northern Ireland to Britain', in P. Scraton (ed.), *Law, Order and the Authoritarian State*. Milton Keynes: Open University Press.

Hirst, P.Q. (1975) 'Marx and Engels on law, crime and morality', in I. Taylor, P. Walton and J. Young (eds), *Critical Criminology*. London: Routledge & Kegan Paul.

Hough, M. and Mayhew, P. (1983) *The British Crime Survey*. Home Office Research Study 76. London: HMSO.

Hunt, A. (ed.) (1977) *Class and Class Structure*. London: Lawrence & Wishart.

Kelly, L. (1988) *Surviving Sexual Violence*. Cambridge: Polity.

Kelly, L. and Radford, J. (1987) 'The problem of men: feminist perspectives on sexual violence', in P. Scraton (ed.), *Law, Order and the Authoritarian State*. Milton Keynes: Open University Press.

Lea, J. and Young, J. (1982) 'The riots in Britain 1981: urban violence and political marginalisation', in D. Cowell, T. Jones and J. Young (eds), *Policing the Riots*. London: Junction Books.

Lea, J. and Young, J. (1984) *What is to be Done about Law and Order?* Harmondsworth: Penguin.

Lemert, E.M. (1967) *Human Deviance, Social Problems and Social Control*. New Jersey: Prentice-Hall.

Lipset, S. (1960) *Political Man*. New York: Doubleday.

Mackinnon, C.A. (1983) 'Feminism, Marxism, method and the state: toward feminist jurisprudence', *Signs*, 8.

Mahony, P. (1985) *Schools for the Boys? Co-education Reassessed*. London: Hutchinson.

Marx, K. (1961) *Capital*, Vols I–III. London: Lawrence & Wishart.

Miles, R. (1982) *Racism and Migrant Labour*. London: Routledge & Kegan Paul.

Miliband, R. (1969) *The State in Capitalist Society*. London: Weidenfeld & Nicholson.

Miliband R. (1977) *Class and Politics*. London: Macmillan.

Millet, K. (1970) *Sexual Politics*. London: Sphere.

Morgan, R. (ed.) (1986) *Sisterhood is Global*. Harmondsworth: Penguin.

Mort, F. (1987) *Dangerous Sexualities*. London: Routledge & Kegan Paul.

Moss, R. (1976) *The Collapse of Democracy*. London: Pan.

Nicolaus, M. (1972) 'The professional organisation of sociology: the view from below', in R. Blackburn (ed.), *Ideology in Social Science*. London: Fontana.

Nightingale, M. (1980) *Merseyside in Crisis*. Liverpool: Merseyside Socialist Research Group.

O'Brien, M. (1981) *The Politics of Reproduction*. London: Rougledge & Kegan Paul.

Oxford, K. (1981) *Report of the Police Committee on Merseyside Disorders* (Evidence to the Scarman Inquiry) [K. Oxford, Chief Constable]. Liverpool: Merseyside Police.

Parsons, T. (1951) *The Social System*. London: Routledge & Kegan Paul.

Poulantzas, N. (1973) 'On social classes', *New Left Review*, 78.

Poulantzas, N. (1975) *Political Power and Social Classes*. London: New Left Books.

PSI Report (1983) *Police and People in London*, Vols I–IV. London: Policy Studies Institute.

Quinney, R. (1970) *The Social Reality of Crime*. New York: Little Brown.

Reiner, R. (1985) *The Politics of the Police*. Brighton: Wheatsheaf.

Rich, A. (1977) *Of Woman Born: Motherhood as Experience and Institution*. London: Virago.

Scarman, Lord (1981) *The Scarman Report: The Brixton Disorders 10–12 April 1981*. Cmnd 8427. London: HMSO.

Scraton, P. (1982) 'Policing and institutionalised racism on Merseyside', in D. Cowell, T. Jones and J. Young (eds), *Policing the Riots*, London: Junction Books.

Scraton, P. (1985) *The State of the Police*. London: Pluto Press.

Scraton, P. (1987) 'Unreasonable force: policing, punishment and marginalisation', in P. Scraton (ed.), *Law, Order and the Authoritarian State*. Milton Keynes: Open University Press.

Scraton, P. (1990) 'Scientific knowledge or masculine discourses? Challenging patriarchy in criminology', in L. Gelsthorpe and A. Morris (eds), *Feminist Perspectives in Criminology*. Milton Keynes: Open University Press.

Scraton, P. and Thomas, P. (1985) *The State v The People: Lessons from the Coal Dispute* (*Journal of Law and Society*, special issue). Oxford: Blackwell.

Scraton, P., Sim, J. and Skidmore, P. (1991) *Prisons under Protest*. Milton Keynes: Open University Press.

Segal, L. (1987) *Is the Future Female? Troubled Thoughts on Contemporary Feminism*. London: Virago.

Segal, L. (1990) *Slow Motion: Changing Masculinities, Changing Men*. London: Virago.

Shaw, M. (1972) 'The coming crisis of radical sociology', in R. Blackburn (ed.), *Ideology in Social Science*. London: Fontana.

Showalter, E. (1987) *The Female Malady. Women, Madness and English Culture, 1830–1980*. London: Virago.

Sim, J. (1990) *Medical Power in Prisons: The Prison Medical Service in England 1774–1989*. Milton Keynes: Open University Press.

Sim, J., Scraton, P. and Gordon, P. (1987) 'Crime, the state and critical analysis: an introduction', in P. Scraton (ed.), *Law, Order and the Authoritarian State*. Milton Keynes: Open University Press.

Sivanandan, A. (1982) 'From resistance to rebellion', *Race and Class*, special issue, XXIII.

Sivanandan, A. (1983) *A Different Hunger*. London: Pluto Press.

Sivanandan, A. (1990) 'All that melts into air is solid: the hokum of New Times', *Race and Class*, XXXI (3).

Smart, C. (1976) *Women, Crime and Criminology*. London: Routledge & Kegan Paul.

Smart, C. (1989) *Feminism and the Power of Law*. London: Routledge.

Smith, D. (1973) 'Women's perspective as a radical critique of sociology', *Sociological Inquiry*, 44.

Smith, (1975) 'An analysis of the ideological structures and how women are excluded', *Canadian Journal of Sociology and Anthropology*, 12 (4).

Smith, D. (1988) *The Everyday World as Problematic: A Feminist Sociology*. Milton Keynes: Open University Press.

Spencer, S. (1985) *Called to Account*. London: NCCL.

Stanko, E. (1985) *Intimate Intrusions*. London: Routledge & Kegan Paul.

Sydie, R. (1987) *Natural Women, Cultured Men: A Feminist Perspective on Sociological Theory*. Milton Keynes: Open University Press.

Taylor, I., Walton, P. and Young, J. (1973) *The New Criminology*. London: Routledge & Kegan Paul.

Taylor-Gooby, P. (1982) *The Welfare State from the Second World War to the 1980s*. D355 Social Policy and Social Welfare, Milton Keynes: Open University Press.

Therborn, G. (1978) *What does the Ruling Class Do when it Rules?* London: New Left Books.

Thompson, E.P. (1975) *Whigs and Hunters: The Origin of the Black Act*. London: Allen Lane.

Walby, S. (1986) *Patriarchy at Work*. Cambridge: Polity.

Walker, A. and Walker, C. (eds) (1987) *The Growing Divide: A Social Audit 1979–1987*. London: CPAG.

Walklate, S. (1988) *Victimology: The Victim and the Criminal Justice Process*. London: Unwin Hyman.

Wilson, J.Q. (1977) 'Crime and punishment in England', in R.E. Tyrrell Jr. (ed.), *The Future that Doesn't Work: Social Democracy's Failures in Britain*. New York:

Doubleday.

Wright, E.O. (1976) 'Class boundaries in advanced capitalist societies', *New Left Review*, 98.

Wright, E.O. (1978) *Class, Crisis and the State.* London: New Left Books.

Wright, Mills, C. (1959) *The Sociological Imagination.* New York: Oxford University Press.

Young, A. (1990) *Femininity in Dissent.* London: Routledge.

Young, J. (1979) 'Left idealism, reformism and beyond: from new criminology to Marxism', in NDC/CSE *Capitalism and the Rule of Law.* London: Hutchinson.

9

Violence against Women and Children: the Contradictions of Crime Control under Patriarchy

Jill Radford and *Elizabeth A. Stanko*

Before engaging with our title subject, we will introduce ourselves and our relationship to the issue of violence against women and children and the academic debates about crime control. Jill Radford, a British feminist, has been active in researching, theorizing and campaigning against violence against women since the late 1970s. Betsy Stanko, an American feminist now working in Britain, founded, along with other women, a shelter for battered women and children in Worcester, Massachusetts, in the late 1970s. Both of us are criminologists and have struggled with issues of men's violence in our own lives.

As feminists we argue that sexual violence is used by men as a way of securing and maintaining the relations of male dominance and female subordination, which are central to the patriarchal social order. We recognize that patriarchy is crossed through and is in interaction with other power structures, namely those of race, class, age and status regarding disability. These shape women's experience of sexual violence and the response of the police and others. We firmly believe that it is through challenging the patriarchal order by increasing women's autonomy that men's violence must be confronted. While this long-term goal is central to our politics, we, like many feminists, are concerned with the need to address the problem in current society. It is these concerns which have drawn us into identifying, naming and working around the problem of male sexual violence. Given that our work links both the immediate problems arising from ongoing sexual violence and the practical strategies to ease women's everyday lives with the longer-term goal of eradicating sexual violence, we anticipate contradictions. This chapter addresses some of the contradictions arising in recent attempts to redefine and address the problem of sexual violence in England and Wales within the paradigms of crime control operant within the policing and legal process.

Our purpose here is to articulate some of the many contradictions facing feminists who attempt to enter the crime control debates.

Although our examples arise largely from the UK and USA, we feel that they illustrate the dilemmas facing feminists in other countries. We begin by examining what we refer to as 'violence against women and children'. Much of this violence is virtually ignored by criminologists and criminal justice policy makers. We then look at the more recent shift in policing sexual violence and domestic assault. The majority of violence against women and children is directed at them by men in their families. Yet dominant professional intervention tactics effectively transform feminist analysis of men's violence to a gender-neutral problem of 'family violence'. We conclude by looking at the attempts to include violence against women under the rubric of crime and the resultant crime control strategies. We argue that it is this redefinition of the problem, from that of men's sexual violence to women, defined through women's experience, to that of crime, as defined by the malestream legal system, which underpins a fundamental contradiction. Throughout, we will ask how possible it is to think seriously about 'crime' to women and attempt to develop 'crime control' strategies that promote women's autonomy and safety.

Violence against women: problems of definition

Over the past 20 years, feminists have once again named and addressed the problem of men's sexual violence from the perspective of women's experience. As has been documented previously:

> ...through the process of naming, women have voiced their anger and expressed their commitment to struggle and survival. 'Men's violence'; 'sexual violence', 'rape', 'incest', 'sexual abuse of women and children', 'woman battering', 'womanslaughter', 'woman killing', 'frawen mishandling', 'the male peril', 'sexual terrorism', 'outrage', 'unspeakable horror', 'sexual harassment' – these are some of the words women in several cultures and at different times in this century have drawn upon to describe their experiences of men's violence. (Hanmer et al., 1989: 1–2)

Through listening to women's experiences of behaviour they found abusive, feminist definitions expanded as women named previously unnamed forms of abuse: 'The development of feminist research and discussion over the past fifteen years can in a very real sense be seen in terms of ever-widening definitions and naming of sexual violence in general and in particular forms' (Kelly and Radford, 1987: 243). A significant illustration of this is Ruth Hall's (1985) use of the concept 'racist sexual violence' to highlight the fact that for black women, racism and sexism are often inseparable.

Another strand in this work is the documentation of women's experience of sexual violence. Survey after survey documents the extent to which women endure various forms of male violence as everyday features of their lives (Stanko, 1988). Sexual harassment, sexual assault, physical battering, childhood sexual abuse and intimidation, obscene phone calls, and the deluge of pornographic popular literature are the backdrop for women's relationships with men.

Kelly (1988) suggests that women's everyday lives exist along a continuum of sexual violence. Radford (1987) endorsed the 'circular spiral of violence', outlined earlier by Hanmer and Saunders (1984), which illustrates the ways in which dominant discourse about public violence impacts on women, often resulting in their becoming isolated within the wider community, retreating into their homes as ostensibly safe havens, where their resultant dependency on men makes them even more vulnerable to abuse.

Stanko (1985, 1990) concludes that women's understanding of physical and sexual safety is so tightly woven with their concern for sexual integrity as to render the concept of safety problematic for women. Rather than take safety for granted, women, she proposes, build strategies of precaution into their everyday lives and speak of situations as less *unsafe*.

In the first comprehensive study of black women's experience of domestic violence, Amina Mama (1989), focuses on the ways in which racism and sexism combine to exacerbate the problems black women face in this situation. In this work, she is also highly critical of previous neglect of black women's experience of violence against women. She points to the part played by racist and sexist immigration laws which define foreign-born wives of British men as dependents with no independent right of residence in the UK:

> The scandalous situation in which British men can call the immigration department to deport wives they have abused, or simply decided they have no further use for, is condemned. So is the use of the immigration service by some men to further terrorise the women with whom they live. Immigration law currently empowers individual men to torture with impunity, women with uncertain or dependent immigration status, because it enables them to have the woman deported, perhaps away from her British born children. (1989: xv)

These and many other feminist studies over the past 15 years have consistently and persistently illustrated the endemic nature of violence within women's lives (Scheppele and Bart, 1983; Russell, 1982, 1984, 1985). The central feminist explanation for the widespread existence of men's violence to women and children is that it is essential to a system of gender subordination (MacKinnon, 1989). Much of violence against women, captured by the feminist surveys, remains outside the realm of criminological thinking about crime. This is a consequence of attempting to locate feminist definitions based on women's experiences into man-made legal categories. Basically they just don't fit. Legal definitions are drawn from dichotomies: lawful as against unlawful; crime and no crime; innocence and guilt; the good polarized against the bad (Smart, 1989). Women's experiences generally, and even more so in relation to violence, are much more complex. The 1970s debates around the limited legal concept of consent/non-consent in the law of rape is one illustration.

While the most frequent and routinized forms of male sexual violence are shielded from public view, lost in the discourse of dysfunctional families and female inadequacies, what does come to the attention of the public are the crimes of the psychopathic stranger, the deranged rapist or the serial killer. The attention drawn to public danger to women is not however a commentary about the gendered nature of this danger (Cameron, 1988; Caputi, 1988), only that it is dangerous for women to be in public. Thus, the bulk of violence to women, that which occurs in private, rarely comes to public attention, is scorned by the police, and the women who ask for police intervention are left neglected and often abused by the very system financed by the state to protect them.

Criminological thinking about crime continues to revolve around the safety of the public and the traditional belief that the proper police role is the policing of public order. Our attention to perceived threats to community life is constantly aimed towards public order problems, to the potential threat from the deranged or evil stranger who wishes to relieve us, forcibly, of our valuables and injure us when out in public, or to the deranged killers or serial rapists striking randomly. The literature analysing risk of criminal victimization recognizes the important contribution made by the lifestyle of the 'victim' to their coming into contact with predatory crime, yet totally neglects how women are so often victimized by those they already know (Hindelang et al., 1978; Cohen and Felson, 1979; Gottfredson, 1984; Hough and Mayhew, 1983, 1985; Mayhew et al., 1989).

What the recent changes in the police response to violence against women and children are about, is the pushing of some of what was classified as non-crime into the crime books. The rise in violent crime in England and Wales, for example, is largely due to the changes in the recording practices of the police concerning domestic violence and rape. In order to explore the crime control and crime prevention strategies about *crime* to women, the reader must keep in mind that, at least in the public discourse, this remains a fraction of the incidences women themselves consider to be *violent* and *threatening* situations.

Keeping feminism alive within debates about controlling violence

Our perspective is not that of dispassionate academics concerned with an anthropological or voyeuristic study of other women, that is with separating or distancing ourselves from our subject. We see the links between the provision of support and safe services, research, theorizing and campaigning as integral and necessary to confronting the oppression of patriarchy within women's everyday lives. Because we conduct our debates within the academic world as well as within the world of the everyday, we live out the contradictions in our social practice. At the same time we have a unique insight into processes through which issues feminists raised about male violence have sparked sudden interest on the part of academics, professional service providers (such as social services, psychologists, psychiatrists and counselling professionals) and also the Home Office (the central British ministry responsible for criminal justice in England and Wales), the police and the legal system.

Within academia, we have become aware of the move to make women's studies respectable, and as a part of this a growth of interest in the subject of violence against women and children. Once established on the agenda of acceptable academic issues, however, feminist concerns are often abandoned as academic success takes priority over feminist praxis. We know, for example, that feminist support services working around violence against women receive many requests from students and tutors at every level from GCSE (the first educational qualification gained by 15–16-year-olds in the UK), through to postgraduate levels to supply information about violence against women, showing interest in drawing on feminist work but without any commitment to the issues or concern for the safety and well-being of all women. Within the academy the personal is divorced from the political and both are divorced from the academic in the rush for academic success and recognition. In this process, we see every day how feminist work is appropriated, but without the feminist commitment which gave it its meaning.

A similar appropriation of feminist concerns can be identified in the belated recognition on the part of some in the caring professions that violence against women and children is a serious and a legitimate area of concern/intervention. While welcoming the fact that these professional carers are recognizing issues feminists have been highlighting as of urgent concern to women, we see very real problems in the form taken by this professional, so-called 'expert', intervention. This is especially important here, because debates about crime control inevitably lead to a diversion of many cases of violence away from the criminal justice system. There is, for instance, serious discussion about the establishment of a family court in England and Wales to handle matters arising within families, including violence and sexual abuse.

We are particularly troubled by the professional redefinition of the problem. Rather than identifying male sexual violence as part of the backdrop of women's lives, conventional intervention models, using the paradigm of victimology, identify it as something that affects only a minority of women, who can then be held in some way responsible for it. This woman-blaming logic of victimology leads many social service providers to conduct support services on their own professional terms – counselling or family therapy directed at reintegrating women and children who have been abused back into active heterosexuality and family life with the abuser with minimum disruption. This is in contrast with feminist women-centred support services developed by and with survivors of male violence, whose response is unconditional support for women and children in whatever strategies they elect. Instead of forwarding women's and children's best interests, we see too many of these professionals containing women within the structures of heterosexuality and the family and building lucrative careers for themselves on the backs of male violence (Kelly, 1989). These academic and professional interventions in the public discourse about violence against women mark two major ideological shifts.

A third major shift has become evident in the Home Office and police forces for England and Wales. Although feminist critiques in the UK and elsewhere through the 1970s and early 1980s constituted a continuing source of embarrassment to those responsible for law enforcement and the judicial process, the recent about-turn in UK policy, we argue, does not stem directly from the pressure of British feminists. Rather, the British police have sought advice and direction from their North American counterparts in dealing with modern management of inner-city riots as well as sexual violence and domestic assault against women. By the 1980s, the crisis in policing could no longer be hidden from public gaze. An urgent need on the part of the police to seek legitimacy from the British public was becoming apparent. After the inner-city uprisings of 1981, followed by the Scarman report, the damning PSI report on the London Metropolitan police (Smith and Gray, 1983), uprisings in Broadwater Farm and Brixton in London in 1985, the police experienced a serious need to renegotiate some consensus in the inner city (Sim et al., 1987).

By shifting attention to the problem of violence against women, in their discourse crime against women, the police in adopting the mantle of protectors to women and children, attempted to renegotiate some legitimacy within the inner city. However this targeting of women in the inner city is problematic for feminists. At the most obvious level, such a move is predicated on the discredited assumption that male violence against women is more prevalent in certain areas, among certain communities, defined with reference to race and class as pathological. Further the unresolved tensions between the police and minority ethnic communities raises a scepticism around police motivation.

The work of North American feminists confronted police practices in relation to woman battering by lobbying for legislative mandates in many US states, and through filing class action law suits in New York and Oakland, condemning the practice of entire police forces. But the individual liability case against Torrington, Connecticut (which resulted in disastrous financial consequences for the municipal government), made police forces take notice: failing to take action in domestic situations could now cost police precious tax resources. These actions opened the doors to scrutinize US policing and police practice (Ferraro, 1989). Changes in the US provided examples of 'good practice' that could be adopted by British police. But the importing of these ideas about 'good' practice left out any possibility of a feminist base.

Identifying women on the one hand as a vocal source of criticism and on the other as a needy target and by drawing on internal police debates on new softer 'community policing' styles of policing (Alderson, 1979), police attention has turned to the long-neglected problem of violence against women. The change of heart has been rapid indeed. For instance, in 1984 Sir Kenneth Newman attempted to shed police responsibility for what he considered 'rubbish work', or non-police matters, naming domestic violence and stray dogs as two such examples. By 1990, police forces compete with each other to find the most creative policy to deal with domestic violence!

But the new interest in violence against women does not include a commitment to promoting women's autonomy, nor does it recognize how policing policy affects women within varying race, class, ethnic and religious contexts. The location of London's first domestic violence units in Tottenham and Brixton, as Amina Mama (1989) states, raises questions about how policing differentially affects women and their communities:

> The establishment of domestic violence response units, staffed by women police officers and resourced to do proper monitoring and follow-up work may be a good idea, but we were concerned to note that these are an initiative so far restricted to areas of black concentration which are already heavily and oppressively policed. This raises the possibility that such units have a hidden agenda, concerned with convicting more black men, underpinning the publicly proclaimed agenda which stresses supporting and following up incidents in the interests of women being subjected to violence. (Mama, 1989: 304–5)

The interest of the political heart of the British ministry in violence to women is widening. The Home Office now recognizes women's 'fear of crime' as a serious problem, and has designed pamphlets to reassure women about their safety in public places. Women's fear of crime is consistently found to be much higher than that of men (Hough and Mayhew, 1983, 1985; Maxfield, 1984, 1988). Hough and Mayhew (1983), the two Home Office researchers responsible for the establishment of the *British Crime Surveys*, speculated that this fear was out of all proportion with their statistically estimated chances of victimization, and therefore potentially 'irrational'. In offering a feminist explanation for women's fear, Stanko (1987: 130) has suggested: 'While women's fear remains an anomoly of perception for criminologists and policy-makers, understanding women's fear of crime – which might also be read as *women's fear of men* – entails understanding the ever-present reality of women's experiences of men's threatening and/or violent behaviour.'

Women's fear of crime, however unfounded to policy makers, has become the focus of a growing number of safety campaigns. The campaigns about safety attempt to reassure women by suggesting ways to minimize the potential threat of public space through the avoidance of dangerous strangers. Exemplified in their 'bolts and bars' approach to crime prevention, the Home Office's focus spotlights street crime, adding to the type of concern voiced by Amina Mama above. John Patten, junior minister of the Home Office and convenor of the ministerial Group on Women, would benefit from adopting a feminist explanation of sexual violence. He recently told a delegation from the Townswomen's Guilds, a group of women similar to the League of Women Voters in the US, that the problem of rape was difficult and so was prosecuting men, who frequently claimed that women 'led them on'. Patten could not suggest a practical solution to preventing rape because it was difficult to foresee, as much of it was 'on the spur of the moment' rape.

If feminism is to remain in the forefront of critiques of crime control, we must not lose sight of our politics. We must not lose sight of our starting point, the experiences of women and children; we must not separate women's experiences of violence and danger from unknown and known men; and we must not forget that men's sexual violence is part of the backdrop of all women's lives and not something experienced by a minority who can be labelled as inadequate and helpless victims. Managing sexual danger is an integral part of being female (Kelly, 1988; Stanko, 1990) and any understanding about crime control must place women's safety at the centre of the debate (see also MacKinnon, 1989). Altering definitions of what is crime, such as changes to the law of rape and encouraging police to treat what comes to their attention as criminal violence are two approaches to confronting crime against women and children. Both strategies, we argue, may lead to some thorny contradictions in resulting approaches to crime prevention, women's safety and crime control. Let us look at the two strategies of change in more detail.

Legislative change

A recent illustration of legislative change is the move towards outlawing rape in marriage in England and Wales. This was the subject of a concerted feminist campaign in the early 1980s in many countries, including the US, Canada, Australia and Sweden. Feminist arguments are arguments of principle, asserting that there could be no equality for married women while in law they could be subjected to sexual violence by their husbands without redress. From a feminist perspective this present state of law represented a clear statement about the nature of marriage and a woman's place within it, and the compulsory nature of heterosexuality itself. Recently, the British government in its decision in January 1990 to refer this matter to the Law Commission, under the supervision of Professor Brenda Hoggett, QC, has indicated its welcome for a change in law. Hoggett's own views are already on the record: 'The difficulties of proving rape are indeed formidable, particularly where a woman knows her assailant well.... There is no reason why the difficulties of proving anti-social behaviour should make us less ready to acknowledge it as a crime' (Atkins and Hoggett, 1984: 72).

What practical benefits this move will bring for women is difficult to know. We do know both that many women will welcome this legal reform and that many women are subjected to this form of abuse. The 1989 Granada Television *World in Action* survey designed by the Centre for Criminology at Middlesex Polytechnic showed that 96 percent of the 1000 women interviewed said there should be a law against rape in marriage. Further, 60 percent reported there had been occasions when they had agreed with reluctance to have sex with their husbands; 15 percent reported having been coerced by their husbands into having sex; 12 percent reported that they had been forced into having sex, despite a clear refusal; and 5 percent reported being beaten before being raped.

From these figures, it is clear that on the face of it there are real practical as well as ideological reasons for criminalizing rape in marriage. However, even Hoggett is concerned that in practice implementing such a law will be difficult. These difficulties were just one of the reasons why previous Law Commission reports have consistently rejected this change. The judiciary has systematically shown its reluctance to convict rapists when they are known to the abused woman. They are also reluctant to convict rapists on the testimony of women alone as shown in the corroboration warning, where judges in rape and sexual assault trials instruct juries to the effect that it is well known that women, like small children, are notorious liars. It seems again that a recommendation for change is largely symbolic. Perhaps the government is more concerned to improve the public image of marriage and heterosexuality, leaving all manner of practical difficulties in place to prevent large numbers of married men – practically one-third, taking the figures above in their most generous interpretation – being convicted of this crime. Removing the legal impediment will not automatically protect women from sexual abuse by their husbands.

Police practice

Feminist concern about the failure of police to protect them from violence is not new. The very inclusion of women within the police force, for instance, is grounded within the belief that women are best able to deal with women and their protection (Radford, 1990; Feinman, 1986). So when feminist criticism angrily attacked police treatment of women who reported rape or domestic violence during the 1970s in the US, the initial defensive reactions were followed by setting up special units in many forces to deal specifically with sexual assault.

Ian Blair's (1985) study of US police practices with respect to sexual assault provided the Metropolitan Police with a structure to ward off increasing public pressure about police treatment of women reporting rape. As the police began to reveal their private face to the public through Roger Graef's BBC documentary series (1982), a number of coterminous events, starkly illustrating the criminal justice insensitivity to women who had been raped, brought remarks even from Mrs Thatcher. Sir Nicholas Fairbairn, Lord Chancellor of Scotland, resigned over a decision not to prosecute three defendants in a horrendous and violent rape case (Jeffreys and Radford, 1984).

Increasingly, the police turned to their US counterparts who had already begun to alter their practice. The establishment of special examination rooms for women victimized by sexual assault, the training of women police officers in taking initial statements from women reporting rape or sexual assault and, in some jurisdictions, the referring of women to Home Office-backed victim support schemes, are examples of recent UK initiatives.

For some feminists, this last point is currently a site of controversy and struggle. Rape Crisis Centres are consciously rooted in feminist principles, women-centred, and have a unique expertise working with women whether or not they rely on police intervention into the violence they experience from men. Victim Support, a voluntary organization, contacts victims of crime through police referrals. Their government support will rise in 1991 to around £4.5 million, a 200 percent increase over 4 years. As the funding to Victim Support increases, Rape Crisis Centres and Women's Aid become starved of funding. At the same time, the majority of domestic physical and sexual assaults are never reported to police, and therefore would never be referred to Victim Support. Despite the commitment of some feminist volunteers within victim support, the philosophy of the national organization, Victim Support, is actively non-feminist. For example, there has been no commitment to guarantee that the support volunteer sent to a sexually assaulted woman be female, a stance that, to feminists, is essential to the process of women coming to terms with the experience of sexual assault. With these moves, the police seem to share an unspoken assumption with policy makers that they have now radically changed their practice and all is currently satisfactory. Police recording of sexual assault complaints has risen, due, perhaps, to careful review of no-criming procedures, encouraged by the damning evidence of the excellent Scottish study of police practices in cases of sexual assault (Chambers and Millar, 1983). Window-dressing reforms then have addressed the most glaring inadequacies in the police response to women reporting rape, public concern is apparently addressed and political debate is relocated elsewhere, but the question of male sexual violence and the police response to it has only been addressed on the most superficial of levels.

Most recently, attention has turned to police practice around domestic assault. Force orders in 1985 and Home Office guidelines concerning violence against women in 1986 and 1990, responded to criticisms from feminists working within the Women's Aid Federation, from feminist activists within Women Against Violence Against Women groups and by the Advisory Committee to Her Majesty's Government, the Women's National Commission report on *Violence against Women* (1986). Academic studies such as that by Susan Edwards (1989) in Islington, north London, showed that police response to complaints of violence within the home largely left women on their own with no legal recourse or protection against violent intimates or former intimates. In London alone, by 1991, over 40 jurisdictions have set up special units to monitor domestic violence and the most recent Home Office guidelines, of July 1990, recommend the establishment of such units in all police forces (Radford, 1990).

Here also the British police looked to their American and Canadian colleagues to witness far-reaching change in policing practice. The studies of London, Ontario (Jaffe et al., 1982), and Minneapolis (Sherman and Berk, 1984) pointed to a more aggressive policing policy to reduce violence in the home. A recent study by Horton and Smith (1988) of the Hampshire constabulary reinforced the need to do something about 'domestics': they reflected 10 percent of police calls in citizen-initiated requests for assistance.

The new policing strategy is to treat the complaints they receive from women about sexual and physical violence more often as criminal violence. To this end, in London, West Yorkshire, Wolverhampton and elsewhere specialist units have been established; some, but not all, staffed by women police officers to supervise officers' handling of 'domestics' and to provide follow-up support services. In addition to recommending that all police forces establish such units, the July 1990 Home Office Guidelines also inform officers that their primary concern should be the safety of the woman and any children involved and that in relation to the man, their first concern should be the possibility of arrest. These measures are new. Their impact has still to be noted, researched and evaluated. An aspect of the new guidelines which is already a subject of controversy is the recommendation that police forces set up a computerized 'at risk' register, naming women reporting domestic violence. This register, it is claimed, will assist the police in protecting the women concerned, yet keeping police files on 'victims' of crime is an entirely new departure and one which raises civil liberties implications. Many women, particularly black women and those whose residence status in this country is uncertain, may be deterred from reporting if they know this will give them a police record. Given the multi-agency approach of the guidelines, such a register, in the hands of social service professionals operating within a victimology perspective, will become a register of pathology listing inadequate women around whom professional intervention can be targeted with a view to retraining and reintegrating them within active family-structured heterosexuality. A vital and urgent task for feminists will be the monitoring of the impact of these new initiatives, particularly in terms of their class and race dynamics.

Criminal violence is private violence

The fact remains that many of women's experiences of coercive sexuality are not recognized in man-made law (Kelly, 1988; Stanko, 1990; Holland et al., 1990). Although the judicial authorities are now seeing more crime than previously, the problem of violence to women, largely located within their relationships with familiar and familial men, is still leading to some conceptual problems in relation to its redefinition in criminal discourse, and discourse concerning remedies and crime control strategies which still revolve around public, not private, violence.

When familial violence is recognized, the old stereotypes around race and class surface. Violence is assumed to be a characteristic of blacks and working-class families, which were then pathologized (see Ferraro, 1989 on the US; Zoomer, 1989 on Holland). If the violence is deemed the norm in 'pathological' families, then either no intervention is called for or alternatively black families are targeted for therapy to bring them into the white, nuclear family 'norm'. Conversely, in white middle-class families, the prevailing myth is that 'nice' professional men don't do it. The strength of this myth is such that some middle-class women find it hard to convince police and other state professionals that they need support.

What is interesting, however, is that the Home Office studies are now beginning to throw some light on the curious reality for women: that their attackers are most likely to be those near and dear rather than the shadowy stranger (Smith, 1989a). The most recent *British Crime Survey* (England and Wales only) found that 56 percent of the assaults against women were 'domestic' in origin. Smith's (1989b) study of rape found that two-thirds of those prosecuted for rape involved men known to the women. Forty-four percent of women killed are killed by their husbands or former lovers; 8 of 10 know their killer, according to a recent analysis of the murders between 1984 and 1988 in England and Wales (Radford and Russell, 1991).

Although there are moves within the Home Office to take this violence seriously, the policy on crime prevention has moved in the opposite direction. Crime prevention advice stems primarily from a perspective that rests prevention on situational deterrence. The 'locks and bolts' solution to crime suggests that adequate security, vigilance, and common sense reduce the likelihood of experiencing crime.

Moving the responsibility for crime prevention to the individual through adequate security and reasonable precaution, means that approaches to preventing crime necessarily focus on the danger of the unpredictable stranger who awaits opportunities for criminal enterprise. (This approach leads up to woman-blaming when protection fails. Not having taken self-defence classes is deemed provocation or negligence inviting attack.) Take for example the £11 million Home Office crime prevention campaign. Now in its third edition, *Practical Ways to Crack Crime* includes a special section advising women about safety. Although there is a paragraph about domestic violence, it appears at the end of a four-page litany addressing women's precautions at home, while on the street, and driving. (The fact that the heading for the section, *Special Advice for Women*, is subsumed under the heading *Your Family* does deserve more than a passing mention.) Women are advised to take care, to protect themselves outside the home and inside the home from outside intrusion.

If one assumes that it is women's safety that is important, then the Home Office campaign on crime prevention misses the mark by a wide margin. So too do the efforts of the newly arrived caring professionals in the field, because, we believe, they do not offer a gendered analysis about violence against women. Physical battering, according to this thinking, is either a reflection of bad marital relations, personality disputes, or intoxicating substances, not the manifestation of unequal power and a need for control. Sexual abuse, following the same line, arises because of some men's uncontrollable lust or miscommunication with women and children, not as an exercise of patriarchal power. Women, in the tradition of victimology, are often blamed as being inadequate wives or as colluding in their own harm and that of their children. The assumption, understandable in childhood, that mothers are all-knowing, is used by professionals to find mothers of abused children guilty of either collusion or 'failure to protect'. These explanations of men's violence succeed in keeping most of the violence against women outside officially used definitions of crime, and away from the only arm of the state mandated to protect – the police and the criminal justice apparatus (Stanko, 1985). Instead diversion programmes, family therapy, and men's counselling groups are the new professional growth industry. Caught up within their own paradigms, the new professionals, confident of the 'cures' they offer, are concerned with the reintegration of women and children within the family, within heterosexuality at whatever risk, and given there is little monitoring of the impact of these uncertain remedies, there must certainly be serious risks.

This then is the heart of the contradiction facing feminists. On the face of it the police and caring professions have responded – albeit for a complex range of reasons – to feminist criticisms of the 1970s, but have done so in a way which has completely negated feminist definitions, politics, research and provision of support services. Not only this, but these interventions are part of a wider attempt on the part of an authoritarian right-wing populist government to win public support for their law and order policies, and these attempts are seductive to some white middle-class women. In terms of policing the velvet glove of a caring police force goes hand-in-hand with the iron fist of riot control and militaristic policing in the 'inner city'. One feminist response has been to monitor these moves, identify and bring together these developments, with a view to understanding at the level of practice as well as ideology. In this chapter we have not attempted to solve these contradictions, but at least to identify them and their complex roots. Identifying a contradiction is a step on the road to resolving it. Certainly, within the politics of feminism, the move into the 1990s has seen a renewed commitment to defend feminist politics and practice and identify and challenge the professional takeover.

Central to the challenge of the professional takeover must be an insistent statement of feminist politics and reinstatement of feminist practice. In relation to violence against women and children, our politics are informed by women's experiences. From feminist support and research work as cited above, we have come to understand that violence, far from being an aberrant experience in our lives or the experience of aberrant women, is in fact the backdrop against which women's lives are lived. We have come to see male sexual violence as one of the defining characteristics of patriarchal societies. While the form and nature of male sexual violence may be situationally defined and thus varied across culture and through time, the presence of male violence is, we argue, a feature of all societies characterized by male supremacy and female subordination – the social relations of patriarchy. It serves as a means of reinforcing women's role as subordinate to men, in the public world, at work and primarily, as both feminist and the Home Office's own research has documented, in the home – in the family.

The family, and the institution of heterosexuality which underpins it, is a central institution in patriarchal society, one in which the private struggles around patriarchal power relations are enacted, and hence one in which violence frequently features as a form of control of the powerless by the powerful. It is not limited to the family, however, as in the public sphere and in paid employment women are outside heterosexuality, or give the appearance of being marginal to it, are those primarily targeted for sexual violence, abuse and harassment, as the amount of violence experienced by lesbians and other women marginal to the white middle-class, ageist and able-bodied image of heterosexual 'normality' status. This is a central point of Adrienne Rich's (1983) classic article, 'Compulsory heterosexuality and lesbian existence'.

Controlling crime against women and children, as we see it, demands policy and practice that confronts men's licence to abuse. However, the state's concern about male sexual violence in the family can be seen as an attempt at policing the family and heterosexuality in order to clean up its public face and to restore its legitimacy as a safe institution for women, by curbing that violence which it can no longer hide. So by moving towards curbing the excesses of male sexual violence within the family and heterosexuality, these sacred institutions of patriarchy are preserved intact and patriarchal gendered relations are reaffirmed, reproduced and represented as in the best interests of women and children. Achieving this requires a silencing of any feminist politics which asks disturbing questions about whether heterosexuality is the natural, normal and only possibility for women, whether it is indeed voluntary or compulsory for women living under conditions of patriarchy and whether it is in our best interests. We will continue to ask: is this new concern with violence to women on the part of the state's police and professional carers a concern with women's interests, a concern for women's autonomy, or is it a last ditch attempt at reinstating the patriarchal status quo by restoring an apparently respectable face to its central institutions, the family and heterosexuality?

References

Alderson, J. (1979) *Policing Freedom: a Commentary on the Dilemmas of Policing in Western Democracies.* Plymouth: McDonald and Evans.

Atkins, S. and Hoggett, B. (1984) *Women and the Law.* Oxford: Basil Blackwell.

Blair, I. (1985) *Investigating Rape.* London: Croom Helm.

Cameron, D. (1988) *Lust to Kill.* Oxford: Polity.

Caputi, J. (1988) *The Age of Sex Crime.* New Mexico: Bowling Green Press.

Chambers, G. and Millar, A. (1983) *Investigating Sexual Assault.* Edinburgh: HMSO.

Cohen, L.E. and Felson, M. (1979) 'Social change and crime rate trends: a routine activity approach', *American Sociological Review*, 44 (4): 588–608.

Edwards, S. (1989) *Policing 'Domestic' Violence.* London: Sage.

Feinman, C. (1986) *Women and Criminal Justice.* New York: Pergamon.

Ferraro, K. (1989) 'The legal response to woman battering in the United States', in J. Hanmer, J. Radford and E.A. Stanko (eds), *Women, Policing and Male Violence.* London: Routledge.

Gottfredson, M. (1984) *Victims of Crime: Dimensions of Risk.* London: HMSO.

Hall, R. (1985) *Ask Any Woman.* London: Falling Wall Press.

Hanmer, J., Radford, J. and Stanko, E.A. (1989) *Women, Policing and Male Violence.* London: Routledge.

Hanmer, J. and Saunders, S. (1984) *Well Founded Fear.* London: Hutchinson.

Hindelang, M., Gottfredson, M. and Garofalo, J. (1978) *Victims of Personal Crime.* Cambridge, MA: Ballinger.

Holland, J., Ramazanlou, C. and Scott, S. (1990) 'Managing risk and experiencing danger: tensions between government AIDS educational policy and young women's sexuality', *Gender and Education*, July.

Horton, C. and Smith, D. (1988) *Evaluating Police Work: An Action Research Project.* London: Policy Studies Institute.

Hough, M. and Mayhew, P. (1983) *The British Crime Survey.* London: HMSO.

Hough, M. and Mayhew, P. (1985) *Taking Account of Crime.* London: HMSO.

Jaffe, P., Wolfe, D., Telford, A. and Austin, G. (1982) 'The impact of police charges in incidents of wife abuse', *Journal of Family Violence* 1 (1): 37–49.

Jeffreys, S. and Radford, J. (1984) 'Contributory negligence: being a woman', in P. Scraton and P. Gordon (eds) *Causes for Concern.* London: Penguin.

Kelly, L. and Radford, J. (1987) 'The problem of men', in P. Scraton (ed.), *Law, Order and the Authoritarian State.* Milton Keynes: Open University Press.

Kelly, L. (1988) *Surviving Sexual Violence.* Oxford: Polity.

Kelly, L. (1989) 'Bitter ironies: the professionalisation of child sex abuse', *Trouble and Strife*, 16, Summer.

MacKinnon, C.A. (1989) *Toward a Feminist Theory of the State.* Cambridge, MA: Harvard University Press.

Mama, A. (1989) *The Hidden Struggle: Statutory and Voluntary Sector Responses to Violence against Black Women in the Home.* Published by The London Race and Housing Research Group, c/o The Runnymede Trust, 11 Princelet St, London E1 6QH.

Maxfield, M. (1984) *Fear of Crime in England and Wales.* London: HMSO.

Maxfield, M. (1988) *Explaining Fear of Crime: Evidence from the 1984 British Crime Survey.* London: Research and Planning Unit Paper No. 43.

Mayhew, P., Dowds, L. and Elliot, D. (1989) *The 1988 British Crime Survey.* London: HMSO.

Radford, J. (1987) 'Policing male violence – policing women', in J. Hanmer and

M. Maynard (eds), *Women, Violence and Social Control.* London: Macmillan.

Radford, J. (1990) 'Sorry, sir, it's domestic. You're nicked', *Rights of Women Bulletin,* Autumn.

Radford, J. and Russell, D.E.H. (1991) *Femicide: The Politics of Woman Killing.* Milton Keynes: Open University Press.

Rich, A. (1983) *Compulsory Heterosexuality and Lesbian Existence.* London: Onlywomen Press.

Russell, D.E.H. (1982) *Rape in Marriage.* New York: Macmillan.

Russell, D.E.H. (1984) *Sexual Exploitation.* Beverly Hills: Sage.

Russell, D.E.H. (1985) *Incest: The Secret Trauma.* New York: Basic Books.

Scheppele, K. and Bart, P. (1983) 'Through women's eyes: defining danger in the wake of sexual assault', *Journal of Social Issues,* 39 (2): 63–81.

Sherman, L. and Berk, R. (1984) 'The specific deterrent effects of arrest for domestic assault', *American Sociological Review,* 49 (2): 261–72.

Sim, J., Scraton, P. and Gordon, P. (1987) 'Introduction', in P. Scraton (ed.), *Law, Order and the Authoritarian State.* Milton Keynes: Open University Press.

Smart, C. (1989) *Feminism and the Power of the Law.* London: Routledge.

Smith, D. and Gray, J. (1983) *Police and People in London.* London: Policy Studies Institute.

Smith, L.J.F. (1989a) *Domestic Violence.* London: HMSO.

Smith, L.J.F. (1989b) *Concerns about Rape.* London: HMSO.

Stanko, E.A. (1985) *Intimate Intrusions.* London: Unwin Hyman.

Stanko, E.A. (1987) 'Typical violence, normal precaution: men, women and interpersonal violence in England, Wales, Scotland and the USA', in J. Hanmer and M. Maynard (eds), *Women, Violence and Social Control.* London: Macmillan.

Stanko, E.A. (1988) 'Hidden violence to women', in M. Maguire and J. Pointing (eds), *Victims of Crime: A New Deal?* Milton Keynes: Open University Press.

Stanko, E. (1990) *Everyday Violence.* London: Pandora.

Zoomer, O. (1989) 'Policing woman beating in the Netherlands', in J. Hanmer, J. Radford and E.A. Stanko (eds), *Women, Policing and Male Violence.* London: Routledge.

10

Abolitionism and Crime Control: a Contradiction in Terms

Willem de Haan

An abolitionist perspective on crime control might seem like a contradiction in terms not unlike a peace research approach to waging a war. Abolitionism is based on the moral conviction that social life should not and, in fact, cannot be regulated effectively by criminal law and that, therefore, the role of the criminal justice system should be drastically reduced while other ways of dealing with problematic situations, behaviours and events are being developed and put into practice. Abolitionists regard crime primarily as the result of the social order and are convinced that punishment is not the appropriate reaction. Instead a minimum of coercion and interference with the personal lives of those involved and a maximum amount of care and service for all members of society is advocated.

The term 'abolitionism' stands for a social movement, a theoretical perspective, and a political strategy. As a social movement committed to the abolition of the prison or even the entire penal system, abolitionism originated in campaigns for prisoners' rights and penal reform. Subsequently, it developed into a critical theory and praxis concerning crime, punishment and penal reform. As a theoretical perspective, abolitionism takes on the twofold task of providing a radical critique of the criminal justice system while showing that there are other, more rational ways of dealing with crime. As a political strategy, abolitionism is based on an analysis of penal reform and restricted to negative reforms, such as abolishing parts of the prison system, rather than providing concrete alternatives.

In this chapter, the abolitionist perspective will be discussed along the lines of this distinction. First, we will deal with abolitionism as a penal reform movement, then as a theoretical perspective on crime and punishment and, more specifically, the prison. Next, a conceptualization of the notions of crime and punishment will be offered in the form of the concept of redress. At the same time, strategies for penal reform will be examined. Finally, the implications of the abolitionist perspective for crime control will be discussed. In conclusion, it will be argued that what is needed is a wide variety of social responses rather than a uniform state reaction to the problem of crime. In policy terms it is claimed that social policy instead of crime policy is needed in dealing with the social problems and conflicts that are currently singled out as the problem of crime.

Abolitionism as a social movement

Abolitionism emerged as an anti-prison movement when, at the end of the 1960s, a destructuring impulse took hold of thinking about the social control of deviance and crime among other areas (Cohen, 1985). In Western Europe, anti-prison groups aiming at prison abolition were founded in Sweden and Denmark (1967) Finland and Norway (1968), Great Britain (1970), France (1970), and the Netherlands (1971). Their main objective was to soften the suffering which society inflicts on its prisoners. This implied a change in general thinking concerning punishment, humanization of the various forms of imprisonment in the short run and, in the long run, the replacement of the prison system by more adequate and up-to-date measures of crime control.

It has been suggested that abolitionism typically emerged in small countries or countries with little crime and 'would never have been "invented" in a country like the United States of America with its enormous crime rate, violence, and criminal justice apparatus' (Scheerer, 1986: 18). However, in Canada and the United States family members of (ex-)convicts, church groups and individuals were also engaged in prisoners' support work and actively struggling for prison reform. More specifically, these prison abolitionists in the United States considered their struggle for abolition of prisons to be a historical mission, a continuation and fulfilment of the struggle against slavery waged by their forebears. Imprisonment is seen as a form of blasphemy, as morally objectionable and indefensible and, therefore, to be abolished (Morris, 1976: 11). To this aim, a long-term strategy in the form of a three-step 'attrition model' is proposed, consisting of a total freeze on the planning and building of prisons, excarceration of certain categories of lawbreakers by diverting them from the prison system and decarceration, or the release of as many inmates as possible.

Originating in prison reform movements in the 1960s and 1970s in both Western Europe and North America, abolitionism developed as a new paradigm in (critical) criminology and as an alternative approach to crime control. As academic involvement increased and abolitionism became a theoretical perspective, its focus widened from the prison system to the penal system, thereby engaging in critical analyses of penal discourse and, in particular, the concepts of crime and punishment, penal practices, and the penal or criminal justice system.

Abolitionism as a theoretical perspective

As a theoretical perspective abolitionism has a negative and a positive side. Negatively, abolitionism is deeply rooted in a criticism of the criminal justice system and its 'prison solution' to the problem of crime. Positively, on the basis of this criticism an alternative approach to crime and punishment is offered both in theory and in practice. Thus, the abolitionist approach is essentially reflexive and (de)constructivist. We will first take a look at the negative side of abolitionism which will be followed by a brief exposé of its positive side.

From the abolitionist point of view, the criminal justice system's claim to protect people from being victimized by preventing and controlling crime, seems grossly exaggerated. Moreover, the notion of controlling crime by penal intervention is ethically problematic as people are used for the purpose of 'deterrence', by demonstrating power and domination. Punishment is seen as a self-reproducing form of violence. The penal practice of blaming people for their supposed intentions (for being bad and then punishing and degrading them accordingly) is dangerous because the social conditions for recidivism are thus reproduced. Morally degrading and segregating people is especially risky when the logic of exclusion is reinforced along the lines of differences in sex, race, class, culture or religion.

For the abolitionist, current crime policies are irrational in their assumptions that: crime is caused by individuals who for some reason go wrong; that crime is a problem for the state and its criminal justice system to control; and that criminal law and punishment or treatment of individual wrongdoers are appropriate means of crime control (Steinert, 1986). Crime control is based on the fallacy of taking *pars pro toto* or, as Wilkins (1984) has put it, crime control policy is typically made by reference to the dramatic incident, thereby assuming that all that is necessary is to get the micro-model right in order for the macro-model to follow without further ado. According to Wilkins, we must consider not only the specific criminal act but also the environment in which it is embedded. It could be added that the same argument holds for punishment and, more specifically, for imprisonment as an alleged solution to the problem of crime.

Abolitionism about prison

For abolitionists, the United States is a prime example of a country suffering from the consequences of a punitive obsession. In the course of a 'get tough' policy of crime control, increasing numbers of people are being sent to prison for longer periods of time. As a result, the prison population in the United States has increased dramatically from roughly 350,000 in the 1970s to 850,000 at the end of the 1980s. Almost 80 percent of the recent increase in prison admissions is accounted for by drugs offenders. By September 1988 about 44 percent of all federal prisoners were incarcerated for drug law violations. According to the 1989 National Council of Crime and Delinquency Prison Population Forecast the impact of the 'war on drugs' will be yet another increase of the prison population 1989–1994 by over 68 percent to a total of 1,133,000 prisoners among whom people of colour will remain strongly overrepresented. With an incarceration rate of 440 prisoners per 100,000 population, the United States will more than consolidate its top rank position in the world. Even with its incarceration rate increasing from about 30 in 1980 to about 50 in the mid-1990s, the Netherlands will remain at the bottom end of the scale. At the same time, the crime problem in the Netherlands can hardly be considered worse than in the United States.

As in the United States, 'street crime' is also considered a major social problem in the Netherlands. In fact, the first International Crime Survey (van Dijk et al., 1990) showed that overall victimization rates 1983–1988 in the United States and the Netherlands were higher than in any other country in the survey. However, there were considerable differences both in the seriousness of the crime problem and the effectiveness of its control. Whereas overall victimization rates in the Netherlands and the United States were similarly high, in the Dutch case this was strongly influenced by the extraordinarily high prevalence of bicycle theft, whereas victimization rates for homicide, robbery and (sexual) assault were particularly high in the United States.

If anything, this proves that the relationship between crime and crime control by imprisonment is much more complex than proponents of the prison solution seem to assume. In terms of protection the 'get tough' approach to crime control has little to offer, and the 'war on drugs' can never be won but has serious repercussions.

Taken together, the prison system is counter-productive, difficult to control, and itself a major social problem. Therefore, abolitionists have given up entirely on the idea that the criminal justice system has anything to offer in terms of protection. They are also pessimistic about the criminal law's potential for conflict resolution. It is felt that the present penal system is making things worse, not better.

In the course of the 'war against drugs' which is currently being waged in the United States and many other countries around the world, the use of ethically problematic techniques for apprehending suspects is being condoned if not required. As a result various forms of organizational complicity undermine the already waning legitimacy of the criminal justice system even further. According to Roshier (1989), the 'war against drugs' must be seen as a forced attempt to reach efficiency in the field of law enforcement or, at least, the appearance of it by using purely technical or even military means of surveillance and policing. It is the criminal justice system that defines, selects, documents and disposes of crime. As a result, legal definitions of suspicion, criminal offence, etc, are being stretched. Thus, the criminal justice system itself increasingly specifies both the nature of the crime problem and what is to be done about it (Roshier, 1989: 128).

Thus, the criminal justice system is part of the crime problem rather than its solution. Not only does it fail to work in terms of its own stated goals and not only are the negative consequences of the infliction of suffering by the state threatening to get out of hand but, more importantly, it is based on a fundamentally flawed way of understanding. Therefore, there is no point in trying to make the criminal justice system more effective or more just. The abolitionist critique of the criminal justice system and its approach to crime control may be summarized by saying that if this is the solution, what is the problem? Or, put differently, crime as a social problem and object of social analysis needs to be rethought.

Abolitionism about 'crime'

The current approach to crime control, the definition of crime and the justification of punishment is 'systemic', that is, based on an instrumentalist point of view and confined within the limits of the criminal justice system. From an abolitionist point of view, these issues require a fundamental reconceptualization in a broader social context. This is where the alternative, positive side of abolitionism starts from. Abolitionists argue that there is no such thing as 'crime'. In fact, 'the very form of criminal law, with its conception of "crime" (not just the contents of what is at a given time and place defined into that category, but the category itself) and the ideas on what is to be done about it, are historical "inventions"' (Steinert, 1986: 26). 'Crime' is a social construction, to be analysed as a myth of everyday life (Hess, 1986). As a myth, crime serves to maintain political power relations and lends legitimacy to the expansion of the crime control apparatus and the intensification of surveillance and control. It justifies inequality and relative deprivation. Public attention is distracted from more serious problems and injustices. Thus, the bigger the social problems are, the greater the need for the crime myth (Hess, 1986: 24–25).

However, not only should the concept of crime be discarded (Hulsman, 1986), but we need to get rid of the theories of crime as well. As Quensel (1987) has pointed out, theories about 'crime' acquire their plausibility largely by virtue of their building on and, at the same time, reinforcing an already-present 'deep structure'. One element of this 'deep structure' is the notion that 'crime' is inherently dangerous and wicked; another is that crime control is a 'value-inspired' call for action against that evil (p. 129).

Abolitionists argue that the crucial problem is not explaining but rather understanding crime as a social event. Thus, what we need is not a better theory of crime, but a more powerful critique of crime. This is not to deny that there are all sorts of unfortunate events, more or less serious troubles or conflicts which can result in suffering, harm, or damage to a greater or lesser degree. These troubles are to be taken seriously, of course, but not as 'crimes' and, in any case, they should not be dealt with by means of criminal law. When we fully appreciate the complexity of a 'crime' as a socially constructed phenomenon any simplified reaction to crime in the form of punishment becomes problematic.

Spector (1981) has argued that when a person offends, disturbs, or injures other people, various forms of social disapproval exist to remedy the situation. The matter may be treated as a disease, a sin, or, indeed as a crime. However, other responses are also feasible like considering the case as a private conflict between the offender and the victim or defining the situation in an administrative way and responding, for example by denial of a licence, permit, benefit or compensation. Our images, language, categories, knowledge, beliefs and fears of troublemakers are subject to constant changes. Nevertheless, crime continues to occupy a central place in our thinking about troublesome people (1981: 154). Spector suggests that, perhaps, 'we pay too much attention to crime because the disciplines that study trouble and disapprove – sociology and criminology – were born precisely in the era when crime was at its zenith' (Spector, 1981; Quensel, 1987).

The concept of 'crime' figures prominently in common sense and has definite effects on it. By focusing public attention on a definite class of events, these 'crimes' can then be almost automatically seen as meriting punitive control. 'Punishment' is thereby regarded as the obvious and proper reaction to 'crime'.

Abolitionism about punishment

Abolitionists do not share the current belief in the criminal law's capacity for crime control. They radically deny the utility of punishment and claim that there can be no valid justification for it, particularly since other options are available for law enforcement. They discard criminal justice as an absurd idea. It is ridiculous to claim that one pain can or, indeed, ought to be compensated by another state-inflicted one. According to them, the 'prison solution' affects the moral quality of life in society at large. Therefore, the criminal justice perspective needs to be replaced by an orientation towards all avoidance of harm and pain (Steinert, 1986: 25). Christie (1982), particularly, has attacked the traditional justifications for punishment. He criticizes deterrence theory for its sloppy definitions of concepts, its immunity to challenge, and for the fact that it gives the routine process of punishment a false legitimacy in an epoch where the infliction of pain might otherwise have appeared problematic. The neo-classicism of the justice model is also criticized: punishment is justified and objectified, the criminal is blamed, the victim is ignored, a broad conception of justice is lacking, and a 'hidden message' is transmitted which denies legitimacy to a whole series of alternatives which should, in fact, be taken into consideration. However, Christie not only criticizes the 'supposed justifications' for punishment, but also claims a decidedly moral position with regard to punishment, which is the intentional infliction of pain which he calls 'moral rigorism'. He deliberately co-opts the terms 'moralism' and 'rigorism' associated primarily with protagonists of 'law and order' and more severe penal sanctions. His 'rigorist' position, however, is that there is no reason to believe that the recent level of pain infliction is the right or natural one and that there is no other defensible position than to strive for a reduction of man-inflicted pain on earth. Since punishment is defined as pain, limiting pain means an automatic reduction of punishment.

More recently, Christie and Mathiesen have both suggested that the expansion of the prison system involves general ethical and political questions such as what could be the effects of all the punishments taken together? What would constitute an acceptable level of punishment in society? What would be the right prison population within a country? How should we treat fellow human beings? And, last but not least, how do we want to meet the crime problem? (Christie, 1986; Mathiesen, 1986).

However, in common-sense and legal discourse alike, 'crime' and 'punishment' continue to be seen 'as independent species – without reference to their sameness or how continuity of both depends on the character of dominating institutions' (Kennedy, 1974: 107). It should be kept in mind, however, that crime comprises but one of several kinds of all norm violations, that punishment is but one of many kinds of reprisals against such violations, that criteria for separating them refer to phenomena external to actual behaviours classed by legal procedure as crime versus punishment, and that even within the criminal law itself, the criteria by which crime is identified procedurally apply with equal validity to punishment (Kennedy, 1974: 108).

Criminology needs to rid itself of those theories of punishment which assume there are universal qualities in forms of punishment or assume a straightforward connection between crime and punishment. Given the perseverance of this conventional notion of 'punishment' as essentially a 'good' against an 'evil', any effort at changing common-sense notions of 'crime' and 'crime control' requires a reconceptualization of both concepts: 'crime' and 'punishment'.

Redress

We need to concern ourselves with the interrelationship and combined effects of crime and punishment. Crime and punishment are closely related with 'social negativity' (Baratta, 1986), destructive developments within contemporary society, in particular, as they affect its already most vulnerable members. In order to formulate a convincing politics of penal reform, crime and punishment should not be seen as action and reaction, but as spiralling cycles of harm (Pepinsky, 1986).

Elsewhere, I have introduced the concept of 'redress' as an alternative to both the concepts of 'punishment' and 'crime' (de Haan, 1990). This seemingly 'obsolete' concept carries an elaborate set of different meanings. The *Concise Oxford Dictionary* offers a wide variety of meanings for 'redress': for instance, to put right or in good order again, to remedy or remove trouble of any kind, to set right, repair, rectify something suffered or complained of like a wrong, to correct, amend, reform or do away with a bad or faulty state of things, to repair an action, to atone a misdeed or offence, to save, deliver from misery, to restore or bring back a person to a proper state, to happiness or prosperity, to the right course, to set a person right by obtaining or (more rarely) giving satisfaction or compensation for the wrong or loss sustained, teaching, instructing and redressing the erroneous by reason (Sixth Edition, 1976: 937).

To claim redress is merely to assert that an undesirable event has taken place and that something needs to be done about it. It carries no implications concerning what sort of reaction would be appropriate; nor does it define reflexively the nature of the initial event. Since claiming redress invites an open discussion about how an unfortunate event should be viewed and what the appropriate response ought to be, it can be viewed as a rational response par excellence. It puts forth the claim for a procedure rather than for a specific result. Punitive claims already implied in defining an event as a 'crime' are opened up to rational debate. Thus, to advocate 'redress' is to call for 'real dialogue' (Christie, 1982). Christie has suggested that social systems be constructed in ways that 'crimes' are more easily seen as expressions of conflicting interests, thereby becoming a starting point for a 'real dialogue' (1982: 11).

The conceptual innovation suggested here offers a perspective for a politics of redress, aimed at the construction and implementation of procedures along the lines of an ethic of practical discourse. As we have seen, the handling of normative conflicts by rational discourse presupposes other procedures than the present criminal ones. In order to increase chances for participation for those involved, procedures based on the rules and preconditions of rational discourse would, therefore, need to be established outside the realm of criminal law; that is in civil law or even in the life world itself. Instead of the panacea which the criminal justice system pretends to provide for problems of crime control, abolitionism seeks to remedy social problems, conflicts, or troubles within the context of the real world, taking seriously the experiences of those directly involved and taking into account too the diversity which is inherent of the social world. The aim of a politics of redress would be to 'arrange it so that the conflict settling mechanisms themselves, through their organization reflect the type of society we should like to see reflected and help this type of society come into being' (Christie, 1982: 113). Social problems or conflicts might be absorbed in order to use them as valuable aids to the social integration of real life and the prevention of social harm.

Abolitionism assumes that social problems or conflicts are unavoidable as they are inherent to social life as such. Therefore, they will have to be dealt with in one way or another. Rather than delegating them to professional specialists, however, they should be dealt with under conditions of mutuality and solidarity. These very conditions will have to be created by social and political action.

The urgent question that remains, of course, is how this might be done. To begin with, no single solution to the problem should be expected. Taking into account the diversity of relevant social phenomena requires the development of a wide variety of forms of social regulation which are not located in or defined by the state but operate (semi-)autonomously as alternative, progressive and emancipatory forms of dispute settlement and conflict resolution.

In reaction to the deeply felt dissatisfaction with the present penal system and, more generally, with the legal system, we see an increasing interest in 'autonomous' forms of conflict resolution and dispute settlement. Other 'styles of social control' (Black, 1976: 4–5) are seen as attractive, promising to provide the parties involved with more chances for participation in settling a dispute or problem.

The aim is compensation rather than retaliation; reconciliation rather than blame allocation. To this end, the criminal justice system needs to be decentralized and neighbourhood courts established as a complement or substitute.

The development of alternative procedures for conflict resolution and dispute settlement faces some rather ticklish questions which have proved intractable in current debates, questions concerning voluntarism versus determinism, 'accountability', 'responsibility' and 'guilt', that is, the moral evaluation of behaviour, the fair allocation of blame and the proper dissemination of consequences. Emphasis on participatory processes of definition or the contextuality of conflicts may be welcome, but it can also lead to problematic outcomes. Among the wide variety of reactions the notion of redress entails there might be sanctions which need to be subjected to legal principles and restraints. For these reasons, legal form is still required to ensure fairness. Just as we need sociological imagination to ensure an open discussion, we need legal imagination to be able to put an end to potentially endless debates as well as allow for the possibility of appeal.

However, by allowing for more complexity in the interpretation of social behaviour, social situations and events, the simplistic image of human beings and their activities currently employed in criminal law and reproduced in criminal justice could be avoided. Through contextualization, the dichotomized character of criminal justice (Christie, 1986: 96) could be replaced with a continuum. Participants would be urged to confront and grapple with complexities around notions of human 'agency', 'intentionality', 'responsibility' and 'guilt' rather than reducing them to manageable proportions by applying the binary logic of criminal law. By dropping the simplistic dichotomies of the criminal law and allowing for differential meanings, justice might finally be done to the complexity of human actions and social events. Such a discourse would feature a concept of 'social responsibility' allowing for interpretations which primarily blame social systems rather than individuals (Christie, 1986: 97).

Abolitionism as a political strategy

Initially, a political strategy had been developed on the bases of the experiences of prison reform groups in their political struggle for penal and social reform. This 'politics of abolition' (Mathiesen, 1974, 1986) consistently refuses to offer 'positive' alternatives or solutions. It restricts itself to advancing open-ended, 'unfinished', 'negative' reforms, such as abolishing parts of the prison system. This requires that they be conceptualized in terms alien to current criminal justice discourse.

More recently, positive alternatives to punishment are also being considered. Various proposals have been made by abolitionists and others to decentralize or even completely dismantle the present penal system in order to create forms of 'informal justice' as an addition to or replacement of the present criminal justice system.

Their implementation also raises many questions, however, concerning allegations about widening the net of social control and, at the same time, thinning the mesh, extending and blurring the boundaries between formal penal intervention and other, informal forms of social control, thereby masking the coercive character of alternative interventions (Abel, 1982: Cohen, 1985).

Fundamental reform of the penal system requires not only imaginative alternatives but, at the same time, a radical change in the power structure. Thus a 'politics of abolition' aims at a negative strategy for changing the politics of punishment by abolishing not only the criminal justice system but also the repressive capitalist system part by part or step by step (Mathiesen, 1986).

A fundamental reform of the penal system presupposes not only a radical change of the existing power structure but also of the dominant culture. However, currently there is no appropriate social agency for any radical reform of the politics of punishment. There seems no immediate social basis upon which a progressive, let alone an abolitionist, strategy of crime control might be spontaneously constructed (Matthews, 1987: 389). Abolitionists tend to refer to the re-emergence of the subcultures of the new social movements with their own infrastructure of interaction and communication and their new ethics of solidarity, social responsibility, and care (Steinert, 1986: 28-9; see also Christie, 1982: 75-80). As Harris argues, the inadequacy of virtually all existing reform proposals lies in the failure to stop outside the traditional and dominant ways of framing the issues. To explore alternative visions of justice we need to consider 'philosophies, paradigms, or models that transcend not only conventional criminological and political lines, but also natural and cultural boundaries and other limiting habits of the mind' (Harris, 1987: 11). According to Harris a wide range of visions of a better world and a better future offer a rich resource for a fundamental rethinking of our approach to crime and justice. The new social movements, in particular the women's movement, have pointed out fundamental weaknesses or biases in criminology's background assumptions, conceptual frameworks, methodology and tacit morality (Gelsthorpe and Morris, 1990). However, the relationship between abolitionism and, for example, feminism is not without stress (van Swaaningen, 1989).

Abolitionism on crime control

Abolitionism argues for a structural approach to the prevention of 'social negativity', or redressing problematic situations by taking social problems, conflicts and troubles seriously but not as 'crime'. Therefore, abolitionism argues for social policy rather than crime control policy. Examples of this structural approach would be dealing with drug problems in terms of mental health, with violence in terms of social pathology, and with property crime in terms of economy.

Abolitionism calls for decriminalization, depenalization, destigmatization, decentralization and deprofessionalization, as well as the establishment of other, informal, participator, (semi-)autonomous ways of dealing with social problems. Problematic events may just as well be defined as social troubles, problems or conflicts due to negligence or caused by 'accident' rather than by purpose or criminal intent. What is needed is a wide variety of possible responses without a priori assuming criminal intent and responsibility.

As we have seen, prison abolition, let alone penal abolition, requires an imaginative rethinking of possible ways of handling problematic situations as social problems, conflicts, troubles, accidents, etc, as well as reconceptualizing punishment and developing new ways of managing 'deviance' on the basis of, at least partial, suspension of the logic of guilt and punishment. Without fixation on individual guilt, responsibility and punishment, 'crimes' would appear as 'conflicts', 'accidents' or 'problematic events' to be dealt with in a more reasonable and caring way by using forms of conflict management which are not exclusively geared towards individuals and confined to the limitations of criminal law in the books as well as in action (Steinert, 1986: 30). Therefore, abolitionists focus instead on extra-legal, autonomous ways for dealing with social problems and conflicts involving offences. The abolitionist challenge to abolish the present prison system now is to construct more participatory, popular or socialist forms of penality (Garland and Young, 1983).

This way of looking at crime and crime control is, of course, controversial. The abolitionist perspective is sometimes criticised for being naive and idealistic. In practice, however, the abolitionist approach turns out to be realistic in that social problems and conflicts are seen as inherent to social life. Since it is illusory that the criminal justice system can protect us effectively against such unfortunate events, it seems more reasonable to deal with troubles pragmatically rather than by approaching them in terms of guilt and punishment. Effectively to prevent and control unacceptable situations and behaviours requires a variety of social responses, one and only one of which is the criminal justice system. Its interventions are more of symbolic importance than of practical value. With some social, technical and organizational imagination 'crime' could be coped with in ways much more caring for those immediately involved. A variety of procedures could be established and institutionalized where social problems or conflicts, problematic events or behaviours could be dealt with through negotiation, mediation, arbitration, at intermediate levels. For dealing with the most common or garden varieties of crime, which is in any case the vast bulk of all recorded criminality, criminal prosecutions are simply redundant.

Certainly for those who are most directly concerned there is little or no benefit. Also in such cases as state or corporate crime where a full abolitionist agenda of dispute settlement – like the criminal justice approach – has profound limitations, it does make sense to look for more workable alternatives to the criminal justice system's mechanisms of apprehension, judgment and punishment. Most of these problems could be dealt with by means of economic, administrative, environmental, health or labour law, rather than by criminal law. Even in cases where a person has become an unacceptable burden to his or her relatives or community, imprisonment could be avoided. Agreements might be reached or orders might be given about temporary or permanent limitations in access to certain people, places or situations. The problems of the really bad and the really mad remain. In these relatively few cases and by way of last resort it might be unavoidable to deprive someone of their liberty, at least for the time being. This exceptional decision should be simply in order to incapacitate and be carried out in a humane way, that is as a morally problematic decision in a dilemma. However, even in these cases it would make sense to look for more just and humane alternatives based on mutual aid, good neighbourliness and real community rather than continue to rely on the solutions of bureaucracies, professionals and the centralized state. Criticism of the inhumanity and irrationality of the prison solution is as valid today as it was 20 or 70 years ago. Therefore, Cohen suggests that three interrelated strategies be followed: first, cultivating an experimental and inductive attitude to the actual historical record of alternatives, innovations and experiments; secondly, being sensitive, not just to failures, co-options and con-tricks, but to success stories – the criterion for success should be, and can be nothing other than, an approximation to preferred values; and thirdly, escaping the clutches of criminology (radical or realistic) by expanding the subject of social control way beyond the scope of the criminal justice system (for example, to systems of informal justice, utopian communes and experiments in self-help) (Cohen, 1988: 131).

In countries with an elaborate welfare system like the Scandinavian countries or the Netherlands, these strategies may seem more reasonable given that their crime problem is less dramatic and, traditionally, their crime control policy is already more cautious. In the context of a relatively mild penal climate with a pragmatic and reductionist penal policy already being implemented, even penal abolition may seem realistic as a long-term goal. However, in those countries where prison populations are enormous and penal institutions are simply 'warehousing' people in order to incapacitate them from reoffending, prison abolition is more acute. When in the early 1970s several commissions and task forces concluded that the American prison system is beyond reform and, therefore, other ways of dealing with criminal offenders need to be developed, the prison population was about one-third of the current one. These criticisms hold true even more, under the present conditions of overcrowding in the prisons. Prisons are places where a lot more harm is done than is necessary or legitimate. Moreover, these institutions contribute to a further brutalization of social conditions. Even in the United States where average prison sentences are much longer than for example in the Netherlands, 99 percent of the prison population will sooner or later hit the streets again. Therefore, there is a definite need not only for prison reform but also for penal reform. Current crime control policy boils down to doing more of the same. In the long run, however, the resulting spiral of harm needs to be reversed in a downward direction. This can only be achieved by doing more rather than less, albeit not more of the same but more of what generally might be called care.

I wish to thank René van Swaaningen for his helpful comments.

References

Abel, R. (ed.) (1982) *The Politics of Informal Justice*, Vols 1 and 2, New York: Academic Press.

Baratta, A. (1986) 'Soziale Probleme und Konstruktion der Kriminalität', *Kriminologisches Journal*, 1: 200–18.

Black, D. (1976) *The Behavior of Law*. New York: Academic Press.

Christie, N. (1982) *Limits to Pain*. Oxford: Martin Robertson.

Christie, N. (1986) 'Images of man in modern penal law', *Contemporary Crises*, 10: 95–106.

Cohen, S. (1985) *Visions of Social Control. Crime, Punishment and Classification*. Cambridge: Polity Press.

Cohen, S. (1988) *Against Criminology*. New York: Transaction Books.

van Dijk, J., Mayhew, P. and Killias, M. (1990) *Experiences of Crime across the World. Key findings from the 1989 International Crime Survey*. Boston: Kluwer.

Garland, D. and Young, P. (1983) 'Towards a social analysis of penality', in D. Garland and P. Young (eds), *The Power to Punish. Contemporary Penality and Social Analysis*. London: Heinemann. pp. 1–36.

Gelsthorpe, L. and Morris, A. (eds) (1990) *Feminist Perspectives in Criminology*. Milton Keynes: Open University Press.

Haan, W. de (1990) *The Politics of Redress. Crime, Punishment and Penal Abolition.* London: Unwin Hyman.

Harris, K. (1987) 'Moving into the new millennium: toward a feminist vision of justice', *The Prison Journal*, 67: 27–38.

Hess, H. (1986) 'Kriminalität als Alltagsmythos. Ein Plädoyer dafür, Kriminologie als Ideologiekritik zu betreiben', *Kriminologisches Journal*, 18 (1): 22–44.

Hulsman, L. (1986) 'Critical criminology and the concept of crime', *Contemporary Crises*, 10: 63–80.

Kennedy, M. (1974) 'Beyond incrimination', in C. Reasons (ed.), *The Criminologist and the Criminal.* Pacific Pallisades: Goodyear. pp. 106–35.

Mathiesen, T. (1974) 'The politics of abolition. Essays', in *Political Action Theory.* London: Martin Robertson.

Mathiesen, T. (1986) 'The politics of abolition', *Contemporary Crises*, 10: 81–94.

Matthews, R. (1987) 'Taking realist criminology seriously', *Contemporary Crises*, 11: 371–401.

Morris, M. (ed.) (1976) *Instead of Prisons: A Handbook for Abolitionists.* Syracuse, New York: Prison Research Action Project.

Pepinsky, H. (1986) 'A sociology of justice', *Annual Review of Sociology*, 12: 93–108.

Quensel, S. (1987) 'Let's abolish theories of crime' in J. Blad, H. van Mastrigt and N. Uitdriks (eds), *The Criminal Justice System as a Social Problem: An Abolitionist Perspective.* Rotterdam: Mededelingen van het Juridisch Instituut van de Erasmus Universiteit. pp. 123–32.

Roshier, B. (1989) *Controlling Crime. The Classical Perspective in Criminology.* Milton Keynes: Open University Press.

Scheerer, S. (1986) 'Towards abolitionism', *Contemporary Crisis*, 10: 5–20.

Spector, M. (1981) 'Beyond crime: seven methods to control troublesome rascals', in H. Ross (ed.), *Law and Deviance.* Beverly Hills: Sage. pp. 127–57.

Steinert, H. (1986) 'Beyond crime and punishment', *Contemporary Crises*, 10: 21–39.

Swaaningen, R. van (1989) 'Feminism and abolitionism as critiques of criminology', *International Journal of the Sociology of Law*, 17: 287–306.

Wilkins, L. (1984) *Consumerist Criminology.* London: Heinemann.

Index

THE ACHIEVEMENT OF T. S. ELIOT

BY THE SAME AUTHOR

Sarah Orne Jewett, 1929
Translation: An Elizabethan Art, 1931
American Renaissance, 1941
Henry James: The Major Phase, 1944
The James Family, 1947
Theodore Dreiser, 1951
The Responsibilities of the Critic, Essays and Reviews
SELECTED BY JOHN RACKLIFFE, 1952

EDITOR OF

Selected Poems by Herman Melville, 1944
Stories of Writers and Artists by Henry James, 1944
Russell Cheney: A Record of His Work, 1946
The Notebooks of Henry James, IN COLLABORATION WITH
KENNETH B. MURDOCK, 1947
The Oxford Book of American Verse, 1950